Grade 10

Grammar *for* Writing

Senior Series Consultant

Beverly Ann Chin
Professor of English
University of Montana
Missoula, MT

Series Consultant

Frederick J. Panzer, Sr.
English Dept. Chair, Emeritus
Christopher Columbus High School
Miami, FL

Series Consultant

Charlotte Rosenzweig, Ed. D.
English Dept. Chairperson
Long Beach High School
Long Beach, NY

Series Editor

Phyllis Goldenberg

Sadlier

Reviewers

John Manear
English Dept. Chair
Seton-La Salle High
 School
Pittsburgh, PA

Cary Fuller
English Teacher
Rye Country Day
 School
Rye, NY

Galen Rosenberg
English Dept.
 Coordinator
Los Altos High
 School
Los Altos, CA

Helen Gallagher
English Dept. Chair
Maine East High
 School
Park Ridge, IL

Rose F. Schmitt
Education
 Consultant
Melbourne, FL

Carolyn Waters
Language
 Arts/Reading 7–12
 Supervisor
Cobb County School
 District
Marietta, GA

Roxanne Hoblitt
English Dept. Chair
Belgrade High School
Belgrade, MT

Dr. Muriel Harris
Former Writing Lab
 Director
English Dept.
Purdue University
West Lafayette, IN

Thomas C. Anstett
English Dept. Chair
Lincoln-Way East
 High School
Frankfort, IL

Patricia Stack
English Teacher
South Park High
 School
South Park, PA

Mel Farberman
Former Assistant
 Principal
 Supervision–English
Cardozo High School
Bayside, NY

Wanda Porter
Former English Dept.
 Head
Kamehameha
 Secondary School
Honolulu, HI

Donna Fournier
English Dept. Chair
 and Teacher
Coyle Cassidy
 Memorial High
 School
Taunton, MA

**Katherine R.
Wilson**
Secondary English
 Coordinator, K–12
North Penn School
 District
Lansdale, PA

Student Writers

Joe Abel
Potomac, MD

Katie Baker
The Lawrenceville
School (a preparatory
school)
Lawrenceville, NJ

Toby Berkman
Newton, MA

Sara Detmering
Gig Harbor, WA

Sarah Fox
Cincinnati, OH

Mike Gradziel
Adams, MA

Fred Hernandez
Coral Gables, FL

Stacey Ho
Cincinnati, OH

Jamie Hui
Potomac, MD

Lauren Keane
San Francisco, CA

Monica McNealy
Coral Gables, FL

**Camilla Ann
Richmond**
Tampa, FL

Tammy Scherer
Jim Thorpe, PA

**Nikole Mandrell
Shipley**
Cincinnati, OH

Chia-Jung Tsay
Lake Grove, NY

Jana Zabkova
Lakewood, OH

Acknowledgments

Every good faith effort has been made to locate the owners of copyrighted material to arrange permission to reprint selections. In several cases this has proved impossible.

Thanks to the following for permission to reprint copyrighted materials.

"Elephants Get Helping Hand from Evolution," by Paul Brown. Copyright © Guardian News & Media Ltd. 1998.

Excerpts from *No Ordinary Time*, by Doris Kearns Goodwin. Reprinted with the permission of Simon & Schuster Adult Publishing Group. From

No Ordinary Time: Franklin and Eleanor Roosevelt: The Home Front in World War II, by Doris Kearns Goodwin. Copyright © 1994 by Doris Kearns Goodwin. All rights reserved.

Excerpt from "Opposition to Female Suffrage in the United States, by Nicole Herz. Copyright © 1992 by *The Concord Review*, 730 Boston Post Road, Suite 24, Sudbury, MA 01776. Reprinted by permission.

"Voters' Ed," (Op-Ed editorial) by John B. Anderson and Ray Martinez III. Copyright © 2006 by *The New York Times*. Reprinted by permission. www.tcr.org.

Credits

Cover Art and Design
Quarasan, Inc.

Interior Photos
Corbis/Digital Stock Corporation:
187 background, 289 background.
Dreamstime.com/Arrr: 171 bottom.
Neal Farris: 171 top, 289. Getty

Images/David Buffington: 115 right;
Chris Clinton: 115 left; Digital
Vision: 47 background; Ryan McVay:
203; Marcus Mok: 20 left; Rubberball
Productions: 187. The Image Works/
Syracuse Newspapers/D Lassman:
221. iStockphoto.com/techzsue: 255
background. Punchstock/Stockdisc:

20 right. Used under license from
Shutterstock.com/ Galina Barskaya:
8, 135, 239; Patrick Breig: 47; Ricard
Coencas: 203 background; Biljana
Kumer: 33; Stephen McSweeny: 151;
Jim Parkin: 275; Nick Stubbs: 95.

ISBN: 978-1-4217-1120-1
4 5 6 7 8 9 RRDW 17 16

Dear Student:

As a student, you are constantly being challenged to write correctly and effectively in a variety of subjects. From homework to standardized tests, more and more assignments require you to write in a clear, correct, and persuasive way.

This new *Enriched Edition* of *Grammar for Writing* has been prepared to help you master the writing and language skills you'll need to be an effective writer, and has been designed to ensure college and career readiness for all students.

The writing section of this book takes you through the writing process and contains **Writing Workshops** with instruction and practice in different types of writing, including the kinds of writing called for on standardized tests and the state assessments.

In the grammar section, **Test-Taking Tips** appear in lessons covering the grammar and usage skills most often assessed on tests, and **grammar and usage practice** in standardized-test formats is included as well.

Of course, there are many reasons to write effectively other than to score well on standardized tests and other assessments. People judge you by the way you write and speak. Your use of English is evaluated in the writing you do in school, on job and college applications, and in many different kinds of careers.

No textbook can make writing easy. Good writers work hard and revise their work often to find just the right words to move their audience. Consequently, in *Grammar for Writing,* you will find many exercises called **Write What You Think**. These exercises are designed to help guide you in developing clear, logical arguments to persuade people that your opinion is right. These exercises will sharpen your thinking as well as your writing skills.

No one has to prove that writing is important—it just *is*. But writing can always be improved, and the best way to improve it is to learn and practice the skills and strategies in this book. *Grammar for Writing* presents the rules of grammar as simply as possible; whether you are refreshing your memory or learning the concepts for the first time, you'll be able to understand the rules and *apply* them to your writing.

All of the skills you learn and practice in this book—grammar, writing, thinking— will last you a lifetime.

Good Luck!
The Authors

CONTENTS

COMPOSITION

CHAPTER 1 The Writing Process **8**
Lesson 1.1 Prewriting: Gathering Ideas 9
Lesson 1.2 Organizing the Ideas and Drafting 13
Lesson 1.3 Revising 15
Lesson 1.4 Editing and Proofreading 18

CHAPTER 2 Writing Effective Paragraphs and Essays **20**
Lesson 2.1 Ideas and Unity 21
Lesson 2.2 Elaborating with Supporting Details 23
Lesson 2.3 Organization and Coherence 25
Lesson 2.4 Types of Paragraphs 28
Lesson 2.5 Writing Expository Essays 31

CHAPTER 3 Writing Effective Sentences **33**
Lesson 3.1 Effective Paragraphs: Varying Sentences 34
*Lesson 3.2 Combining Sentences: Compound Subjects and Compound Verbs 36
Lesson 3.3 Combining Sentences: Inserting Phrases 38
*Lesson 3.4 Combining Sentences: Using Subordinate Clauses 40
*Lesson 3.5 Eliminating Short, Choppy Sentences 42
*Lesson 3.6 Eliminating Wordiness 44
     Revising and Editing Worksheet 46

CHAPTER 4 Writing Workshops **47**
Lesson 4.1 Narrative Writing: Biographical Essay 48
Lesson 4.2 Persuasive Writing: Editorial 53
Lesson 4.3 Writing About Literature: Analyzing Poetry 61
Lesson 4.4 Expository Writing: Cause-and-Effect Essay 67
Lesson 4.5 Expository Writing: Research Paper 74
Lesson 4.6 Practical Writing: Workplace Writing 86
*Lesson 4.7 Writing a Timed Essay 91

GRAMMAR

CHAPTER 5 Parts of Speech **95**
Lesson 5.1 Nouns 97
Lesson 5.2 Pronouns 99
Lesson 5.3 Verbs 101
*Lesson 5.4 Adjectives 103

* Denotes lessons with skills most commonly assessed on standardized tests.

*Lesson 5.5 Adverbs.. 105

Lesson 5.6 Prepositions... 107

Lesson 5.7 Conjunctions and Interjections 109

Lesson 5.8 Determining a Word's Part of Speech.......................... 111

Revising and Editing Worksheet.. 113

Chapter Review.. 114

CHAPTER 6 Parts of a Sentence 115

*Lesson 6.1 Complete Sentences 117

Lesson 6.2 Subject and Predicate 119

*Lesson 6.3 Correcting Sentence Fragments 121

Lesson 6.4 Finding the Subject 123

*Lesson 6.5 Correcting Run-on Sentences 125

Lesson 6.6 Direct and Indirect Objects 127

Lesson 6.7 Predicate Nominatives and Predicate Adjectives 129

Revising and Editing Worksheets 131

Chapter Review.. 133

CHAPTER 7 Phrases 135

Lesson 7.1 Prepositional Phrases: Adjective and Adverb Phrases...... 137

Lesson 7.2 Appositive and Appositive Phrases 139

Lesson 7.3 Participles and Participle Phrases............................. 141

Lesson 7.4 Gerunds and Gerund Phrases 143

Lesson 7.5 Infinitives and Infinitive Phrases 145

Revising and Editing Worksheets 147

Chapter Review.. 149

CHAPTER 8 Clauses 151

Lesson 8.1 Independent Clauses and Subordinate Clauses.............. 153

Lesson 8.2 Subordinate Clauses: Adjective Clauses 155

Lesson 8.3 Subordinate Clauses: Adverb Clauses 157

Lesson 8.4 Noun Clauses 159

Lesson 8.5 Four Types of Sentence Structures........................... 161

*Lesson 8.6 Effective Sentences: Parallel Structure 163

Revising and Editing Worksheets 165

Chapter Review.. 167

Cumulative Review, Chapters 5–8.. 169

USAGE

CHAPTER 9 Using Verbs... 171

Lesson 9.1 Regular Verbs 173

Lesson 9.2 Irregular Verbs 1 175

Lesson 9.3 Irregular Verbs 2... 177

* Denotes lessons with skills most commonly assessed on standardized tests.

*Lesson 9.4 Verb Tense... 179

Lesson 9.5 Using the Active Voice 181

Revising and Editing Worksheets................................ 183

Chapter Review... 185

CHAPTER 10 Subject-Verb Agreement **187**

*Lesson 10.1 Agreement in Person and Number........................... 189

*Lesson 10.2 Agreement with Intervening Phrases and
Inverted Subjects 191

*Lesson 10.3 Agreement with Indefinite Pronouns 193

*Lesson 10.4 Agreement with Compound Subjects 195

*Lesson 10.5 Other Problems in Agreement 197

Revising and Editing Worksheets................................ 199

Chapter Review... 201

CHAPTER 11 Using Pronouns... **203**

Lesson 11.1 Using Subject Pronouns 205

Lesson 11.2 Using Object Pronouns... 207

*Lesson 11.3 *Who* or *Whom*?.. 209

Lesson 11.4 Appositives and Incomplete Constructions 211

*Lesson 11.5 Agreement with Antecedent 213

*Lesson 11.6 Clear Pronoun Reference....................................... 215

Revising and Editing Worksheets................................ 217

Chapter Review... 219

CHAPTER 12 Using Modifiers **221**

Lesson 12.1 Forming the Degrees of Comparison........................... 223

*Lesson 12.2 Using the Degrees of Comparison 225

*Lesson 12.3 Illogical Comparisons and Double Negatives 227

*Lesson 12.4 Misplaced Modifiers 229

*Lesson 12.5 Dangling Modifiers... 231

Revising and Editing Worksheets................................ 233

Chapter Review... 235

Cumulative Review, Chapters 9–12 237

MECHANICS

CHAPTER 13 Punctuation: End Marks and Commas **239**

Lesson 13.1 End Marks and Abbreviations 241

Lesson 13.2 Commas in a Series.. 243

Lesson 13.3 Commas with Compound Sentences and
Introductory Elements.. 245

*Lesson 13.4 Commas with Sentence Interrupters and
Nonessential Elements.. 247

* Denotes lessons with skills most commonly assessed on standardized tests.

Lesson 13.5 Other Comma Uses 249

Editing and Proofreading Worksheets 251

Chapter Review 253

CHAPTER 14 Punctuation: All the Other Marks **255**

Lesson 14.1 Colons 257

*Lesson 14.2 Semicolons 259

Lesson 14.3 Underlining (Italics) 261

Lesson 14.4 Quotation Marks 263

Lesson 14.5 Punctuating Dialogue 265

Lesson 14.6 Apostrophes 267

Lesson 14.7 Hyphens, Dashes, and Parentheses 269

Editing and Proofreading Worksheets 271

Chapter Review 273

CHAPTER 15 Capitalization **275**

Lesson 15.1 Proper Nouns and Proper Adjectives 277

Lesson 15.2 Titles; Greetings 279

Lesson 15.3 First Words, Groups, Organizations, Religions,
School Subjects 281

Lesson 15.4 *I* and *O*; Historical Events, Documents, and Periods;
Calendar Items; Brand Names; Awards 283

Editing and Proofreading Worksheets 285

Chapter Review 287

CHAPTER 16 Spelling **289**

Lesson 16.1 Using a Dictionary 291

Lesson 16.2 Spelling Rules 293

Lesson 16.3 Prefixes and Suffixes 295

Lesson 16.4 Noun Plurals 297

Editing and Proofreading Worksheets 299

Chapter Review 301

Cumulative Review, Chapters 13–16 303

STANDARDIZED TEST PRACTICE

SAT Practice: Identifying Sentence Errors 306

SAT Practice: Improving Sentences 311

SAT Practice: Improving Paragraphs 317

ACT Practice 320

Practice Test 326

Commonly Confused Words 342

Index 345

* Denotes lessons with skills most commonly assessed on standardized tests.

The Writing Process

Prewriting: Gathering Ideas

▶ **Prewriting** is everything you do before you begin to develop paragraphs. It consists of thinking, planning, listing, brainstorming, and organizing.

If you're like most writers, these two questions burden you: "What will I write about?" and "What will I say?"

As you start to think about writing, choose a topic that interests you, that is important to you, or that you know a lot about. Limit your topic, or narrow it, so that you can cover it completely.

TOO BROAD   The Academy Awards
LIMITED   How the Academy Awards got started
             Why this year's best picture won
             What makes the Academy Awards show so popular?

Here are five useful strategies that will help you discover topics, develop main ideas, gather supporting details, and elaborate on ideas. The last four strategies can also help you take a big idea and narrow it.

PREWRITING STRATEGIES

1. **Writer's Notebook** Devote a print or digital journal just to ideas for writing. Use it to jot down anything and everything that interests, delights, inspires, or puzzles you. You might include quotations, jokes, interesting word choices, or lines of poetry.

Later, you may turn these notes and jottings into essay ideas, topic sentences, or descriptive details. While you're recording them, though, don't worry about their form or "correctness." Just get them down on paper.

WRITING HINT

Most of the prewriting strategies covered in this lesson help you to narrow a topic. Narrowing a topic is a key to successful writing. How can you tell if a topic is too broad, too narrow, or just right?

- If you can break your topic down into more than five subtopics, it may be too broad. Consider one of the narrower subtopics to write about.

- If you cannot break your topic down into more than two subtopics, it may be too narrow already. Think more broadly.

Writing Model

Watched the awards last night—it went on forever. So many commercials! Everyone just wants to watch those big award shows at the end, like for best picture and best actress. How did this thing ever get started? Why do I keep watching it?

2. Brainstorming To brainstorm, choose just one word or topic, and then
write down everything that comes to mind when you think about it.

As you brainstorm, don't worry whether each suggestion is a good one; just keep writing.
When you've run out of thoughts, go back and choose the topics that you could write
about. Circle the ones that seem most promising. When you brainstorm with a partner
or group, have one person do the writing as everyone else calls out ideas as fast as they
can think of them.

Writing Model

TOPIC: The Academy Awards
BRAINSTORMING NOTES:

members of the Academy	high television ratings	host
actors, filmmakers, producers	appeals to broad range	spectacle
writers, studio execs	big media hype	big party
costume designers	What/Who is Oscar?	
others in film business	those little trophies	
everyone dressed-to-kill	too many tuxedos!	
some people don't go	great film clips	

---

3. Freewriting When you freewrite, you brainstorm in phrases, sentences, or
even paragraphs. As with brainstorming, you choose a key word, phrase, or
idea, but you set a time limit of three to five minutes. Once you begin, the
goal is to write nonstop, stringing together words and ideas without
judgment or reconsideration. Just keep going—even if you have to keep
writing the same word several times—until a new idea develops.

When you're done, look for a center of focus in the writing, or pull out ideas
worth saving or developing. Here is just a small portion of a freewriting exercise,
which might go on for pages.

Writing Model

TOPIC: The Best Picture Oscar

So what makes a best picture? The one that the most people go see, whether it's
really good or not? The one that makes plenty of money? Some best pictures in the
past weren't so great. Would they win now? What made them win then? Do studio
execs lobby to make sure their picture wins?

---

4. **Clustering** (also called **webbing** or **mapping**) To do this kind of prewriting, write your topic—or any word or phrase—in the center of a piece of paper, and circle it. Think of ideas that are related to the center word, topic, or phrase. Then circle these ideas, and draw lines to connect the circles to the first idea you wrote. You can make one of these new circles the center of another cluster or web and repeat this process until you run out of ideas. Later, you can turn these notes into essay ideas, topic sentences, or descriptive details.

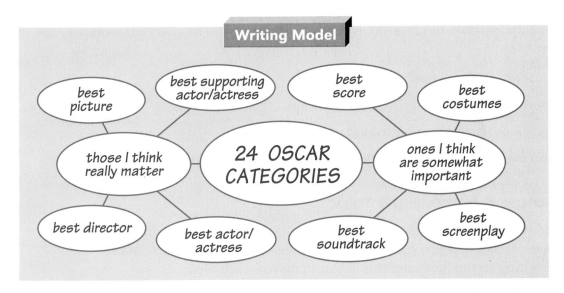

5. **5-W and How? Questions** Use this method to explore a topic you have already discovered. Ask questions about your topic by beginning with the words *Who? What? When? Where? Why?* and *How?* You can ask any number of questions that begin with the same word, and you do not have to use every question word. What you should do, however, is concentrate on probing your topic, prodding it and poking it, to see what you can discover about it.

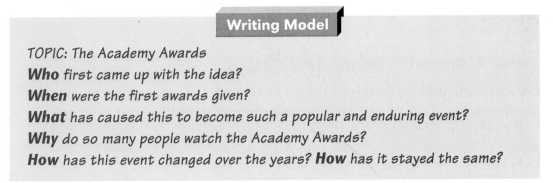

EXERCISE 1 Starting a Writer's Notebook

If you haven't already started a writer's notebook, start one now. Create one or more entries. Jot down notes about experiences, thoughts, and observations that you would be willing to share with a writing group.

EXERCISE 2 Finding Topics

For each idea below, use the prewriting strategy suggested in parentheses to come up with two or more topics to write about. Be sure to save your work for later use.

1. A sport, game, or hobby (brainstorming)

2. Something that bothers you (freewriting)

3. A season, holiday, or school vacation (clustering)

4. An event that occurred at school or at home (*5-W and How?* questions)

EXERCISE 3 Narrowing a Topic

Choose four of the broad, general topics below. For each topic, suggest three limited topics that you could cover in a three-page paper. Use any of the prewriting techniques from this lesson to narrow each topic.

TOO BROAD	Bicycling
LIMITED	What a beginner should know
	How to buy a mountain bike
	Bicycle safety

1. Tornadoes   5. Computers   9. Entertainment

2. After-school clubs   6. The environment   10. Careers

3. Football   7. Music

4. FM radio   8. Cars

EXERCISE 4 Gathering Supporting Details

For one of the limited topics you identified in Exercise 3, use brainstorming, clustering, and/or the *5-W and How?* questions to gather details about that topic.

Organizing the Ideas and Drafting

▷ Now that you've gathered your ideas, think about the order in which you want to present them. Decide whether the best way to sequence your ideas would be, for example, chronological order, order of importance, or cause and effect.

▷ **Drafting** occurs when you put your thoughts and ideas into sentences and paragraphs.

▷ Sometimes during prewriting or drafting, writers develop **outlines**. An outline is a plan for a piece of writing that tells its most important points. Some writers need an outline—either written down or in their minds—before they can begin to develop ideas in writing. Others find that a general outline begins to emerge after they start drafting. Even a rough outline, such as the one at the right, can help writers make decisions about what ideas to include in a draft as well as in which order to present them.

While making outlines may be useful before or during drafting, you should think about your **audience** and **purpose** early in the writing process. Your audience is the person or persons who will read what you write. Your purpose may be to inform, to entertain, to narrate, to persuade, or any combination of these goals.

Consider what your audience already knows and what new information you need to share. Then select the relevant details from your prewriting notes. As you draft, keep your purpose in mind and choose the details that will help you support and develop your ideas.

DRAFTING STRATEGIES

When you are ready to develop sentences and paragraphs, these strategies may help you with your task.

1. **Write the Big Idea** Remember your writing purpose and audience, and draft a sentence that expresses the main idea of your paragraph or essay. This sentence is usually stated directly or implied near the beginning of an essay. Decide where you will put yours.

2. **Grab Your Reader** Start out with a "hook," or a statement or question that will make your reader want to continue reading.

Writing Model

*A Rough Outline:
Roaring Twenties*

I. *Fueled by thriving economy*
   A. *Billions spent on recreation*
   B. *Entrepreneurs respond*

II. *Booming popular culture*
   A. *New-found money*
   B. *Radio, jazz, movies, dance crazes*
   C. *Spectator sports, sports heroes*
   D. *Reaction to fast-moving events*

III. *Great Depression follows*

---

3. **Stay Flexible** Follow the general direction of your organizational plan, but feel free to make appropriate changes and add or drop details if necessary. Don't worry about mistakes when you draft. Concentrate on getting your ideas down on paper.

4. **Create an Ending** Conclude your writing in the final paragraph by including one or more sentences that restate your main idea. A good conclusion wraps up your writing logically and gracefully and can contain a call to action, a quote, or a final thought on the subject.

Below is a first draft based on the outline on page 13. The writer's purpose was to inform history classmates about the Roaring Twenties. Remember, when you're drafting, don't stop your flow of ideas to fix mistakes. You'll have time for that during the next two steps in the writing process: revising and editing.

Writing Model

Does the writer use a hook to grab your attention?

Which sentence is redundant and can be deleted?

Does the writer include a memorable ending?

Remember, drafting is just one part of the writing process.

The years following World War I were a time of hope and lots of money for many Americans. Fueled by a thriving economy and the quick response of entrepreneurs, Americans developed a great wish for recreation. A period of leisure activities began. Dance crazes grabbed public attention, aided by radio music and the growing popularity of jazz. Movies now had sound, and theaters were built everywhere. People went to baseball games, boxing matches, horse races, and other sports. People were into watching the action.

Although it was the age of play, not everyone took part. In an attempt to hang on to old values during this fast-paced period, not only fundamentalists and rural clergy, but teachers of all faiths protested the dancing and new styles of dress and behavior.

Then, with little sense of tragedy, all the optimism came to an end with the Stock Market Crash of 1929 and the Great Depression that followed.

EXERCISE 5 Drafting a Paper

Working Together

Write a first draft of your own. Use the prewriting notes you made for Exercise 4 on page 12. With a partner, decide on your intended audience and purpose, and then develop a rough outline. When you're ready to draft, keep in mind the strategies presented in this lesson.

Revising

▥➡ When you **revise**, you look for ways to make your writing better. By concentrating on issues such as ideas and unity, organization and coherence, and sentence variety, you determine how well you've already achieved your purpose and what work still needs to be done.

REVISING STRATEGIES

When you revise, try this four-step strategy. Reread your draft four separate times, concentrating on only one of the issues below during each reading.

1. **Ideas and Unity** When you revise for ideas and unity in writing that explains, informs, or persuades, check each paragraph for a clear statement of a main idea and sufficient supporting details. In all kinds of writing, look for places where your writing is less focused, and ask yourself whether adding or deleting details will improve the draft. Also ask yourself whether you have included enough information, and if so, whether what you have written is clear.

2. **Organization and Coherence** Does the opening sentence grab the reader's attention? Is information presented in a logical order, an order that makes sense to the reader? To better organize your writing, you may need to delete or move paragraphs. In addition, you should look for places to add or improve your transitional words and phrases. Use them not only to link paragraphs but also to show how ideas and sentences are connected. Check your draft to make sure the last sentence brings closure to it.

3. **Sentence Variety** Have you varied the beginnings, lengths, and structures of your sentences? Would some sentences sound better combined?

4. **Word Choice** Ask yourself whether you have kept the members of your audience in mind by giving them the information they need to understand your points and by tailoring your approach specifically to them. This is a matter not only of *what* you say but also of *how* you say it: your word choice. Is your tone right? Depending on your purpose and audience, do you sound appropriately formal or informal, subjective or objective? Can you delete unnecessary words or phrases? Look for general, vague words, and replace them with precise ones. If you've used a cliché or an overworked word, such as *very* or *great*, think of a new way to express the same idea.

Below is the first draft on the Roaring Twenties from Lesson 1.2. Notice the revisions the writer has made to it.

Writing Model

Has the writer improved the draft by inserting more vivid verbs, precise nouns, and effective modifiers?

The years following World War I were a time of hope and *prosperity* ~~lots of money~~ for many Americans. Fueled by a thriving economy and the quick response of entrepreneurs, Americans developed a great *thirst* ~~wish~~ for recreation. A period of leisure activities began. Dance crazes *, such as the Charleston,* grabbed public attention, aided by radio music and the growing popularity of jazz. Movies now had sound, and theaters *sprang up* ~~were built~~ everywhere. People *flocked* ~~went~~ to baseball games, boxing matches, horse races, and other sports. ~~People were into watching the action.~~

Do you see any new ideas in this revision?

What do you notice that is different about this revision and the draft?

Although it was the age of play, not everyone took part. In an attempt to hang on to *traditional* ~~old~~ values during this fast-paced period, not only fundamentalists and rural clergy, but teachers of all faiths protested the dancing and new styles of dress and behavior.

How does the writer create a conclusion?

Then, with little sense of *impending* tragedy, all the optimism came to an end *abruptly* with the Stock Market Crash of 1929 and the Great Depression that followed. This period of gloom and economic woe replaced the Roaring Twenties.

When you're revising, getting the advice of another reader or a small group can be invaluable. **Working with a writing partner** involves giving feedback to a classmate and getting help from him or her on your works in progress. Writing partners give positive feedback, telling the writer what they like best about his or her writing. They also make specific suggestions for improving a paper and ask questions about anything that is unclear.

EXERCISE 6 Revising a Letter to the Editor

Use the four-step revising strategy in this lesson to improve a classmate's letter to the editor below. The readers of your local newspaper are your audience. Your purpose is to persuade. There is no single correct way to revise this letter, so feel free to include additional details. You might also delete sentences or ideas, add transitions, and combine sentences.

> To the Editor:
>
> On Saturday, March 22, the town of Allendale will hold its annual cleanup day. These cleanup days have been very successful in the past. These cleanup days have been sponsored by the Kiwanis Club and the Junior Kiwanis. We hope everyone turns out for this nice activity to make Allendale beautiful. We hope everyone can make it.
>
> If you're interested, please show up on the lawn in front of the town library at 9:30 A.M. Work teams will be formed. Assignments will be given. You can join us for the day, a half-day, or even just an hour.
>
> Mei-Ling Mitchell
> Allendale Junior Kiwanis

EXERCISE 7 Revising a Paper

Find a paper you've written for English or for another class. Choose one you think needs revising. Remind yourself of your original audience and purpose, and then, one step at a time, work through the revising steps given on page 15 of this lesson.

EXERCISE 8 Working with a Writing Partner

1. Revise the paper you drafted in Lesson 1.2, Exercise 5. Use the revising strategies in this lesson to improve your draft.

2. Work with a partner to revise your paper. Allow your partner to read your paper without your feedback. Your partner should respond to your writing using the revising strategies on page 15 as a guide.

3. Review your writing partner's comments on your paper, and incorporate those that you feel will improve your writing. You may need to rewrite some sections.

Editing and Proofreading

▐▌▌▶ When you **edit** or **proofread** (these words refer to the same task), you search for and correct mistakes in spelling, punctuation, capitalization, and usage.

Edting is an important process with a big payback. Readers often find errors in spelling or punctuation to be distracting. Use the following strategies to eliminate all the blemishes in your paper.

EDITING STRATEGIES

1. **Spelling** Even if you've used a spell checker, check every word. When in doubt, consult a print or online dictionary. If you are curious about a form, such as a past participle or a plural, a dictionary will list any irregular form with the related entry word. Also, remember to watch out for homophones and other often confused or misused words.

2. **Capitalization** Do proper nouns and proper adjectives begin with a capital letter? If you're in doubt about whether something needs to be uppercase or lowercase, consult a dictionary.

3. **Punctuation** Look at every punctuation mark, but look especially closely at dialogue and quotations. Also, remember to check for both beginning and end quotation marks, parentheses, and brackets.

4. **Sentence Correctness** Are there any fragments, run-ons, or misplaced modifiers?

5. **Verbs** Do all present tense verbs agree with their subjects? Are verb tenses consistent and correct?

6. **Pronouns** Do all the pronouns agree with their antecedents? Are pronoun references clear?

7. **Usage** Are adjectives modifying nouns and pronouns? Are adverbs modifying verbs, adjectives, and other adverbs? Are comparisons clear and complete? Are *-er/more* and *-est/most* forms used correctly?

When you edit/proofread, you may find it helpful to use the proofreading symbols in the chart on page 19.

▐▌▌▶ **Publishing** means sharing or presenting what you've written. You can publish your work by personally sharing it with family and friends, or you can use a computer and the Internet to share it with an even wider audience. See page 19 for publishing suggestions.

Refer to the lessons in Chapter 16 for spelling help.

Refer to Chapters 13 and 14 for rules about punctuation.

Proofreading Symbols

CORRECTION	SYMBOL	EXAMPLE
Delete (remove).	ℓ	"Stop that know!" he be shouted.
Insert.	^	This is the new mille*n*ium.
Transpose (switch).	⌐⌐	I only received one postcard.
Capitalize.	≡	We spent our vacation in the northwest.
Make lowercase.	/	Isn't Spring early this year?
Start a new paragraph.	¶	¶Jess replied, "Of course, I do!"
Add space.	#	Please take this to the postoffice.
Close up space.	⌣	Parent hood is a big responsibility.

Exercise 9 Proofreading a Passage

Find and correct every error in the following passage. Use the proofreading symbols.

[1]How did the bull dozer get it's name? [2]The frist form of this word appeared in america in 1875. [3]The word, or compound term, used than was *bull dose*. [4]This term refered to a flogging, the "dose, or amount ofthe flogging that was supposed to be strong enough for a bull. [5]By 1875, the form of term this had changed to *bulldoze*; by then, it had the same meaning, more or less as *steamroll*. [6]it wasn't until 1890 that the name was applied to themachine on tank treads that has a Large steel blade for moving Earth and for clearing growth and rubbish. [7]That name, of course, has not changed since 1890. [8]Today, the the verb *bulldoze* means both "to oprate a bulldozer" and "to come on strong.

Publishing Suggestions

WRITTEN WORDS

Magazine of student writing

School or local newspaper

Local or national poetry, story, or essay contest

Class anthology

Writing portfolio

Letters

SPOKEN WORDS

Speech

Audio recording

Oral interpretation

Radio broadcast

Reader's theater

Interview

Debate

DIGITAL

E-mail

E-book

Web site

Blog

Podcast

Video recording

Writing Effective Paragraphs and Essays

Ideas and Unity

▐▶ Paragraphs that inform, explain, or persuade have **unity** (or are unified) when all of their sentences focus on a single main **idea**.

As you draft a paragraph, concentrate on developing one main idea. When you revise and edit, you'll have another opportunity to achieve unity by dropping sentences and details that wander away from the main idea.

▐▶ A **topic sentence** states the main idea of a paragraph.

A topic sentence can appear anywhere in a paragraph, but it is most often in the first sentence. In this position, it introduces—and sometimes even organizes—everything that follows. When the topic sentence is the last sentence in the paragraph, it summarizes the ideas that have preceded it.

Not all paragraphs have a topic sentence that directly states the main idea. Instead, the main idea of the paragraph may be implied. When you are drafting, you should have a topic sentence for each paragraph clearly in mind. When you are revising, you should be able to identify the topic sentence of each paragraph whether it is directly stated or not.

▐▶ A paragraph that starts with a topic sentence may end with a **clincher sentence** that restates or summarizes the main idea.

Clincher sentences can be particularly effective in persuasive paragraphs. For creating an effect, however, they are best used sparingly.

The following paragraph about how President Franklin D. Roosevelt ran the country during World War II is unified.

WRITING HINT

The topic sentence of a paragraph and the clincher sentence often work together. (The following example leaves out all of the supporting details that develop the main idea of the paragraph.)

There are seemingly countless variations of the name *Jane*, which is itself a feminine form of *John*. . . . From *Gianina* to *Zaneta*, you'll find that *Jane* is not so plain after all.

Writing Model

¹To be sure, there were errors in Roosevelt's wartime leadership. ²A precious year was lost in 1940–41, when the mobilization process was not pushed hard enough, when, as Washington lawyer Joe Rauh noted, "the arsenal of democracy was more democracy than arsenal." ³Indeed, had it not been for the period of borrowed time provided by the heroic resistance of the British and the Russians, the United States might not have been able to overcome the head start of the Axis in time to influence the course of the war. ⁴And once the mobilization got under

Topic sentence states the main idea

First example of an error

Explanation of the possible cost of such an error

Second example of an error

Explanation of the lasting effects

> way, he failed to protect small business against the military's tendency to lavish its contracts on the nation's industrial giants. [5]It was during the war years that the links were forged that would lead to the rise of the "military-industrial complex" in postwar America.
>
> —Doris Kearns Goodwin, *No Ordinary Time*

Skills for Maintaining Unity

Paragraph unity depends primarily on your topic sentence, how you develop the related ideas, and how well you link your clincher sentence—if you include one—to the paragraph as a whole.

1. **Topic Sentence** Goodwin states her topic sentence at the beginning of the paragraph. It is direct, clear, and to the point. It focuses the reader's attention.

2. **Effective Development of Ideas** Goodwin's paragraph sticks to the main idea. Although she spends much of her book praising Roosevelt, when she does present some weaknesses, she focuses solely on that topic.

3. **Clincher Sentence** Goodwin could have chosen to sum up her paragraph with a clincher sentence, but it clearly is not necessary.

Exercise 1 Choosing a Topic Sentence

Use a separate piece of paper to answer the following questions.

1. Which of the following sentences would work in place of the topic sentence that Goodwin wrote? Give reasons for your choice.
   a. Roosevelt's leadership during the war was not perfect.
   b. Roosevelt helped get the "military-industrial complex" off to a good start.
   c. Roosevelt's wartime leadership suffered from bad timing and lack of foresight.

2. Which of the following sentences could most easily be added to Goodwin's paragraph without detracting from its unity? Explain your choice.
   a. The "military-industrial complex" played an important role in the economic development of postwar America.
   b. Roosevelt, who did not fear regulation, could have imposed rulings to make small businesses more competitive, but he did not.
   c. The Axis powers—Germany, Italy, and Japan—waged war on several fronts.

Elaborating with Supporting Details

▌▶ **Elaboration** is the process of adding details that support a main idea.

Develop, or support, a paragraph's main idea with the following kinds of details: **facts**, **statistics**, **quotations**, **definitions**, **anecdotes** or **incidents**, **examples**, **reasons**, and **comparisons**. You can develop an effective paragraph by using just one type of detail or a combination of types.

The writer of the following paragraph realized that her first draft did not contain enough specific details to support the topic sentence. Notice the details she added during revision.

Writing Model

¹The skeleton of an elephant reveals a great deal about it. ²An elephant's skeleton is immediately recognizable because of its tusks.
These long, pointed teeth are used for fighting and also for digging.
³Tusks are actually front teeth that have grown to be enormous. ⁴A key
These leg bones must support the elephant's enormous weight.
part of an elephant's skeleton is its long, heavy leg bones. ⁵It also has
If the toe bones were not flat, the great weight of the elephant would probably break them.
toe bones that are flat on the ground. ⁶It has a short neck.
This shows that an elephant does not feed by grazing. Instead, an elephant uses its trunk to carry food to its mouth.

EXERCISE 2 Improving Unity and Adding Details

Work with a partner or small group to revise the following paragraph. Cross out any words or sentences that damage the paragraph's unity. Then from the list below the paragraph, select the details that you think would improve the paragraph. (Some of the details can be inserted as phrases and clauses.) Write the letter of the detail where you think it belongs in the paragraph. Then write your revised paragraph on a separate piece of paper.

¹Three features of the cat's skeleton reveal a great deal about this animal. ²A cat is a vertebrate. ³It is also a favorite pet. ⁴First, it has a small skull with very large eye sockets. ⁵Second, it has two long, sharp teeth.

Enriching Your Vocabulary

The word *nocturnal*, used on page 24, comes from the Latin word for night, *nox*. Both bats and owls are *nocturnal* hunters; they sleep during the day.

[6]Third, it has a long tail made up of many bones.

[7]The tail bones of a fish are also very revealing,

primarily because of the fin bones near it.

Details

A. This long tail is critical for balance; it suggests that the cat can jump from place to place easily.
B. This suggests the presence of large eyes that probably let in a lot of light and allow the animal to hunt at night.
C. These may be used for grabbing or killing prey.
D. All these clues combine to suggest that the cat is an agile nocturnal hunter.

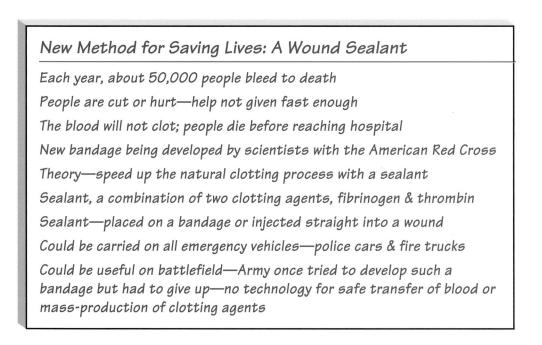

WRITING HINT

The type of details you use or add depends on the idea you want to develop. For example:

• To support an opinion, use facts, statistics, or quotations.

• To describe a person, use sensory details or anecdotes.

• To explain a concept, use examples or incidents.

EXERCISE 3 Writing Paragraphs from Notes

On a separate piece of paper, write two or more unified, well-developed paragraphs based on the information in the notecard below. You do not need to use all of the information. Begin your paragraph with a clear topic sentence.

New Method for Saving Lives: A Wound Sealant

Each year, about 50,000 people bleed to death

People are cut or hurt—help not given fast enough

The blood will not clot; people die before reaching hospital

New bandage being developed by scientists with the American Red Cross

Theory—speed up the natural clotting process with a sealant

Sealant, a combination of two clotting agents, fibrinogen & thrombin

Sealant—placed on a bandage or injected straight into a wound

Could be carried on all emergency vehicles—police cars & fire trucks

Could be useful on battlefield—Army once tried to develop such a bandage but had to give up—no technology for safe transfer of blood or mass-production of clotting agents

---

Organization and Coherence

▶ When a paragraph is **organized** and **coherent**, each word, phrase, and sentence in it works together to present the ideas in a sequence that makes sense to the reader.

STRATEGIES FOR WRITING COHERENTLY

1. **Be clear.** Express your thoughts simply and directly.

2. **Guide the reader.** Wherever they are helpful, use the transitional words and phrases found in the chart on page 26. Also, repeating key words and providing synonyms can help readers link later ideas with those that precede them. Clear pronoun reference also helps ideas cohere, or "stick together." Finally, to make your writing coherent, do not shift tense or person unnecessarily.

3. **Put your thoughts in order.** Organization is one of the most important parts of coherence. Below are four common methods for organizing paragraphs and essays.

   • **Chronological Order** Organize your writing in time order, or chronologically, when you want to tell about events in the order in which they occurred. Chronological order is effective for writing about a historical event and for explaining steps in a process. Chronological order is used in fictional stories as well as true ones, such as autobiographies, biographies, and eyewitness accounts.

   • **Spatial Order** Organize your writing spatially when you want to describe the appearance of a person, an animal, a place, or an object. Describe details in an orderly way. For example, you might present them from left to right, top to bottom, near to far, or inside to outside.

   • **Order of Importance** Organize your writing in order of importance when you are trying to persuade your audience. State the least important reasons and details first, and end with the most important ones—or the reverse.

   • **Logical Order** Organize your writing to give information in the order that a reader needs to know it. Use common sense to decide which details to group together or where to insert background or explanatory information.

The revisions in the following model show how one writer improved organization and coherence in response to a writing partner's notes.

Enriching Your Vocabulary

Cohere comes from the Latin verb *cohaerere*, which means "to stick together." Hail stones are formed when ice and snow *cohere* in the clouds.

Alert reader to method of organization

Use spatial order

Use pronouns

Repeat terms already used

Do not shift person

Add transition/ Use pronoun

Writing Model

From head to toe,
[1]My Dalmatian, Dots, is a fast, strong, good-looking dog. [2]At the top of her head are her high ears, which taper to a rounded point. *Her* [3]A matching black nose has a tinge of pink around its edges. *Her* [4]A long, arched neck leads to a pair of powerful shoulders, the first sign of how ~~lean and well-balanced~~ *fast and strong* she is. [5]~~The~~ *Her* eyes are sparkling and lined all around with jet black. [6]Even though it is not wide, her chest is deep, and ~~you can just barely see~~ the ribs of her ~~muscular~~, black-and- *are just barely visible. Finally, her* white spotted body, [7]~~The~~ legs are straight and heavy, and they are supported by small but strong feet.

Some Common Transitional Words and Expressions

Time		Order of Importance		Position		Cause-Effect	
after	first	above all	first	above	here	accordingly	for
afterward	later	to begin	second	across	in front of	as a result	since
already	next	to conclude	third	after	inside	because	so
before	soon	equally important		before	next to	consequently	so that
finally	then	more (most) important		behind	outside	if . . . then	therefore
following				between	over		
		Contrast		beyond	under	**Similar Ideas**	
Examples		although	but			also	as
for example	namely	however	still	**Emphasis**		and	similarly
for instance	that is	in contrast	though	for this reason	again	just as	too
in addition		nevertheless	unlike	moreover	in fact	like	likewise
in other words		on the contrary		most important		equally important	
		on the other hand					

EXERCISE 4 Revising a Paragraph for Organization and Coherence

Working Together

Work with a partner or small group to improve the organization and coherence of the following paragraph. Try adding transitional words and expressions, reordering information, and combining sentences. Make any other changes that you think will improve the paragraph. Write your revised paragraph on a separate piece of paper.

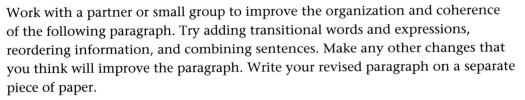

[1]John Jacob Astor, when he died in 1848, was the richest man in America. [2]He was the son of a German butcher. [3]He was twenty when he came to the United

States in 1783. [4]He worked for a fur trader. [5]He learned the business. [6]He began trading furs himself in 1786. [7]Trading furs with Native Americans was an important part of our economy. [8]This was just after the American Revolution. [9]He used his fur profits to buy real estate in New York City.

EXERCISE 5 Writing an Organized, Unified Paragraph

Choose one of the following assignments, and write an organized, unified paragraph.

1. Study a pair of sneakers that you or someone else is wearing. Write an accurate, orderly, and detailed description of them.

2. Explain how to perform a title search in your library's electronic database or card catalog.

3. Your local board of education is considering phasing out the high school library and devoting the resources to the computer labs. Write what you think about this idea. Give reasons to support your opinion.

EXERCISE 6 Writing a Paragraph from Notes

Write an organized, unified paragraph based on the following notes. Include a topic sentence.

Martha Gellhorn, 1908–1998

One of the most notable American war correspondents of the 20th century

Covered the Spanish Civil War, World War II, Vietnam, and Arab-Israeli wars

Covered the D-Day landings and the liberation of Dachau concentration camp in Germany

Wrote passionately about the effects of war on the innocent

Began her career in 1937; last assignment more than 50 years later in Panama

Lived abroad a great deal: France, Cuba, Mexico, Italy, Kenya

Also a novelist—The Honeyed Peace and The Trouble I've Seen

Was once married to Ernest Hemingway

Types of Paragraphs

Most paragraphs have more than one purpose. For example, a paragraph that narrates often also describes; a paragraph that persuades often also explains. Learning how to develop a paragraph that has a single purpose, however, will help you focus on coherent and unified elaboration. The following suggestions will help you write for different purposes.

DESCRIPTIVE

When you are describing the appearance of a person, an animal, a place, or an object, use the following suggestions.

- Use **sensory details** to appeal to the reader's five senses (sight, hearing, smell, touch, and taste) and to create a **main impression** or **mood**.

- Use **spatial order** to present the sensory details from left to right, top to bottom, near to far—or in reverse. Use appropriate transitions. (See page 26.)

Writing Model

Main idea or impression

Sensory details

Comparisons

Transitions signal spatial order

Sensory details

[1]Nothing about the outside of an avocado prepares you for the pleasant surprise inside. [2]The skin covering the avocado's pear or oval shape is a wrinkled green or black. [3]In fact, some avocados have textures somewhere between the skin of an elephant and the skin of a crocodile. [4]On the inside is a very large seed that seems to take up way too much of the entire fruit. [5]Between the seed and the skin is a firm, yellowish-green, melt-in-your-mouth fruit. [6]It takes on and enhances the flavors of anything you serve it with, from tomatoes or salsa to sandwiches or salad. [7]An avocado adds a creamy, almost buttery, texture as well as a subtle flavor.

NARRATIVE

When you are telling a true or fictional story, use the following suggestions.

- Use **specific details** to help make the reader an eyewitness to events.

- Use **chronological order** (time order) to relate events in the order in which they occur. Use appropriate transitions. (See page 26.)

Event 1	**Writing Model** ¹I shook Andrew from his sleep and told him we were going
Specific details	to the pond. ²"Lemme sleep!" he moaned pleadingly in his little-brother voice. ³I was a sister on a mission. ⁴I knew we would see that
Transition signals Event 2	blue heron again if only we would just be there once at dawn. ⁵A few minutes later, in the half-light of early day, we made our way
Specific details	down the winding, dew-covered path. ⁶As we rounded the last
Transition signals Event 3	bend, I silently called the heron to us.

Writing Model

Event 1   ¹I shook Andrew from his sleep and told him we were going to the pond. ²"Lemme sleep!" he moaned pleadingly in his little-brother voice. ³I was a sister on a mission. ⁴I knew we would see that blue heron again if only we would just be there once at dawn. ⁵A few minutes later, in the half-light of early day, we made our way down the winding, dew-covered path. ⁶As we rounded the last bend, I silently called the heron to us.

Event 1

Specific details

Transition
signals Event 2

Specific details
Transition
signals Event 3

EXPOSITORY

When you are writing an exposition, you are explaining or informing. Exposition includes comparing or contrasting; explaining cause and effect; defining, classifying, or analyzing; and giving instructions or explaining the steps in a process. For any of these specific purposes, use the following suggestions.

• State your **main idea** as early and as clearly as possible.

• Use **facts**, **examples**, **quotations**, **statistics**, and **definitions** as supporting details to develop the main idea.

• Present the details or the steps in **logical order**—in a way that makes sense to the reader. Use appropriate transitions. (See page 26.)

Writing Model

Main idea   ¹*Gothic* describes a type of church architecture. ²This style
Fact   arose nine hundred years ago in Europe. ³Before that time, churches
Transition/   were built with thick, heavy walls and low, heavy roofs. ⁴In contrast,
comparison   Gothic churches soared upward, as if reaching for heaven. ⁵They had
Example/   pointed ribbed vaults to support the weight of the roof. ⁶They also
explanation   had a new feature called flying buttresses, arches on the outside of
   the building that provided support. ⁷This newer, more graceful
Statistics   architecture became so popular that almost five hundred Gothic
   churches were built in Europe between 1170 and 1270.

PERSUASIVE

When you are trying, in a single paragraph, to convince someone that your opinion is correct or to persuade someone to take action, use the following suggestions.

- Begin with a sentence that is an **attention grabber**.

- Include a **thesis statement,** or **claim,** that clearly expresses your point of view.

- Supply **reasons** and other **evidence** (facts, statistics, anecdotes, quotations) to suport your opinion.

- Arrange the supporting details in **order of importance**—from most to least important, or the reverse.

- Include a **call to action** that tells the reader what to do.

Topic sentence, with transition and link to thesis, or claim

Reason

Statistic

Explanation

Writing Model

¹Another reason to restore funding to the high school football program is that it helps build a strong link between the high school and the community. ²Football games are an event that anyone in town can enjoy. ³In fact, a survey conducted at last season's final game showed that almost twenty percent of those attending had no children on the team or even in the high school. ⁴Instead, they were people who felt allegiance to the school because of the football program. ⁵Many of these individuals are the same people who pay the school taxes to support our system.

EXERCISE 7 Writing for Varying Purposes

Write two paragraphs that have different purposes. You may use the topics suggested below or choose a topic of your own.

- A persuasive paragraph for or against tougher licensing standards for beginning drivers

- A descriptive paragraph about a place you loved as a child or a place that is special to you now

- A narrative paragraph about a race, contest, or competition

- An expository paragraph giving information about a local place of interest or about a useful product or invention

Writing Expository Essays

▐▐▐▶ An **essay** is a piece of writing on a limited topic. Most essays have three common elements: an **introduction**, a **body**, and a **conclusion**.

INTRODUCTION

The beginning of a persuasive or expository essay should accomplish two purposes: It should create interest, and it should present the overall idea of the essay.

The **thesis statement** of an essay is its overall idea. It is also called a **claim** or a **controlling idea**. A thesis statement is for an essay what a topic sentence is for a paragraph.

When you write, remember that your thesis statement, or claim, controls the direction of your paragraphs. Each paragraph must be directly related to the thesis statement. Whether stated or implied, the topic sentence of every paragraph should support, demonstrate, or explain the thesis. In fact, sometimes, the thesis statement not only signals the content of an essay, but it also reveals its organization, as this example shows.

THESIS STATEMENT, OR CLAIM	The war in Vietnam was difficult for the United States because U.S. troops were fighting a guerrilla war in jungle terrain, because popular support for the Vietcong increased even as the U.S. waged war, and because the Vietcong were supported by outside forces, including China and the Soviet Union.
TOPIC SENTENCE OF BODY PARAGRAPH 1	The United States was not prepared to fight a guerrilla war, and its troops had insufficient knowledge of the terrain.
TOPIC SENTENCE OF BODY PARAGRAPH 2	Meanwhile, the Vietcong grew more—not less—popular as the war raged.
TOPIC SENTENCE OF BODY PARAGRAPH 3	In addition, the United States was not the only foreign power involved in the war: The Vietcong were receiving strong support from China and the Soviet Union.

The side column lists some effective ways to begin an essay. Avoid these less effective beginnings.

> I will write about . . .
> This paper will explain . . .

Some Ways to Begin an Essay

- an anecdote
- a quotation
- a question
- an interesting statement or fact
- a direct invitation or address to the reader
- a statement of a writer's stand on an issue

WRITING HINT

Remember that text features, such as headings and formatting, can help clarify an essay's organization. Graphic elements, such as tables, charts, and images, can help your audience better understand complex information.

BODY

In the body of your essay, you develop your thesis, or claim. This will require several paragraphs and a logical organization that makes sense to readers. Follow these guidelines when you draft the body.

1. **Turn main ideas into paragraphs.** Think of each paragraph as a single main idea that explains and develops your thesis. You will support each idea with relevant facts, definitions, details, quotations, examples, and other information that is related to your topic.

2. **Organize your ideas.** Arrange body paragraphs logically, in a way that is easy for readers to follow. Use appropriate transitional words and phrases to link your ideas and create a cohesive essay. For example, in a compare-contrast essay, you might use *similarly*, *likewise*, and *however*. In a cause-effect essay, you might use *as a result* and *therefore*.

3. **Stay focused.** As you write, be sure to focus on your claim and the main idea discussed in each body paragraph. Use precise language and vocabulary that is specific to your topic and at the appropriate level for your audience. Maintain a formal style and objective tone as you write. Also remember to avoid unnecessary wordiness and repetition.

CONCLUSION

When you've developed your main points, stop writing. A strong conclusion follows logically from the body of the essay, without repeating too much information or introducing new points. Give your audience a sense of closure by limiting your concluding section to a final point or insight about the topic. Try using one of the strategies listed in the side column.

Some Ways to End an Essay

- a brief but fresh restatement of the main idea
- a comment on the importance of the topic
- a quotation
- a question
- a prediction
- a call to action

EXERCISE 8 Writing a Thesis, or Claim

Expand one of the paragraphs you wrote for Exercise 7 in Lesson 2.4 into a three-page essay. Write a thesis statement, or claim for the essay using the suggestions in this lesson.

EXERCISE 9 Writing an Introduction and a Conclusion

Write an introduction and a conclusion for the essay you wrote in Exercise 8. Remember that your introduction must include a thesis statement.

Writing Effective Sentences

Effective Paragraphs: Varying Sentences

▐▐▶ For variety, begin some of your sentences with a subordinate clause.

Subordinate, or dependent, clauses are an important tool for varying sentence beginnings. Here is the same idea expressed in two ways.

ORIGINAL   Many colonists came to the New World for religious freedom, but they did not accept people with other beliefs.

SUBORDINATE CLAUSE   **Although many colonists came to the New World for religious freedom,** they did not accept people with other beliefs.

In the example above, more than just the beginning of the sentence changes. The sentence structure also changes from compound to complex. When you are writing paragraphs, vary your sentences in these three ways:

1. Vary beginnings.

2. Vary sentence structures. Use a mixture of simple, compound, complex, and compound-complex sentences.

3. Vary the lengths of your sentences. Place short sentences between longer ones. Use short sentences for emphasis at key places in your paragraphs.

All three kinds of sentence variation appear in the following paragraph. The symbols **S** (simple), **CD** (compound), **CX** (complex), and **CD-CX** (compound-complex) identify the structure of preceding sentences. Subordinate clauses are underlined.

Because the Puritans were seeking religious freedom, they left England and settled in Massachusetts, where they were able to practice their own religion in peace; however, other groups did not find life among the Puritans to be peaceful. (**CD-CX**) Instead, they sought to escape the rigid laws that the Puritans made them live by. (**CX**) Escaping Puritan intolerance, these groups started the colony of Rhode Island. (**S**) Intolerance was not unique to Massachusetts. (**S**) In Maryland, Catholics could not hold public religious services, and Jews could not even vote in most colonies. (**CD**) The Puritans, while seeking religious freedom for themselves, fell short of extending it to others. (**CX**)

EXERCISE 1 Revising a Paragraph

Work with a partner or small group to revise the following paragraph. Vary the sentence structures, the sentence beginnings, and the sentence lengths. You may combine sentences and change words.

[1]Most Roman towns were small. [2]Some contained just a few thousand people. [3]Towns were laid out on a grid. [4]A network of streets created the grid. [5]The streets were all at right angles to one another. [6]This created blocks. [7]Roman blocks were called *insulae*. [8]Each block was made up of different kinds of buildings. [9]There might be homes, workshops, and shops on one block. [10]A forum was in the center of each town. [11]A forum is a marketplace. [12]It was a place to shop. [13]It was a place to get together and conduct business. [14]The business of government went on there. [15]The most important temples in the town were also in the forum. [16]The number of public buildings in the forum depended on the size of the town.

EXERCISE 2 Writing a Paragraph

Use the notes below to write a paragraph on a separate piece of paper. Be sure to vary sentence beginnings, sentence structures, and sentence lengths.

Tundra

Like cold desert; gets less than 25 cm/year of rain

Located at the northernmost extremes of land—along Arctic Ocean & North Pole

Water on tundra gets locked in ice

Layer of soil called permafrost—permanently frozen, except tiny bit at surface in summer; permafrost stops large trees from growing

Flowers bloom in summer; also mosquitoes, birds, grass

Large musk oxen live there; also lemmings

Lichens—plantlike organisms

Caribou eat lichens; wolves eat caribou

Combining Sentences: Compound Subjects and Compound Verbs

Coordinating Conjunctions

and	but	or
nor	yet	so

Correlative Conjunctions

both . . . and
either . . . or
just as . . . so (too)
neither . . . nor
not only . . . but also
whether . . . or

Repetition, such as in the example below, wastes space and wears out your reader.

ORIGINAL   Whales are mammals. Bears are mammals. Dogs are mammals.

A compound subject solves the problem.

REVISED   Whales, bears, and dogs are mammals.

The word *compound* means "two or more of something." Any sentence part can be compound.

▶ A sentence with a **compound subject** has two or more subjects sharing the same verb. Use a conjunction to join the separate subjects. See the list of conjunctions in the side column.

SEPARATE SUBJECTS   Mushrooms are fungi. Molds are fungi. Yeasts are fungi.

COMPOUND SUBJECT   Mushrooms, molds, and yeasts are fungi.

SEPARATE SUBJECTS   Mushrooms are plantlike, but they have no chlorophyll. Molds are plantlike, but they have no chlorophyll.

COMPOUND SUBJECT   Mushrooms and molds are plantlike, but they have no chlorophyll.

▶ A sentence with a **compound verb** has two or more verbs sharing the same subject. Use a conjunction to join the separate verbs.

SEPARATE VERBS   Molds grow on foods. Molds multiply on foods.

COMPOUND VERB   Molds grow and multiply on foods.

SEPARATE VERBS   People view common bread mold with horror. People welcome the blue-green mold penicillium.

COMPOUND VERB   People view common bread mold with horror but welcome the blue-green mold penicillium.

P.S. Combining ideas comes naturally in speech. In writing, however, you may have to make a conscious effort to combine subjects, predicates, and other sentence parts. It's worth the effort to end up with smoother-sounding sentences.

Exercise 3 Combining Sentences

On a separate piece of paper, combine the sentences in each numbered item into a single sentence with a compound subject or a compound verb. Change words or forms of words as needed. In your revised sentences, underline the subject(s) once and the verb(s) twice. Do not underline the conjunction.

1. Native American words are the sources of many American place names.

   European history is the source of many American place names.

2. *Iowa* comes from a Native American word. *Kentucky* comes from a Native

   American word. *Idaho* comes from a Native American word.

3. *Mississippi* is a Native American word. *Kissimmee* is a Native American word.

4. *Maryland* is named after a European queen. *Virginia* is named after a

   European queen.

5. *Carolina* and *Georgia* come from the names of kings. Carolina and Georgia

   were given these names to honor those kings.

Exercise 4 Revising a Report

Work with a partner or small group to revise the following passage from a report. Look for ways to combine sentences, using compound subjects and compound verbs. Write your revised report on a separate piece of paper. Compare your revised passage with those of other pairs or groups.

[1]The orangutan is an example of an endangered species. [2]The giant panda is an example of an endangered species. [3]The macaw is an example of an endangered species. [4]As the world's population increases, people need more land to live on. [5]They need more land to grow their food. [6]Houses take some of this land. [7]Farms take some of this land. [8]Roads take some of this land. [9]As growth continues, streams sometimes disappear. [10]Wetlands sometimes disappear. [11]Sometimes, huge forests are cut down. [12]They are destroyed forever. [13]When this happens, an animal's habitat may be radically changed. [14]It may even be completely lost. [15]Because of this loss of habitat, the animal's food supply diminishes. [16]Sometimes, the food supply disappears. [17]In addition to the loss of habitat, overfishing causes some animals to be endangered. [18]Hunting causes some animals to be endangered. [19]Poaching causes some animals to be endangered.

Combining Sentences: Inserting Phrases

In addition to combining sentences by creating compound sentences, compound subjects, and compound verbs, writers combine sentences by inserting phrases.

▐▐▐➡ Combine related sentences by inserting a phrase from one sentence into another sentence. Sometimes, you need to change slightly the phrase you move from one sentence to another. Other times, you can just select a phrase from one sentence and insert it into another without any change. Usually, there is more than one way to combine two sentences.

ORIGINAL   Knights trained for years. They spent years practicing with swords and running at each other with lances.

COMBINED   Knights trained for years **by practicing with swords and running at each other with lances**. [prepositional phrase, gerund phrase]

ORIGINAL   Knights protected their lord. They defended the castle.

COMBINED   **To protect their lord**, knights defended the castle. [infinitive phrase]

ORIGINAL   Knights fought in tournaments. These are a series of mock battles. They spanned many days.

COMBINED   Knights fought in tournaments, **a series of mock battles spanning many days**. [appositive phrase, participial phrase]

EXERCISE 5 Combining Sentences

On a separate piece of paper, use phrases to combine the sentences in each numbered item below. Change or add words, as needed, to create prepositional, appositive, participial, gerund, or infinitive phrases. Don't forget to add commas where they belong. **Hint:** For some items, several answers are possible.

EXAMPLE   Rosa Parks sparked the Montgomery bus boycott. She refused to give up her seat on a bus.
         Rosa Parks sparked the Montgomery bus boycott by refusing to give up her seat on a bus.

1. Oliver Brown challenged the Board of Education in Topeka, Kansas. Oliver Brown said it violated his daughter's rights.

2. Linda Brown was denied admission to an all-white elementary school. The school was in her neighborhood.

3. Chief Justice Earl Warren wrote the decision. Justice Warren concluded that the idea of "separate but equal" did not belong in education.

4. One Southern town hit the national news when students tried to desegregate a school there. The town was Little Rock, Arkansas.

5. The angry mobs had to be stopped there. The National Guard was called out.

6. Protests called freedom rides were part of the civil rights movement. These rides were made by civil rights activists.

7. Before the freedom rides, the Supreme Court had made a decision. The Supreme Court banned segregation on buses and in bus terminals.

8. Buses and riders were attacked, and a firebomb was tossed into one bus. The firebomb set the bus on fire.

9. President Kennedy sent U.S. marshals. The U.S. marshals' job was to protect the freedom riders.

10. During sit-ins throughout the South, student protesters sat at segregated lunch counters. The students refused to move.

EXERCISE 6 Writing a Report Working Together

Use information on the timeline below and from Exercise 5 to write a report of several paragraphs about some of the key events of the civil rights movement. Order your report chronologically. When you have completed a draft, exchange it with a partner, and make suggestions for improving each other's report. As you revise or make suggestions for revision, combine related sentences by inserting phrases.

1954 Supreme Court orders desegregation of public schools in Brown v. Board of Education.

1955 Montgomery bus boycott begins.

1956 Supreme Court outlaws bus segregation.

1957 Dr. Martin Luther King, Jr., and other leaders founded the Southern Christian Leadership Conference (SCLC).

1957 African American students integrate Little Rock's Central High School.

1960 Students stage a sit-in at a Woolworth's lunch counter in Greensboro, North Carolina. This movement spreads rapidly throughout the South.

1960 The Student Nonviolent Coordinating Committee (SNCC) is formed.

1961 Freedom rides begin.

1963 March on Washington, D.C.; Martin Luther King, Jr., delivers his "I Have a Dream" speech.

Combining Sentences: Using Subordinate Clauses

▶ You can combine two sentences by turning one sentence into an adjective clause.

Begin the adjective clause with *who, which, that,* or another word from the list on page 155. Then insert the adjective clause to modify a noun or pronoun in the remaining sentence. If you create a nonessential adjective clause, don't forget the commas.

ORIGINAL   Madison Central won the debate. Madison is my high school.
COMBINED   Madison Central, **which won the debate,** is my high school.

ORIGINAL   The captain of the team is Sam Lin. He is very quick on his feet.
COMBINED   The captain of the team is Sam Lin, **who is very quick on his feet**.

▶ You can combine two sentences by turning one sentence into an adverb clause.

Use a subordinating conjunction to turn one sentence into an adverb clause. Then attach the adverb clause to the remaining sentence. Choose a subordinating conjunction that shows how the ideas in the two sentences are related. For example, *because* and *so that* show a cause-effect relationship. *While, when, before, after, until,* and *since* show a time relationship. In the margin is a list of subordinating conjunctions.

ORIGINAL   We took the ferry. The bridge was closed for repairs.
COMBINED   We took the ferry **because the bridge was closed for repairs**.

ORIGINAL   The bridge will reopen. It will have two additional lanes.
COMBINED   **When the bridge reopens**, it will have two additional lanes.

EXERCISE 7 Combining Sentences with Adjective Clauses

Combine each pair of sentences on the following page into a single sentence that contains an adjective clause. For the first two sentences, a word has been suggested in parentheses following each sentence; use this word to introduce the adjective clause. Write your combined sentences on a separate piece of paper, and underline the adjective clause. Remember to set off nonessential clauses with commas. **Hint:** As in the example, there may be more than one way to combine sentences.

Subordinating Conjunctions

Time
after	since
as long as	until
as soon as	when
before	while

Place
where	wherever

Cause
because	since

Comparison
as	than
as much as	whereas

Condition
although	though
as long as	unless
as if	while
even though	
provided that	

Purpose
so that	that
in order that	

EXAMPLE   Alexander Graham Bell invented the telephone. He was educated at
home. (who)
*Alexander Graham Bell, who invented the telephone, was educated
at home.*
*Alexander Graham Bell, who was educated at home, invented
the telephone.*

1. Bell was educated by his mother. She was hearing-impaired. (who)

2. She taught him the manual alphabet. He used it for communication with
her. (which)

3. Elisha Gray came close to inventing the telephone before Bell. His ideas
were similar to Bell's.

4. Both Bell and Gray did a series of experiments. The experiments were nearly
the same.

5. Gray is not credited with the invention. Gray was apparently every bit as
talented and capable as Bell.

EXERCISE 8 Combining Sentences with Adverb Clauses

Work with a partner to combine each pair of sentences into a single sentence
that contains an adverb clause. Choose a subordinating conjunction that
shows the relationship between the ideas. You may have to add, delete, or
change words. Write your combined sentences on a separate piece of paper,
and underline the adverb clauses. Remember to set off nonessential clauses
with commas.

EXAMPLE   Alexander Graham Bell was born in Scotland. Bell is one of the United
States' most well-known inventors.
*Although he was born in Scotland, Alexander Graham Bell became one of
the United States' most well-known inventors.*

1. All the elements needed for the creation of the telephone had been known for
forty years. Alexander Graham Bell put them together to make a phone.

2. Bell brought his ideas to the patent office. Elisha Gray brought his ideas to the
patent office a few hours later.

3. Both men could have easily been credited as the inventor. Bell got to the patent
office first.

4. Gray knew the human voice could be reproduced. He knew the correct number
of tones needed to be sent over a wire at the same time.

5. We think of Alexander Graham Bell. We think of the invention of
the telephone.

Eliminating Short, Choppy Sentences

One short sentence after another can be very boring. Combine short, choppy sentences by inserting the key word or words from one sentence into another sentence.

ORIGINAL The children played at the party. The children were young. They played contentedly. It was a birthday party.

COMBINED The **young** children played **contentedly** at the **birthday** party.

The combined sentence above sounds more interesting because it doesn't have unnecessary repetition. Moving the adjectives and adverb helped pick up the pace.

STEP BY STEP

Combining Sentences

Follow these steps in order.

1. Identify the sentence that gives the central information.
2. In other sentences, find key words and phrases that you can insert into the sentence you identified in Step 1.
3. Change key words as needed to create a smoothly flowing sentence.
4. Read the combined sentence to see if it sounds natural.

When you combine sentences, you sometimes change the form of a word or the order of modifiers. In the first example below, *constant* and *forceful* become *constantly* and *forcefully*. In the second example, *erupt regularly* becomes *regularly erupting* and *bubble and boil* become *bubbling, boiling*.

ORIGINAL Patrick Henry criticized England. He was a patriot. His criticism was constant and forceful.

COMBINED The **patriot** Patrick Henry **constantly** and **forcefully** criticized England.

ORIGINAL Yellowstone Park has geysers and hot springs. The geysers erupt regularly. The hot springs bubble and boil.

COMBINED Yellowstone Park has **regularly erupting** geysers and **bubbling, boiling** hot springs.

EXERCISE 9 Combining Sentences

Work with a partner to combine each group of sentences into a single sentence. Use a separate piece of paper if necessary. Compare your revised sentences with those of other pairs.

1. Madeleine Albright advised the President. She was Secretary of State. She advised the President of the United States.

2. She gave advice on political situations. These situations were international. They were often critical.

3. Albright came to this country as an immigrant. She was eleven. Her native country was the former Czechoslovakia.

4. Her father had criticized the government in his homeland. It was a Communist government. It was a newly formed government at the time.

5. She has also been the U.S. representative to the United Nations. She was appointed to that post.

EXERCISE 10 Revising a Paragraph

With a partner, improve the following paragraph. Look for opportunities to combine sentences. Compare your revised paragraph with those of other pairs.

[1]The widespread use of computers has introduced some new health problems. [2]These problems are serious. [3]A computer screen can be bad for your eyes. [4]This is true if the light from the screen is flickering. [5]It is true if the light is too bright. [6]It is true if the screen is too close to your eyes. [7]Use of the keyboard can be bad for your wrists. [8]This is especially true if you use the keyboard for long periods. [9]Another problem results from how your hands are positioned. [10]Fingers should not be too curled. [11]Wrists should not drop below the level of your fingers.

Eliminating Wordiness

Writing is most effective when it is direct and clear and when it is not weighed down with unnecessary words and phrases. Here are ways to achieve clarity in your writing.

▸ **Eliminate Extra Words.** Don't pad your writing with extra words to make it longer. Use words and phrases that make your writing succinct. In addition, avoid using empty words and phrases, which can obscure the points you wish to make.

ORIGINAL   Biologists, I know, have never doubted for an instant that elephants, young and old, can readily hear all kinds of airborne sounds from both near and far, but until recently, these scientists did not realize that these mighty giants of the Animal Kingdom can detect underground vibrations as well.

REVISED   Biologists have never doubted that elephants can readily hear all kinds of airborne sounds, but until recently, they did not realize that these animals can detect underground vibrations as well.

▸ **Eliminate Unnecessary Repetition.** In public speaking, repeating words or phrases can be a powerful way to persuade listeners. But unnecessary repetition in writing is simply another kind of padding. Avoid redundancy.

ORIGINAL   No matter what their breed's initial, original purpose or function was, many dogs today are dogs bred for shows or bred to be family pets.

REVISED   No matter what their breed's original purpose was, many dogs today are bred for shows or to be family pets.

▸ **Write in Your Own Voice.** Don't try to impress your audience with complicated sentences or with vocabulary you do not understand. Write what you mean as simply and as directly as you can.

ORIGINAL   Krill are diminutive invertebrates that feed nightly in the oceans' abundantly stocked surface waters and then, as they have done for eons, descend to unfathomable depths.

REVISED   Krill are small invertebrates that feed nightly in the oceans' rich surface waters and then descend to deep water.

EXERCISE 11 Revising Sentences

On a separate piece of paper, revise the following wordy sentences.

1. Reaching lengths of more than forty feet, the whale shark is the world's biggest, largest fish in the sea.

2. Unlike some of their more belligerent, aggressive relatives, whale sharks have gentle, docile dispositions.

3. The opportunity to swim with whale sharks has spawned lucrative money-making ecotourism industries in locales where these docile whale sharks congregate.

4. The lumbering slowness of whale sharks and their tendency to swim close to the water's surface make these elephantine creatures not only a favorite of snorkelers but also frequent victims of collisions with fishing trawlers, pleasure cruisers, and other kinds of ocean-going vessels, including naval ships, both flat-bottomed and otherwise.

5. I want to mention that, although surprisingly little is known about whale sharks, human interaction with these gargantuan sea creatures has been growing substantially and considerably in recent years.

EXERCISE 12 Revising a Paragraph to Eliminate Wordiness

On a separate piece of paper, revise the paragraph below to trim wordy expressions and make the writing as clear and economical as possible. Make any other changes that you think will improve the paragraph.

[1]Bursting, practically overflowing, with designated wetlands and waterfowl parks, the Canadian province of New Brunswick is a birdwatcher's idea of true paradise, an ideal place. [2]For example, up to 95% of the world's sandpipers calls the mudflats of the Bay of Fundy home. [3]Anyone would be awestruck by the awesome sight of seeing these birds airborne; when they coordinate their flying movements, the birds are nearly indistinguishable from a school of fish in flight, flying in the sky. [4]That's what some people claim who have witnessed the spectacle. [5]Birdwatchers also would not want to miss New Brunswick's Grand Manan Island because it exhibits not only eagles, but ospreys and puffins, too, which are quite riveting.

Revising and Editing Worksheet

Improve the following draft by revising for ideas, organization, word choice, and sentence variety. After revising, edit the draft for errors in spelling, capitalization, punctuation, and usage. Write your revised and edited version on a separate piece of paper. Compare your changes with those of a writing partner.

[1]The earliest methods of keeping time were based upon observations of the cycles of the sun. [2]They were based on observations of the cycles of the moon. [3]And they were also based on observations of the cycles of the stars. [4]By recording the periods in which these cycles took place, people were able to forecast natural events. [5]Natural events, as one might expect, affected their daily lives. [6]By recording these periods people were able to determine the intervals by which the measurement of time was based.

[7]Sundials, water clocks, and astrolabes were among the instruments of time measurements people used before the invention of the mechanical clock toward the end of the thirteenth century. [8]Astrolabes are devices for positioning celestial bodies. [9]Many of these early devices were designed primarily to perform two key functions. [10]The first function was to establish a calendar. [11]On this calendar, the dates of significant civil and religious ceremonies could be determined. [12]The calendar also showed the optimum time when planting crops could be scheduled. [13]It also showed the best time to harvest crops, in addition. [14]The second function of the calendar was to separate the periods of daylight and darkness. [15]This was a key function, too.

[16]Several early civilizations marked the beginning of the day by sunrise. [17]They marked the end of the day by sunset. [18]In ancient Egypt and in ancient Greece, both the period of daylight and the period of darkness were divided into twelve equal parts. [19]The hours of daylight and the hours of darkness varied in length according to the time of the year. [20]They were equal in length only on the first days of spring and fall. [21]These hours were called temporal hours. [22]They were in general use in Western civilization until the increased use of mechanical clocks. [23]These made it more practical for countries to gradually adopt a 24-equal-hour timekeeping system.

Writing Workshops

Narrative Writing: Biographical Essay

A biography tells a life story; a biographical essay usually zooms in on just one event or moment in a life or on one related series of events. It also conveys the significance of the event or related incidents.

The following excerpt is from Doris Kearns Goodwin's *No Ordinary Time*. The excerpt focuses on Eleanor Roosevelt, showing how she and her husband Franklin worked together as a team, each enriching the effectiveness of the other. Though part of a larger historical work, this excerpt works by itself as a biographical essay.

from No Ordinary Time
by Doris Kearns Goodwin

Introduces the topic

[1]During the past seven years in the White House, Eleanor [Roosevelt] . . . traveled more than 280,000 miles around the United States, the equivalent of nearly a hundred cross-country trips. [2]Franklin called Eleanor his "will o' the wisp" wife. [3]But it was Franklin who had encouraged her to become his "eyes and ears," to gather the grass-roots knowledge he needed to understand the people he governed. [4]Unable to travel easily on his own because of his paralysis, he had started by teaching Eleanor how to inspect state institutions in 1929, during his first term as governor [of New York].

Defines/limits topic

[5]"It was the best education I ever had," she later said. [6]Traveling across the state to inspect institutions for the insane, the blind, and the aged, visiting state prisons and reform schools, she had learned, slowly and painfully, through Franklin's tough, detailed questions upon her return, how to become an investigative reporter.

First incident

Presents concrete detail through dialogue

[7]Her first inspection was an insane asylum. [8]"All right," Franklin told her, "go in and look around and let me know what's going on there. [9]Tell me how the inmates are being treated." [10]When Eleanor returned, she brought with her a printed copy of the day's menu. [11]"Did you look to see whether they were actually getting this food?" Franklin asked. [12]"Did you lift a pot cover on the stove to check whether the contents corresponded with this menu?" [13]Eleanor shook her head. [14]Her untrained mind had taken in a general picture of the place but missed all the human details that would have brought it to life. [15]"But these are what I need," Franklin said. [16]"I never remembered things until Franklin taught me," Eleanor told a reporter. [17]"His memory is really prodigious. [18]Once he has checked something he never needs to look at it again."

Second incident

[19]"One time," she recalled, "he asked me to go and look at the state's tree shelter-belt plantings. [20]I noticed there were five rows of graduated size. . . .

Presents concrete detail through dialogue

[21]When I came back and described it, Franklin said: 'Tell me exactly what was in the first five rows. [22]What did they plant first?' [23]And he was so desperately disappointed when I couldn't tell him, that I put my best efforts after that into missing nothing and remembering everything."

[24]In time, Eleanor became so thorough in her inspections, observing the attitudes of patients toward the staff, judging facial expressions as well as the words, looking in closets and behind doors, that Franklin set great value on her reports. [25]"She saw many things the president could never see," Labor Secretary Frances Perkins said. [26]"Much of what she learned and what she understood about the life of the people of this country rubbed off onto FDR. [27]It could not have helped to do so because she had a poignant understanding. . . . [28]Her mere reporting of the facts was full of [a] sensitive quality that could never be escaped. . . . [29]Much of his seemingly intuitive understanding—about labor situations . . . about girls who worked in sweatshops—came from his recollections of what she had told him."

Sums up the significance by means of a quotation

Critical Thinking   After you read the biographical incident, answer the questions below.

1. What do you think is the purpose of Goodwin's writing? Who do you think is her audience?

2. What do the two incidents show about Eleanor and her eagerness to learn? How do they show that Eleanor and Franklin worked as a team?

3. What does the dialogue contribute to each incident?

4. Choose one of the two incidents that Goodwin reports, and pay close attention to how she relates it. Analyze (a) the order and (b) the amount of space given to each of the following: background information, setting, dialogue, and report of what happened. What kinds of details does Goodwin omit?

5. With a partner, read one of the incidents aloud. Analyze the sentences for variety in lengths, structures, and beginnings.

Build Your Vocabulary. Underline the words in the selection that you do not know. Use a dictionary to find each word's meaning, and write a brief definition in the margin or in your notebook. The following list may help: *asylum* (sentence 7), *prodigious* (sentence 17), *graduated* (sentence 20), *poignant* (sentence 27), *mere* (sentence 28), and *intuitive* (sentence 29).

Writing Strategies   The purpose of writing a biographical essay is not only to retell what happened but also to convey its significance. Your audience will be other students who are interested in your topic.

1. **Introduce your subject.** Anyone—someone you may or may not know personally—who interests you can be a subject for a biographical essay. Engage your reader by introducing your subject as a character, and set the scene by describing events, settings, and other characters with whom your subject interacts.

2. **Use narrative techniques.** As you write, use narrative techniques, such as description and dialogue, to develop experiences, events, and characters. Use precise language to paint a vivid picture of your subject, and make sure your word choice is appropriate for your audience. Research to find relevant quotations from your subject to enliven the biography and give it depth. Using a person's own words helps reveal the subject's unique voice and character.

3. **Think in chronological, or time, order.** In most cases, biographical events are retold in the order in which they occurred, but not always. Use transition words and other techniques, such as foreshadowing or flashbacks, to sequence events so that they build on one another to create a coherent narrative.

4. **Ask questions.** Your readers will want to know *Who? What (happened)? Where? When? Why?* and *How?* (For more about these questions, see page 11.) Be sure to provide enough background information to capture the character of your chosen subject.

5. **Reveal the significance.** Each detail and event you describe will help the reader understand the significance of your subject. Reflect on why the subject is important to you by including your own thoughts and feelings.

6. **Wrap up concisely.** Conclude in a way that reflects briefly on the subject, the experiences, and the observations you described in the narrative. Make sure you show why your subject is important to you, and leave your readers with a final thought, impression, or insight.

WRITING HINT

If you know the subject of your biography, your approach may be more personal, and your tone may be less formal and distant than, say, that of a professional biographer telling about the life of a president. Even if your subject is famous, however, it's fine to let your attitudes and opinions slip into the picture. You can do this through your tone, which may be friendly, respectful, harshly critical, or full of wonder.

EXERCISE 1 Choose a Subject

Think of a person who interests you. Select someone familiar or someone about whom you know a great deal; otherwise, be prepared to do some research. Then use brainstorming, clustering, freewriting, or asking *5–W and How?* questions to begin focusing on an event or related series of incidents in that person's life. You might talk about lessons learned. You might also zero in on a specific incident that is funny, embarrassing, sad, or heartwarming. Continue to explore people and to employ prewriting techniques until you have come up with a person and an event or a related series of events.

EXERCISE 2 Plan Your Biographical Essay

Use the planner below—or create one like it—to organize your ideas or to outline your biographical essay. Adapt it for your biographical essay: In other words, if setting is not important in your story, there is no reason to include it; on the other hand, if there is a conflict, then note it. Similarly, if there are four key events in your "story," add more events to the Body section of the organizer.

Introduction
- Introduce subject

   Identify setting

Body
   Event 1

   Event 2

   Event 3

Conclusion
   Overall statement
   of significance

EXERCISE 3 Draft Your Biographical Essay

Using your organizer from Exercise 2 as a guide, draft your essay for an audience of your classmates. As you develop each body paragraph, keep your purpose in mind to help your classmates "see" or better understand your subject. As you draft, make sure you do the following:

- **Introduction** Create interest by starting off with an attention-grabbing quotation, an intriguing question, or a vivid image. Introduce the subject of your essay in a striking way. Set the stage by providing any necessary information about time and place.

- **Body** As you introduce events, bring them to life with specific sensory details. Add dialogue if it is interesting and helps reveal character, conflict, or significance. Tell events in order, and use transitional words and phrases to clarify their relationships. Keep your audience in mind: Remember to put down on paper everything that the audience needs to know to understand these events and their significance.

- **Conclusion** Sum up the significance that these events had for your subject. Consider using a quotation to strengthen your conclusion.

EXERCISE 4 Revise Your Biographical Essay

Try reading your paper aloud to yourself. Revise so that the organization is clear, and rewrite as needed so that your sentences read smoothly. Then—or at the same time—focus on your word choice. See if you can find precise words to replace vague, general nouns and verbs. Revise your essay to eliminate repetition and unnecessary words. When you are satisfied with your paper, share it with a partner, and ask for comments, questions, and suggestions.

EXERCISE 5 Edit and Publish Your Biographical Essay

Check your revised paper for errors in grammar, usage, spelling, punctuation, and capitalization. Exchange papers with a partner—or several partners—to see if you've missed anything.

Share your biographical essay with any students who are interested in the person you have written about. You may even want to write more "chapters" about this person to create—at least eventually—a full-length biography. You may also want to write a biography of an older relative, friend, or neighbor to preserve his or her memories for younger members of the family or community.

Persuasive Writing: Editorial

When you write to persuade, you try to make your reader agree with your opinion. To do so, you present an **argument:** a thesis statement, or claim, followed by a logical presentation of reasons and evidence that support and develop the claim.

You build an argument based on the **logical appeals** of reasons and evidence. You may also add **emotional appeals** to persuade by influencing your reader's feelings. An editorial is an argument that appears on special pages of a newspaper. As you read the editorial below, think about how the writer tries to persuade you. Look for the place-ment of the claim and the kinds of reasons and explanations used to support the claim. Listen to the writer's tone. Also, think about the word choices. Remember that all words have **denotations**, the meanings found in dictionaries, and that many words and expressions also have **connotations**, or emotional associations. These are often called **loaded words**. One way that writers appeal to readers' emotions is by choosing words with positive or negative connotations.

Voters' Ed

by John B. Anderson and Ray Martinez III

from *The New York Times*, April 6, 2006

[1]High school seniors already have a lot on their minds: SAT's, college acceptance letters, job applications. [2]But our democracy should demand something else of these 18-year-olds: that they prepare to cast their first-ever vote in this fall's Congressional elections.

Grabs reader's attention

States position in thesis statement, or claim

[3]Unfortunately, all too many young people will graduate from high school without registering to vote and without even taking a class on the basics of voting. [4]We need a new "leave no voter behind" policy.

States the problem

Restates position

[5]There is precedent for us to build on. [6]In 1993, Congress passed the National Voter Registration Act, which promoted voter registration at motor vehicle and social service agencies. [7]A recent survey by the federal Election Assistance Commission measured steady increases in voter registration since passage of the law.

Recalls an earlier partial remedy for the problem

[8]Still, only 72 percent of eligible citizens were registered to vote in 2004, according to the Census Bureau. [9]And the registration rate among 18- to 24-year-olds was a dismal 58 percent, which helps explain why voter turnout for this age group in the presidential election was far below the national average. [10]That's simply unacceptable.

Supports position with statistics

[11]We propose automatic voter registration for all high school seniors; our goal is the registration of all eligible students before they graduate.

Proposes a solution to the problem

Makes an emotional appeal [12]This approach would be a change from relying on private, nonprofit organizations to register most voters. [13]But it's a change worth making. [14]High schools, after all, are the ideal environments in which to introduce young Americans to voting and to impress upon them the importance of active participation in our democratic system.

Supports position with statistics and additional factual information [15]Some jurisdictions have, in fact, already taken steps to establish school-based voter registration programs. [16]In New York City, public high school graduates get registration forms with their diplomas. [17]Hawaii allows citizens to pre-register at 16, making it easier to achieve 100 percent student registration. [18]And in Vermont, Secretary of State Deborah L. Markowitz has designated a "high school voter registration week."

Supports position with additional factual information [19]Many high schools require students to fulfill a certain number of community service hours to graduate. [20]Under our plan, that community service could include working in election offices. [21]The hope here is that we would be training the next generation of election administrators and, equally important, providing poll workers who are comfortable with computers—a desirable qualification given our increasingly modern voting systems.

[22]Finally, high school government or civics classes should not only explain to students how to vote in their community but also emphasize the value of lifelong voter participation.

Addresses a counterargument [23]Some election officials might worry that automatic voter registration would create more work. **Refutes counter- argument with analysis of factual information** [24]But systematically registering students in classes would decrease the number of errors on registration forms, teach students about how best to change their addresses and get absentee ballots, and ease the burden of processing new registrations near Election Day. [25]New statewide voter registration lists should also help reduce the likelihood of duplicate names. [26]Ultimately, election officials would save time and money.

Restates claim in conclusion [27]Of course, voter registration is no guarantee of turnout, but it is the first —and often, most difficult—step. [28]There is perhaps no better place to begin this critical task than our high schools. [29]By improving our registration and education efforts, we will not only help protect the voting preferences of younger Americans but the long-term vitality of our participatory **Concludes with a call to action** democracy. [30]Let's not leave any voters behind.

John B. Anderson, a candidate for president in 1980, was the chairman of FairVote, which promotes fair elections. Ray Martinez III serves on the United States Election Assistance Commission.

Critical Thinking   After you read the editorial, answer the questions below.

1. Who is the audience for this editorial? What is its purpose?

2. Briefly outline the editorial. What is the writers' opinion on the issue?

3. Do you agree with the statement in sentence 14: "High schools, after all, are the ideal environments in which to introduce young Americans to voting and to impress upon them the importance of active participation in our democratic system"? Explain your answer.

4. In sentence 23, the authors write "Some election officials might worry that automatic voter registration would create more work." Do the authors address this concern effectively? Why or why not?

5. Is this piece of persuasive writing effective? Why or why not?

Build Your Vocabulary. List at least two words or phrases from the editorial that you consider to be "loaded." Explain the connotations these words or phrases carry that go beyond their literal, dictionary meanings.

Writing Strategies   When you write persuasively, you present your opinion on a topic or on an issue that you feel strongly about. The audience is, typically, people who do not share your opinion. Your purpose is to sway the members of your audience so that they can see your point of view. To write persuasive pieces effectively, keep the following strategies in mind.

1. **Present your opinion clearly in your claim.** State your **claim** as clearly as you can in a single sentence or two. Use precise language and an objective tone to focus your argument. In an argument, the claim usually comes in the introduction—but not always.

2. **State reasons for your claim.** A **reason** is a statement that tells why you hold your **claim**. Usually, two or three strong and distinctly different reasons are the minimum number required to support a claim. Include a new paragraph for each new reason, and state the reason clearly in the paragraph's topic sentence.

3. **Support your reasons with relevant evidence.** Use the strongest evidence to support your relevant evidence. Don't stick to just one kind of evidence—use several different kinds.

- A **fact** is a statement that can be proven. Make sure that you get your facts from reliable reference sources. One effective way to introduce such facts is to begin with a reputable or known source, as in "According to historian Stephen E. Ambrose in *Undaunted Courage*, . . ."

- Use **expert** opinions and quotations. Be sure to identify the expert and, when you are quoting, use his or her exact words. Again, you may want to introduce such expert opinion in this way: "As Ira Glass noted on National Public Radio, . . ."

> ## STEP BY STEP
>
> Build an argument this way:
> 1. Present your claim.
> 2. Support it with your first reason. Develop that reason with evidence, including facts, examples, statistics, and other support.
> 3. Repeat the process with your second and third reasons.
> 4. End strongly, restating your claim. Add a call to action, when appropriate.

- **Statistics** are facts expressed in numbers, such as "In the 2012 presidential election, only fifty-seven percent of all registered voters showed up at the polls."

- A **definition** is a statement of meaning. You can use definitions for clarification, as reminders of your focus, or as a way to express your point of view.

- An **example** is a particular type or instance used as an illustration. For a paper on why dress codes don't work, the writer might say, "A dress code was instituted at Liberty High in January 2004, but it has never had a favorable reaction from students."

- An **anecdote** is a brief true story; it sometimes introduces the writer's personal experiences or observations. An interesting anecdote can have an emotional impact, but use it only when it fits your topic and audience.

4. **Use emotional appeals sparingly.** Persuasive writers sometimes appeal to a reader's fears, hopes, wishes, or sense of fairness. Loaded words—words with clear positive or negative connotations—can sway the reader's emotions. They can also make the writing sound like unsubstantiated opinion or advertising copy. Use emotional appeals selectively.

5. **Anticipate and refute counterarguments.** A **counterargument,** or **counterclaim,** is a viewpoint that is the opposite of your opinion and claim. Address a counterargument by first acknowledging its strengths and some possible weaknesses in your own argument. Then refute the counterargument by using logical reasoning and evidence to reveal its weaknesses or limitations. Ideally, use your logical response to the counterargument as further evidence that your argument is more convincing.

6. **Include transitions.** Use a variety of transitional words and phrases to link your ideas. Connect claims to reasons, link reasons to evidence, and distinguish claims from counterclaims. Transitions can also connect ideas across paragraphs and help readers follow your argument.

7. **Establish a formal style and objective tone.** Your style and tone, or your attitude toward your subject, is crucial in winning your reader's respect. Maintain a formal style and confident, objective tone to suggest you are reliable and knowledgeable about your topic. Keep your tone reasonable and respectful, particularly when refuting counterarguments.

8. **End with a call to action.** End your argument with a concise conclusion that supports your claim and follows logically from the evidence presented. Some kinds of persuasive writing, like editorials, end with a **call to action** that urges the reader to do something—write a letter, donate money, or participate in an event, for example.

EXERCISE 6 Choose a Topic

Work with a partner or small group to brainstorm at least six topics for a persuasive essay. Use these hints.

- Decide on something you feel strongly about. Consider things you wish you could change in your own school or neighborhood. You might even think about things you would like to change in your state or country or in the world.

- Make sure your topic is arguable. No one would say that the environment is not important, for instance. But people would argue strongly about the best ways to protect it, as well as the degree of protection or intervention required.

- Keep in mind that not every topic is suitable for a school assignment. Check with your teacher if you are unsure about the appropriateness of your topics.

EXERCISE 7 Analyze Claims

With a small group, analyze each of the following three claims.
Decide which is strongest, and tell why. Give suggestions for improving the others.

(a) Everyone should see *Citizen Kane* by Orson Welles; this is the best movie that was ever made.

(b) Cutting funding for the high school band is a mistake for many reasons. It will diminish one of the greatest assets of Concord High and therefore

reduce school pride and spirit; it will send a message to our students and
our community that music is not important; and it will hurt students
currently in the program.

(c) In my opinion, the student council needs to be reorganized because it is
operating poorly, not benefiting anyone at Millbrook High.

EXERCISE 8 Write a Claim

Choose one of the topics you brainstormed in Exercise 6. On a separate piece of
paper, state your claim on your chosen topic in one or two clear sentences.
You might draft several versions of your claim and then choose the best one.

EXERCISE 9 Consider Your Audience

Before you begin drafting, be sure you have given adequate thought to your
audience and the relationship of your topic to that audience. On a separate
piece of paper, answer the following questions.

1. Why should your audience care about this issue?

2. In what ways can your audience help solve the problem or take the action you
   are calling for?

3. How well informed is your audience on this topic? What might the members of
   that audience not know? What do they already know well? How can you deepen
   their understanding of the issues?

4. Can you see a weakness in your argument or some strength in the opposing point
   of view? What counterarguments can you offer?

5. In what other ways can you sway your audience to accept your point of view?

EXERCISE 10 Develop Your Argument

Be sure your reasons are both strong and persuasive. Once you have gathered
information on your topic, use the organizer on page 59 to plan the body of
your persuasive essay. Remember that each topic sentence should be directly
related to your claim. For evidence, be sure to include specific examples, facts, and
statistics from reliable sources. Keep in mind other types of evidence as well, including
quotations and definitions.

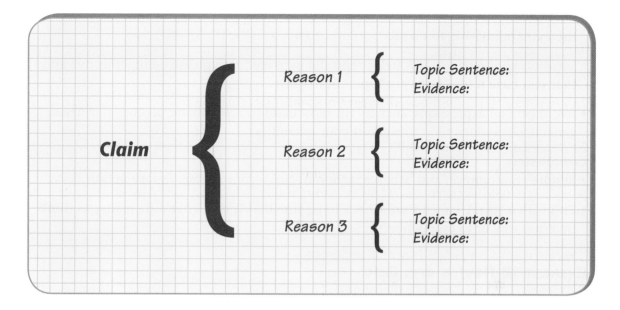

EXERCISE 11 Draft Your Persuasive Essay

As you draft your persuasive essay, be clear and stay focused. Make sure that your claim, reasons, evidence, and counterarguments are logically organized. Each of your reasons should clearly support your claim, and each piece of evidence should clearly support your reasons. Use precise language, and avoid including irrelevant evidence or unnecessary repetition. Also keep the following guidelines in mind:

Introduction
• Grab your reader's attention.

• State your claim clearly. Briefly introduce the strong and persuasive reasons that you will develop in each body paragraph.

• Give the reader helpful cues, perhaps by mentioning the number of reasons you will develop ("I oppose the dress code for three reasons . . .") or by providing a guide to your method of organization ("First, I'll start with the most important reason . . .").

Body
• Begin each paragraph with a topic sentence, which should be a clear statement of each reason. Make sure each reason strongly and directly supports your opinion.

• Use transitional words and phrases such as *first, second, in addition,* and *furthermore* to link paragraphs and sentences.

- Provide ample support for each reason. The more support you give for each reason, the more persuasive you'll be.

- Mention your sources. This helps send the message that you are being objective and that you have researched your topic thoroughly.

- Avoid general expressions, such as "in most cases . . ." or "many people. . . ." These general expressions tend to weaken your reliability.

Conclusion
- Restate your opinion and, when appropriate, urge your readers to take action.

- End with a strong conclusion. Check to be sure that it challenges the reader to think in a new way or to take action on an issue.

EXERCISE 12 Revise and Edit

Revise your essay by adding, deleting, or moving content. Eliminate unnecessary words, vary sentence structures, and add more transitions where they are needed. This will help you tighten your argument. Also, evaluate your reasons and your use of supporting details. Be sure your details are both substantial and clear. Also make sure your arguments aren't too emotional. Although emotional appeals can add force to your argument, you cannot rely on them exclusively. Remember that a persuasive writer should appear logical, reasonable, and well informed. After revising, edit your essay to correct mistakes in spelling, punctuation, capitalization, and usage.

EXERCISE 13 Publish Your Persuasive Essay

Share your essay with a writing group, or use the following publishing suggestions.

- Send your persuasive essay to a school or community official, or to another local or national leader who might act on the issue you've discussed. You might also post it to a related blog.

- Submit your essay to a local television or radio station that may be interested in publicizing your issue.

Writing About Literature: Analyzing Poetry

There are many different ways to write about a poem. Here are three of the most typical.

1. In a **personal response** essay, you write about how you felt and what you thought as you read; about the lines, images, or ideas that seemed particularly meaningful; and about other works that the poem brought to mind.

2. In an **evaluation**, you discuss the weaknesses and strengths of the poem. To do so, you use objective **criteria**, or standards commonly used to measure the worth of poetry. For example, you might base your evaluation on how fresh the images are, how well the poet uses his or her form, and how well the poem conveys an idea or creates a dominant impression.

3. In a **literary analysis**, you discuss one or more of the **elements** or features of the poem. These elements include form, the manner or style of literary composition; sound devices such as rhythm, rhyme, assonance, alliteration, and consonance; the speaker; the setting; and the language, including figurative language, symbolism, imagery, and connotations. You might also discuss what a poem means or what it reflects about the poet.

The following literary analysis treats the freshness and newness of E. E. Cummings's poetry. The writer focuses on just one poem, "The Cubist Break-Up," to show how Cummings embraced and recreated Cubism in his own characteristic and refreshing way. Cubism, led by Pablo Picasso, was an art movement in early twentieth-century Europe that embraced the idea that the artist's conception of a subject, not its outward appearance, is its entity.

Enriching Your Vocabulary

The root of the noun *enigma* and its adjective form used on page 62, *enigmatic*, is the Greek verb *ainissesthai*, meaning "to speak in riddles." An *enigma* is a baffling or inexplicable person or situation. The bicycle at the bottom of the swimming pool was an *enigma* to the lifeguards.

E. E. Cummings and Cubism
by Wendy R. Diskin

[1]What is equally as amazing as E. E. Cummings's style of writing is his wide range of subjects. [2]The reader gets the sense that nothing in Cummings's public or private life has been left unwritten. [3]Indeed, sometimes it seems that what unites two poems such as "in Just—" and "somewhere I have never travelled,gladly beyond" could only be the distinctive lowercases, spaces, and misspelled words. [4]But that is not entirely correct; there is something throughout all his subjects that is alike even beyond their arrangement on

— Attention grabber

Quotation	the page. [5]Richard S. Kennedy, in *Dreams in the Mirror*, describes Cummings's quality best as "his joyous acceptance of whatever life will bring" (xvii). [6]Cummings, in other words, attacks each subject with a vivacity and playfulness that is unique and refreshing.
General statement	[7]"The Cubist Break-Up" demonstrates several things that are characteristic of Cummings. [8]There is, most obviously, the poem's physical composition on the page: its lines are broken up and spaced somewhat
Examples and explanation	randomly on the page. [9]Cummings, as Kennedy explains (31–33), was a great admirer of Picasso's Cubist work. [10]Consequently, it is likely that Cummings strives to duplicate the confusion and symmetry of Cubist paintings in this poem.
General statement	[11]The words in the poem convey the blending and contorting effect of Cubism. [12]Oxymorons, such as "the awful beauty" (l. 13) and "the becoming
Words from the poem with line numbers	garden of her agony" (l. 18), bend conventional meaning and ask the reader to find new interpretations of recognizable words and objects. [13]A Cubist painting asks the same thing of its viewer.
General statement Explanation	[14]The joy that Cummings had for whatever life will bring is also apparent in this poem. [15]Cummings embraced Cubism because of its newness, its daring, its willingness to try the impossible. [16]Almost needless to say, there are many even today who turn away from experiments such as Cubism (or Cummings's style) because of this same enigmatic quality.
Lines from the poem with line numbers	[17]Cummings was not afraid, however. [18]His love for this new perspective is evident in these lines: "As/peacefully,/lifted/into the awful beauty/of sunset/the young city/putting off dimension with a blush" (ll. 10–16). [19]Cummings recognizes the beauty of the clamor, crackle, and collapse of jutting planes in Picasso's paintings; I believe the reader can find the same beauty in the sag, splintering, and rasp of Cummings's poetry.

Works Cited

Kennedy, Richard S. *Dreams in the Mirror: A Biography of E. E. Cummings*. New York: W.W. Norton & Company, 1980.

Critical Thinking   After reading the literary analysis, answer the questions below.

1. What is the writer's thesis, or claim? Is it stated or implied? How would you improve it?

2. How does the writer back up the thesis? Identify the kinds of explanation and supporting details used.

3. How does the writer introduce the essay? What do you find effective or ineffective about this introduction?

4. How does the writer conclude the essay? What do you find effective or ineffective about this conclusion?

Build Your Vocabulary. Underline the words in the selection that you do not know. Use a dictionary to find each word's meaning, and write a brief definition in the margin or in your notebook. The following list may help: *vivacity* (sentence 6), *symmetry* (sentence 10), *oxymoron* and *conventional* (sentence 12), *perspective* (sentence 18), and *clamor* and *rasp* (sentence 19).

Writing Strategies   The purpose of writing a literary analysis of poetry is to explain your interpretation of a poem, usually by focusing on just one or two elements of it. Use the following strategies as you write.

1. Choose a poem. You might look for a poem that surprised or disturbed you, a poem that helped you see something in a new way, or a poem that expressed some of your own thoughts and feelings. You might simply choose a poem that you feel you understand well or one that you know you have something to say about.

2. Decide on a focus. Although there is a wide range of things you can write about in a literary analysis, often it's best to focus on just one or two elements. To find your focus, try answering these sets of questions:

Sound Is there alliteration (repeated initial consonant sounds, as in *a tale of terror*) or assonance (repeated internal vowel sounds, as in *high tide*)? If there is onomatopoeia (the use of words to suggest sounds, as in the **howling** *of the wind*), what effect does it create? What is the rhyme scheme (the pattern of the matching of final vowel or consonant sounds in two or more words)? Is the rhythm (the recurrence of accent or stress in lines of verse) slow and stately, bouncy, dancing, jangling, or syncopated? Is free verse (poetry without a regular pattern of meter or rhyme) used? Why?

Speaker Who is speaking? How much or how little do you learn about this person? Is the poem about the speaker? Remember that the speaker may not be the same person as the poet.

Form Is the poem divided into stanzas? If not, why not? Has the poet used a familiar form such as a haiku or a sonnet, and if so, how does this form affect the meaning of the poem?

Figurative Language What is personified, and why? What comparisons are made by means of metaphors and similes? How does the figurative language help make the meaning, or the expression of the meaning, new and fresh?

Other Uses of Language What can you hear, see, touch, taste, or feel? Is there a pattern of imagery, as in the use of color? Does the poem contain symbols? What do they mean? How has the poet built in multiple word meanings or connotations?

Theme (Meaning) What central idea does the poem convey? How do the other elements illustrate this idea? Is there an insight into life that intrigues you?

3. **Prewrite.** In addition to answering the questions above, remember that you can brainstorm, cluster, or freewrite.

4. **Write your draft.** Throughout the entire essay—and whenever you refer to characters, events, or themes in literature—use the **literary present tense**.

> In A. E. Housman's "When I was one-and-twenty," the speaker **remembers** when he was twenty-one. The message **is** one of wisdom gained over time.

In addition, be sure your style and tone are formal. Avoid contractions, sentence fragments, and slang. Keep this advice in mind as you draft each part of your literary analysis.

5. **Write the introduction.** Identify the poem and the poet. Very briefly introduce what the poem is about, such as "the suffering of the soldiers in World War I." Present a thesis statement, or claim, about one or more of the poetic elements that you think are significant in the poem. As with any thesis statement you write, be as specific as possible about why the element is important and about what you will say about it in the body of your paper.

> See
> **Mechanics**,
> Lessons 14.4
> and 14.5, for
> help with
> punctuation of
> quotations.

6. **Write the body.** Each paragraph should make at least one clear, general statement about the poem. Within each paragraph, provide strong support for each general statement, using phrases or lines from the poem to support your claims. Enclose quoted words and lines in quotation marks followed by parentheses containing the line number(s) in which they are found. For example, you might write, "When Housman refers to the 'wise man' (l. 2), . . ." In this case, you are referring to just one line, and the abbreviation is "l." When you are referring to many lines, place a slash (/) between each, and write "ll." for *lines* ["And I am two-and-twenty,/And oh, 'tis true, 'tis true" (ll. 15–16)]. You may also quote or summarize what an expert has to say—as long as you properly introduce and document your source.

WRITING HINT

When you are quoting from a poem:

- be sure you quote the exact words.
- enclose single words, phrases, and lines in quotation marks. Follow each quotation with the line number or numbers in parentheses.
- use a slash within quotations to show where one line ends and a new one begins.
- follow the capitalization used in the poem.

7. **Write the conclusion.** In a new and fresh way, restate, summarize, or reflect on the meaning of the poem or the importance of the element(s) you have just analyzed.

EXERCISE 14 Prewriting: Choose a Topic

Choose a poem that you have already read and want to write about. Use the questions from Strategy 2 on pages 63–64 about the elements of poetry to help you choose one literary element to write about. Of all the elements, connotation, imagery, and figurative language tend to yield the best topics; however, each poem is different. Sometimes, it may be the speaker that sets a poem apart; at other times, it may be the symbolism or sound.

EXERCISE 15 Prewriting: Major Points and Supporting Details

1. Reread the poem carefully. The more times you read a poem, the more likely you are to develop a good understanding of it. Ask yourself questions, and use a dictionary to explore the possible multiple meanings or obscure meanings of words. Take notes.

2. Write your two or three main points—your general statements—on the organizer below.

3. From the main points, draft a thesis statement, or claim, a single sentence that expresses what you will cover in your essay. Don't agonize about it; you can change it later.

4. List specific details (quotations, incidents, examples) that prove each main point, and mark the strongest details with a check.

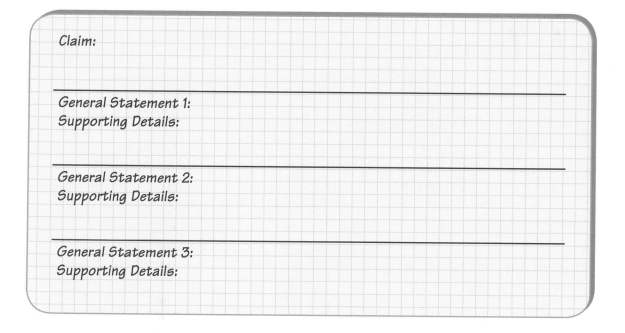

Claim:

General Statement 1:
Supporting Details:

General Statement 2:
Supporting Details:

General Statement 3:
Supporting Details:

Exercise 16 Draft Your Literary Analysis

Use the organizer from Exercise 15 as a guide when you draft. It will help you write part of your introduction (the thesis statement) as well as the body of your analysis. Be sure also to add a conclusion, as well as a title that suggests both the work and your essay's focus. As you write, remember to provide the words and phrases that will create transitions and help readers make the connections between your ideas. Keep in mind, however, that your draft does not have to be perfect. At this point, it is better simply to get your ideas down on paper than to worry about things such as spelling and grammar.

Exercise 17 Revise Your Essay

Let your draft sit awhile. Then use the revision strategies suggested in Lesson 1.3. Read for ideas and content, clear organization, and appropriate word choice for your purpose and audience. As you and your writing partners revise, ask these questions.

- Have you written in a unified and coherent way? Do all the general statements (your main ideas) relate to the thesis statement? Is each general statement backed up with specific information and text evidence?

- Are the general statements clear and concise?

- Have you elaborated each general statement by quoting or directly referring to the text?

Exercise 18 Edit and Publish Your Essay

Double-check each quotation for accuracy and also for correct punctuation. When you are satisfied that you have corrected all errors in grammar, usage, and mechanics, exchange papers with a partner who will check for any errors you might have missed.

You might also form a reading group with others who wrote about the same poem or about a different poem by the same poet. Take turns reading your papers aloud. See where you agree and disagree, justify or modify your views, and discuss the variety of elements you chose to focus on.

You might compile a "lit crit" anthology of everyone's essays analyzing poetry. Share it with other English classes.

Expository Writing: Cause-and-Effect Essay

When you write a cause-and-effect essay, you explain the relationship between an **effect** and the event or events that preceded it or the **causes** that led up to it. You might explain just one cause and its many effects or just one effect and its many causes. Whether the causes and effects are single or multiple—and whether you are focusing more on causes or more on effects—your purpose is the same: to make a clear connection between results and causes.

The following newspaper article is a cause-and-effect essay that details a number of causes and effects. See how many you can identify as you read.

Evolution Shortens Tusks
by Paul Brown

[1]Evolution is saving elephants in Africa by producing herds with tiny tusks or none at all—which provides no profit for poachers and thus ensures the survival of the species.

States cause→effect→cause

[2]The phenomenon has been noticed in all parts of Africa where hunting has been going on longest, with both trophy hunters and poachers always shooting elephants with the biggest tusks.

[3]A survey in the Queen Elizabeth National Park in Uganda in the 1930s showed that only 1 percent of adult elephants were without tusks. [4]Then it was regarded as a rare mutation.

Uses statistics to back up claim

[5]This year Eve Abe, of the Ugandan wildlife authority, found that 30 percent of adult elephants in the same area were without tusks.

[6]Richard Barnwell, World Wide Fund for Nature conservation officer for Africa, said the trend toward elephants having smaller tusks or none had been noticed all over the savannah area of West Africa, where elephants had been hunted the longest.

Introduces expert who clearly relates the cause and effect

[7]"All the elephants with genes that produce big tusks have been taken out of the population. [8]Those that remain either have small tusks or none at all." [9]He said it was now rare to find a big tusker in Cameroon, Nigeria, Ghana, the Ivory Coast, Niger, or Mali.

[10]Another attribute aiding elephant survival is bad temper. [11]Elephants were hunted almost to extinction in South Africa at the end of the nineteenth century. [12]One small herd in what is now the Addo National Park on the edge of the Indian Ocean survived, however. [13]Barnwell said this was partly because these elephants were known to be very bad-tempered and did not have particularly large tusks. [14]"Elephants are very intelligent and can be very dangerous if they are prone to bad temper. [15]Hunters decided that trying to kill

Second cause→effect

them was not worth the risk, so being bad-tempered is a survival technique, too."

Explanatory cause-and-effect support

[16]Poaching in the Queen Elizabeth National Park reduced elephant numbers from 3,500 animals in 1963 to 200 in 1992. [17]Now the population is 1,200 and is growing quickly. [18]The difficulty of finding an elephant with large enough tusks is defeating commercial poaching.

[19]Lack of tusks is not all good news for elephants, however. [20]Bulls, male elephants, fight for the right to mate with females, and in this respect large tusks are a big advantage. [21]This is why bulls with big tusks developed in the first place.

Further explanation of causes and effects

[22]An additional advantage is that tusks are used as tools, particularly in the dry season for digging in river beds [when elephants are] looking for water. [23]Barnwell said this did not particularly matter in Queen Elizabeth National Park because water was plentiful, but for dry savannah elephants, it could be crucial.

[24]In parts of central Africa, elephants are hunted for their value as meat, so even being without tusks is no help.

[25]He added: "The fact is that elephants with big tusks would come back if we stopped hunting them. [26]Large tusks are an adaptation that took place to help survival. [27]The message of all this is that we are forcing a change in elephants which is not necessarily to their advantage. [28]If they are to survive, we need to look after them."

Critical Thinking   After you read the cause-and-effect essay, answer the questions below.

1. What is the purpose of this article? Who do you think is the audience?

2. What, in your own words, is the main idea of the article?

3. What does the author use to help explain the connection between the cause, having big tusks, and the effect, being hunted? What else is used to explain and support this relationship?

4. The main effect that is examined and explained in this article is the increasing survival rate of elephants. What else, besides small tusks, is contributing to, or partly causing, this survival? Why?

5. The evolutionary effect of smaller tusks is itself a cause of other problems. What are they?

6. Working with a partner, draw a graphic organizer to represent the various causes and effects discussed in this article. Use arrows, circles, or boxes. See the graphic organizers on page 70, for example.

Build Your Vocabulary. Look for the following words in context, and discuss what each word means: *poachers* (sentence 1), *mutation* (sentence 4), *attribute* (sentence 10), *extinction* (sentence 11), and *adaptation* (sentence 26). If you can't define or aren't sure of any word's meaning, check a dictionary, and add the word to your vocabulary notebook.

Writing Strategies   The purpose of writing a cause-and-effect essay is to analyze the connection between causes and/or effects of a particular situation or event. The audience may be any that you choose or any that would have an interest in your topic. Use the following suggestions as you write.

1. Choose a topic. Look for something that is changing now or has changed over time. This can be something in your daily experience at home or at school—or it can be something far away. As topics come to mind, probe them by asking *Why? What caused this?* or *What's the result? What effect has this had or does it have?*

2. Gather information. If the topic is a personal or everyday one, gather information through your own experience or from people around you. If the topic is something outside your daily experience, use print and digital sources from the library or the Internet. As you gather information, you may begin to deal with multiple causes and/or multiple effects. Don't worry. A good cause-and-effect essay can connect them all.

> **WRITING HINT**
>
> As you explore connections between causes and effects, avoid the **false cause-effect fallacy**. Just because one event follows another, don't assume that the first event is the cause of the second. For example, if you get sick after a meal, you could incorrectly assume you ate something bad. In reality, a stomach virus may have caused your sickness.

3. Create a diagram. It will help if you can see what you're about to say. See page 70 for some possibilities for visually representing cause-and-effect. Choose or adapt the graphic organizer that best suits your topic.

> For help with punctuating introductory sentence elements, parenthetical elements, words such as *therefore*, and other transitional expressions, see Lessons 13.3 and 13.4.

4. Write your thesis statement, or claim. Once you have represented the causes and effects visually, you can use your diagram to write your thesis statement, or claim. The best thesis statement will clearly but briefly state causes and effects. It might also cue the reader in to your organization by stating, for example, "three main results." Alternatively, you might suggest multiple effects or interrelated effects with a thesis statement, such as "this led to a chain of

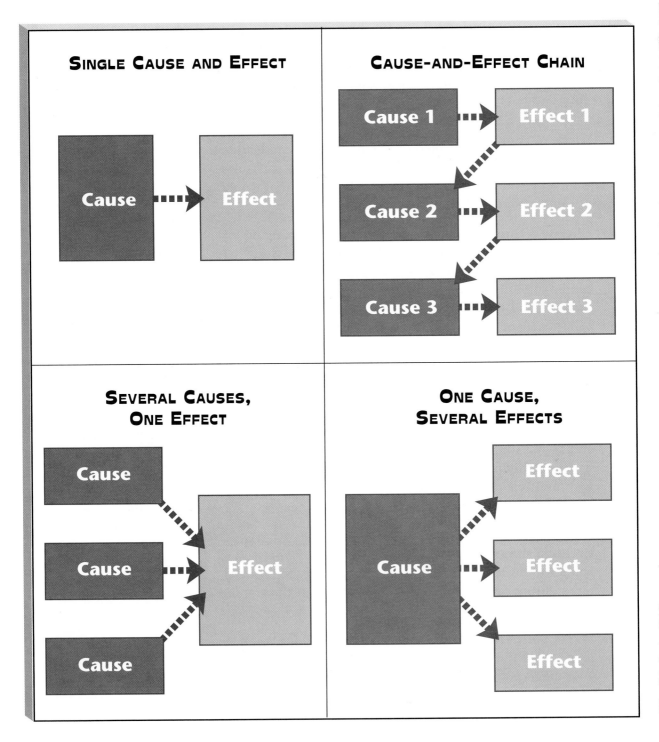

effects and generated new causes such as. . . ." Always embed cause-and-effect signal words in your thesis statement as well as in your essay. The most common of these words are *cause, effect, result, leads to, therefore, because,* and *for this reason.* In these examples of good thesis statements, signal words are italicized.

> The collision of tectonic plates *causes* the formation of volcanoes along the collision line. (Single Cause, Single Effect)
>
> The passengers on the *Mayflower* sought both religious freedom and the chance to start a new life; *therefore*, they risked the perilous journey across the ocean to an unknown land. (Multiple Causes, One Effect)
>
> Robotics in factories streamline many processes in manufacturing. More important, they *result* in a significant shift in employment patterns in manufacturing communities. (Single Cause, Multiple Effects)
>
> The huge oil spill in Alaska *caused* record environmental damage; this in turn *led to* stiff penalties and tougher laws. (Related Causes and Effects)

5. **Organize and develop your essay.** Use your own thesis statement as a guide to organize your essay. For example, if you're dealing with a historical topic, chronological order (events presented in the order in which they occur) may be the best method for organizing your supporting details. With other topics, you will want to use order of importance (details presented from the least important to the most important, or the reverse). Develop your cause-and-effect essay with relevant facts, details, quotations, and examples. Be sure to include any key terms and definitions your reader will need to know to understand your topic and follow your explanation.

EXERCISE 19 Explore Possible Topics

Look back at your writer's notebook for a topic, or use one of the prewriting strategies discussed in Lesson 1.1. Focus generally on a situation or a condition about which you can ask *Why? What caused this?* or *What's the result?* Jot down possible topics. You may want to stay away from personal topics. When you are finished, circle the one that you think you can explain most clearly.

EXERCISE 20 Gather Information

Once you have decided on a topic, you'll probably have to do some research. Take notes and record details. Use the suggestions on the following page.

If you have chosen a topic from everyday life, consider these methods of gathering information:

- **Make observations.** Take detailed notes as you actually look at, listen to, or otherwise observe your subjects.

- **Conduct interviews.** Gather information from people who have experienced the various causes, effects, or both.

If you have chosen a topic that is remote from your own experience, conduct research. Consider the following approach:

- **Begin with an encyclopedia article.** An encyclopedia article—either online or in a printed volume—will provide you with a broad overview.

- **Turn next to other reference sources and books.** These sources will lead you to more specific information and more detailed discussions.

- **Use periodicals.** For recent, up-to-date information, look up specialized periodicals and journals at the library. Archives for many print periodicals are also available online.

- **Use the Internet.** Also consider other sources of information that you can access through online databases at your library or through search engines on the Internet. Web sites and other digital media offer up-to-the-minute coverage on many topics.

EXERCISE 21 Create a Diagram

Represent your topic and information visually. Use or adapt one of the diagrams shown on page 70, or find another way to show the relationship you are presenting. Refer to your diagram as you draft your cause-and-effect essay.

EXERCISE 22 Analyze Thesis Statements, or Claims

With a small group, analyze each of the following thesis statements, or claims. Decide which is strongest, and tell why. Give suggestions for improving the others.

(a) As a result of many recent changes and developments, the Pacific Rim has become a great influence on American culture and economy.

(b) Michael Faraday's experiments in electromagnetic induction led to Edison's development of the first practical incandescent light bulb.

(c) In order to further conserve our fossil fuels and reduce our dependence on oil, it should be mandatory for all automobile makers to offer a selection of hybrid cars.

EXERCISE 23 Write a Thesis Statement, or Claim

Using your diagram as a guide, write your thesis statement in one or two clear sentences. Remember that your thesis statement should use words that signal a cause-and-effect relationship and guide the reader to expect, for example, a single cause and effect or a cause-and-effect chain. You might draft several versions of your thesis statement and then choose the best one.

EXERCISE 24 Draft Your Essay

Remember the three key parts of an essay: introduction, body, and conclusion.

1. **Introduction** Begin by creating interest in your topic. Then introduce the cause-and-effect relationship in a clearly stated thesis statement.

2. **Body** Begin each body paragraph with a topic sentence. Develop your support logically, using chronological order or order of importance, as appropriate. Link paragraphs, sentences, and ideas with transitional words and phrases. Use precise language to avoid wordiness, and be sure to include key vocabulary terms that are specific to your topic. Use an objective tone, and maintain a formal style by avoiding slang and following the conventions of standard English.

3. **Conclusion** In a new and fresh way, restate, summarize, or reflect on the importance of the relationships or connections that you have just explored.

EXERCISE 25 Revise and Edit Your Essay

Read your paper aloud to small group. Ask your group members to take notes as they listen. Can they identify the cause-and-effect relationship that you are exploring? If not, go back and revise your thesis statement or your supporting paragraphs—or both. Also be sure you have provided enough support and explanation to make cause-and-effect connections clearer. Once you have revised your essay, edit your paper for grammar, usage, mechanics, and spelling.

EXERCISE 26 Publish Your Essay

Create a class anthology of cause-and-effect essays. Work with your classmates to sort the essays by subject area, such as history and science. Then develop a table of contents that organizes the essays for potential readers. Consider creating an online version of your anthology that you can share with other classes in your school.

Expository Writing: Research Paper

A **research paper** is based on a thorough investigation of a limited topic, often a specific question or problem. Sometimes, a research paper is assigned, in English as well as in other classes, as a final project. It reflects thinking, studying, and writing as a process undertaken and refined over a period of many weeks. In fact, a research paper is sometimes called a term paper because a term (often a quarter) is the time given to complete it. There are five main types of research papers:

1. The most common type of research paper **summarizes** or **explains** information that you have collected from several different sources. In it, you **synthesize** (combine to form a new, coherent whole) what others have reported. Your report is generally based on information found in books and periodicals.

2. An **evaluation** paper is also based on information you have gathered, but it adds a solution to a problem or offers a statement judging the worth or value of certain decisions or courses of action. For example, in an evaluation, you might discuss an issue that is troubling state officials and evaluate the effectiveness of several possible solutions or responses to that issue. Such a paper may be based on information from current periodicals and news reports.

3. In an **original research** paper, you not only write a paper but also conduct the research that forms its basis. You might formulate a question that you can answer through observation and analysis. If you are doing scientific research, your paper should begin with your hypothesis (the theory you are testing), and you should explain how you controlled your experiments. Your paper should also include a survey of the literature that led you to your investigation.

4. In a **combination** paper, you merge original research with the research of respected authorities. You combine information from books, periodicals, and other sources with information gathered from your own correspondence, interviews, and visits.

5. An **I-Search paper** focuses on a topic that you, the writer, personally wish to address; and in it, you narrate the story of your search and findings. For example, you might wonder whether a career in law is for you. As a result, you volunteer after school in a law office for two weeks. What do you find out? In your paper, you present not only what you discovered but also why you chose that topic, how you conducted your research, and what you experienced along the way.

On the following pages you will find excerpts from a high school student's research paper, printed in *The Concord Review*, that explains and synthesizes what other writers have written about the Anti-Suffragist Movement, a movement that tried to keep women from voting in the late nineteenth and early twentieth centuries in America. The research paper also states the claim that this movement, sometimes overlooked in the history of the era, has much to tell us about the values of the times. The paper includes parenthetical references to its sources and ends with a Works Cited list. Later in this workshop, you will find a discussion of both of these key elements of research writing. This research paper and Works Cited list are formatted according to MLA (Modern Language Association) style.

4-line heading: Name/Teacher/ Class/Due Date —

Nicole Herz
Dr. Charles Orson Cook
United States History
12 Dec. 2012

Title (centered)

Opposition to Female Suffrage in the United States

Introduces topic —

[1]Although scholars have produced an abundance of information about the women's movement, one aspect of the post-Civil War era has been largely neglected: the anti-suffrage resistance. [2]Anti-suffrage ideology provides the historian with a rich source of information about the age's moods and mentality. [3]Anti-suffragists (or as suffragists called them, "antis") did not rely on one vague, all-encompassing rationale in their protest. [4]Rather, they appealed to society's already solid conceptions of women, men, and the relationship between the two sexes.

Should be one-half-inch margins on all sides and one-half-inch paragraph indents per MLA style

Explains importance of topic

[5]Women's suffrage would violate the cherished cult of domesticity dominant in both Europe and America during this period, they claimed. [6]It would also give power to the "undesirable" portions of society, a complaint stemming from the bourgeois tone of the movement. [7]"Antis" asserted that suffrage would also sever the chivalric ties between men and women, as well as go against the word of God, as written in the Bible. [8]Using all these arguments, anti-suffragist men and women managed to hold back the passage of the Nineteenth Amendment, as well as a change in American society's attitude about women, for generations. [9]A steadfast and persistent social force in America, the anti-suffragists' ideology and power contain historical clues to social norms deserving much closer attention. [10]In addition, the examination of anti-suffragist propaganda helps to place much greater perspective on a turbulent and complex age in American history.

Thesis statement, or claim, ends introduction

Herz 2

Intoduces first key
aspect of
anti-suffragist
"propaganda"

Quotation
provides support
and explanation

Writer integrates
quotations with
comments and
explanations

Elaborates on
anti-suffragist
"propaganda"

Quotations
provide support
and explanation

(Some of
the writer's
development has
been omitted)

Introduces second
key aspect of anti-
suffragist stance

[11]The Victorian cult of domesticity in the United States rapidly developed as modernization produced a wealthy, conservative middle class. [12]The image of the domestic wife was both a symbol of decent womanliness and the only female occupation worthy of prestige or reverence. [13]An anti-suffragist Florida Congressman remarked that woman "was made man's helper, was given a servient place (not necessarily inferior) and the man dominant (not necessarily superior) in the division of labor" (Kraditor 14). [14]Therefore, all middle class women were destined from birth to be full-time wives and mothers. [15]To dispute this eternal truth was to challenge "true biology" and "true sociology" (Kraditor 13). [16]Male and female anti-suffragists reasoned that the domestic duty and inevitability of motherhood left women no time or energy for the "monstrous oppression and injustice" of female suffrage ("Address" 1). . . .

[17]"Antis" maintained that women were forever bound exclusively to the affairs of home and family and that they should feel proud and content about it. [18]They asserted that women's suffrage "would lead to the neglect of children by politically active mothers, and thereby, to increased juvenile delinquency" (Kraditor 16). [19]One rather puerile flyer entitled "Household Hints" read, "Housewives! You do not need a ballot to clean your sink spout . . . Good cooking lessens alcoholic craving quicker than a vote on local option" (Kraditor 17). [20]This condescending rebuke struck a nerve at the movement's strong roots in the temperance movement. [21]Despite quick and varied rebuttals by suffragists, the overwhelming desire to keep women in their place by mainstream American male and female anti-suffragists made the cause for women's suffrage impossibly difficult at the turn of the nineteenth century. [22]"Close to the heart of all anti-suffragist orators," observed historian Aileen Kraditor, "was a sentimental vision of Home and Mother" (12). [23]Besides the childlike sentimentality and the paternalistic argument that accompanied it, there was always the underlying fear that the goal of the suffragists would result in "large-handed, big-footed, flat-chested, and thin-lipped" women (Kraditor 23). [24]"Antis" perceived the ballot as the evil that would either freeze the feminine warmth of home or cause the unsuspecting housewife to neglect her numerous duties to home and husband. . . . [25]In fact, the idea that suffrage would lead to problems in the family and even to divorce was so persistent that Alice Stone Blackwell felt compelled to instruct all pro-suffragists on how to counter it most effectively (Blackwell 161–202).

[26]Another strong theme in the anti-suffragist movement had to do with a traditional, Biblical argument. [27]According to anti-suffragists, women's suffrage would not only wreak havoc on women's domestic sphere, but it would go against God's will as well. [28]"Those who seek to protect the older

Herz 3

order of things as they relate to woman reverently appeal to the division of Divine purpose," Grover Cleveland said, linking the domestic sphere with ostensibly anti-suffragist implications of Genesis (Kraditor 13). . . . [29]Almira Seymour, an anti-suffragist pamphleteer, claimed woman's enclosure in the home was created "in recognition of the essential divinity of her nature" (Seymour 11–12). [30]Anti-suffragist rhetoric often likened the idea of the housewife to the priestly service for a temple. [31]Senator Peter Frelinghuyson of New Jersey agreed when he said, "Women have a higher and holier function than to engage in the turmoil of public life" (Oates 138). [32]The moral specialization of women succeeded in furthering their separation from men in public life. [33]The "Restorer of lost Eden" had no business voting or participating in city government (Seymour 12). [34]Often using Biblical imagery, anti-suffragists pleaded to the public and Congress as God's children attempting to save America from the evil of woman suffrage. [35]"Let us labor earnestly," preached one 'anti,' "to save women from the barren perturbations of American politics. . . . Let us pray for the deliverance from female suffrage" (Parkman 16).

[36]Women's suffrage also seemed to threaten a less specified chivalric tie between men and women. [37]Twentieth-century historian John Morton Blum pointed out that the sentimental vision of Lady Guinevere "persuaded self-conscious Lancelots that the right to vote was male as well as white" (Blum 116). [38]The idealists among the male "antis" wished to preserve women from the disagreeable task of public responsibility, hoping they could clean up politics without feminine help. [39]One representative of Florida commented only five years before [the passage of] the amendment of 1920: "I do not wish to see the day come when the women of my race in my state shall trail their skirts in the murk and mire of partisan politics" (Kraditor 18).

[40]Coupled with this "knight in shining armor" notion was the continuation of women's social isolation. [41]Mrs. Barclay Hazard, an active twentieth-century anti-suffragist, insisted that women were not deprived of anything, but rather protected from the vileness of politics (Hazard 22). [42]Professor Kraditor made the distinction by noting, "It was wrong to say that [a woman] did not have the right to vote; rather, she had the right not to vote" (19). [43]Suffragist Gerrit Smith observed about anti-suffragists at the time, ". . . [T]hese ladies . . . are so perverted and befooled by their ladyism as to shrink from the vulgarity of voting" (Kraditor 20). [44]Smith had pinpointed the image of the "damsel in distress" exploited in anti-suffragist propaganda. [45]If women invaded the masculine sphere, they would forfeit their right to chivalry, that mode of male behavior which "antis" and the mainstream public considered the ennobling characteristic of society. . . .

Ties together
ideas with fresh
restatement

Herz 4

[46]The motives and rationales behind the anti-suffragist arguments demonstrated with unabashed lucidity the American mentality concerning women and men, the prejudices of the period, and the essentially conservative consensus of the middle class. . . . [47]Buried in the heap of discarded history, the anti-suffragists truly provide the historian with clear insight into a complicated transition in America.

Herz 5

Works Cited

Indent turnover
lines of
each source
one-half inch

"Address to the Voters of the Middle West." Chicago: Illinois Association Opposed to the Extension of Suffrage to Women. 1900. Print.

Blackwell, Alice Stone. "Objections Answered." *Woman Suffrage: History, Arguments, and Results*. Eds. Frances M. Borkman and A. Poritt. New York: National Woman Suffrage Publishing, 1915. 161–202. *The Douglas Project*. Web. 30 Nov. 2012.

Blum, J. Morton. *Woodrow Wilson and the Politics of Morality*. Boston: Little, 1956. Print.

Hazard, Mrs. Barclay. "How Woman Can Best Serve the State." Chicago: Illinois Association Opposed to the Extension of Suffrage to Women, 1907. *Harvard University Library Open Collections Program*. Web. 30 Nov. 2012.

Kraditor, Aileen S. *The Ideas of the Woman Suffrage Movement 1890–1920*. Garden City, NY: Doubleday, 1971. Print.

Oates, Stephen B., ed. *Portrait of America*. 5th ed. Vol 2. Boston: Houghton, 1991. Print.

Parkman, Francis. "Some of the Reasons Against Woman Suffrage," 1883. *Harvard University Library Open Collections Program*. Web. 30 Nov. 2012.

Seymour, Almira. "Home, the Basis of the State." Boston: A. Williams, 1869. Print.

Writing Strategies   The following specific strategies apply to all of the types of research papers. You must also use the writing strategies in Chapter 1 and the general advice for writing essays in Lesson 2.5.

1. Choose and limit a topic. Think carefully before you choose. Choose a topic that interests you, not the first one that comes to mind. Remember that you will spend weeks or more developing this paper, so finding the most suitable topic is crucial. Once you limit yourself to a topic that interests you, be sure to narrow or broaden it, if necessary.

TOO BROAD:	Knighthood
TOO NARROW:	Gauntlets (metal gloves)
LIMITED AND WORKABLE:	Armor in Medieval France

2. **Schedule your time.** Imagine you have a total of five weeks. By the end of week one, you should have chosen your topic, limited it, and found your sources. By the end of week two, you should have taken all your notes. By the end of the week three, you should have your draft done. That leaves two weeks for extensive revision, careful documentation, proofreading, and preparation of your final manuscript.

3. **Find a variety of print and digital sources.** You may be required to use both primary and secondary sources. A **primary source** is any original text, such as a novel or poem, a diary, letters, or a historical document. A **secondary source** presents someone else's view of, or comments on, an event or person. Examples of secondary sources include biographies, literary criticism, history and science textbooks, and all kinds of magazine articles and news reports that interpret and re-create events and information.

For many subjects, a computer is your most valuable research tool. If you have not yet discovered your local library's databases, now is the time to do so. These may include everything from InfoTrac, the online equivalent of the *Readers' Guide to Periodical Literature*, to your local newspaper. You can also search the Internet for information.

4. **Evaluate your sources.** Before you take a single note, take a close look at your sources. If you have a timely topic, such as strides toward equal pay for women, don't use outdated sources. Even if you are researching something historic (the role of women during the Roman Empire, for example), remember that newer sources reflect the most timely, up-to-date viewpoints and research. Look at each author's credentials, too. Be sure that he or she actually is an expert in the field. Also, be sure that others respect this source; one easy way to do that is to see if any of your other sources refer to the source or include it in their own bibliographies.

For sources on the Internet, be especially careful. Anyone can post information on a Web page; no publisher decides its worth; no one corrects it; no one, in many cases, makes sure it is accurate or fair. Your best bet is a *.gov* (government) site. Check government sites for all kinds of statistical information, including population and other census data. For American history and government, visit the Library of Congress online. Its main government page, Thomas

(*thomas.loc.gov*) provides access to every part of the federal government. For access to the Library's holdings, go to its American Memory site (*memory.loc.gov/ ammem/amhome.html*). Another good bet on the Internet is sites followed by *.edu* (education): These are often university sites, and they are typically more reliable than commercial sites or personal sites. Once you reach a site, see if you can find the author's credentials and documentation of sources. If you can't find them, move on to the next site.

5. **Record your sources.** Be sure to make a numbered source card, or bibliography card, for every source you use. (The number comes in handy when you make multiple notes from one source. Then you don't have to record all the bibliographic information each time; instead, you record just the number.) Or if you prefer, keep track of your sources electronically. Add a new entry for each new source.

SAMPLE SOURCE CARD

1   **Number of source**
Blackwell, Alice Stone. "Objections Answered." <u>Woman Suffrage: History, Arguments, and Results.</u> Eds. Frances M. Borkman and A. Poritt. New York: National Woman Suffrage Publishing, 1915. 161–202. <u>The Douglas Project.</u> Web. 30 Nov. 2012.

6. **Take notes.** When you find information you think you may want to use, you have three choices for how to record it.

- **Summarize it.** This is an ideal note-taking technique since it involves boiling down large amounts of text to brief, concrete statements. It ensures that information goes into your paper in your own words.

- **Quote it.** In note taking, use this technique far more sparingly than summarizing. In fact, quote only when:

   (a) the words of the source are so perfect that there is no better way to say it, and

   (b) you are recording unique information that must be attributed to its source.

After you copy the quotation, go back to the source and check it word for word. Make sure you got it absolutely right. Record the page number(s) where the quote appears.

- **Paraphrase it.** It's also best to use this technique somewhat sparingly. In a paraphrase, you use your own words to express someone else's thinking. With this approach, it's easy to cross the line into **plagiarism**—passing off someone else's ideas as your own. When you paraphrase, double-check yourself to be sure you have changed more in a sentence than, say, just the verb. Ask yourself, "Does this still sound like my source? Or have I used enough of my own words and phrasing?"

WRITING HINT

When you introduce a quotation by naming its author, you do not have to repeat the name in the parenthetical reference. Instead, provide only the page number.

The best way to avoid plagiarism—which is sometimes a criteria for failing a paper or, later in life, losing a job—is to take care at the note-taking stage. If you're working hard here to distinguish between what belongs to you and what doesn't, you won't have to trouble yourself with changes and rewrites when you get to the drafting and revision stages.

The following note card summarizes what was read. Its author records the main idea at the top of the note card and then underlines it.

SAMPLE NOTE CARD

1

Pamphlet: Takes arguments against suffrage and meets them one by one, such as women don't need to vote because their husbands, fathers, and brothers already represent them; and men know more about business and, therefore, make better voters. Counterargument: Women need their own voice to communicate specific concerns to policymakers.

Identifies and summarizes work

Lists arguments that might be treated as anti-suffragist topics

7. **Write a thesis statement, or claim, and organize your ideas.** Write a thesis statement, a sentence or two that states the controlling idea of your paper. Then start sorting your notes to identify the main ideas that will support your thesis, or claim. Another approach for getting started is to put your note cards in an order that makes sense and then try to come up with a thesis statement. Sort note cards that might work together as groups of ideas or paragraphs. At this stage, consider writing an outline. Use the style of outline you are most comfortable with: formal, informal, or sentence. (See Lesson 1.2 for more on outlines.) Even if your thesis statement or your first stabs at organizing ideas are not perfect at this point, they will give you a starting point for drafting. Because you're just starting, don't discard any note cards at this stage, even if they don't seem to fit anywhere. They may come in handy later, or they may help you rethink and revise.

8. **Document your sources.** A research paper shows where your information comes from. Be sure to acknowledge each source whenever you (1) quote a phrase, sentence, or passage directly or (2) summarize or paraphrase another person's ideas in your work. You do not have to document common knowledge, basic knowledge you might find about a subject in any source. For example, most experts on nineteenth-century U.S. immigration will suggest some of the same reasons for this influx of Europeans—for example, the potato famine in Ireland (1845–1847) and pogroms (organized massacres of Jews in 1882) in Russia. They will supply the same dates; they will tell where certain groups headed; they will cite the same conditions in Europe that led groups to emigrate to America. Information such as this that can be found in any source does not need a citation.

One common method for documenting sources is called **parenthetical documentation**. Developed by the Modern Language Association (MLA), this method is shown in the sample research paper on pages 75–78. In this method, the author's name and the page number in the source appear in parentheses after each quotation. This abbreviated citation is a reference to the **Works Cited** list at the end of the paper, which gives complete information about each source.

There are many acceptable methods of documentation, and what you use may depend on your teacher and your subject area. If you are asked to use MLA style, your best guide to it is the *MLA Handbook for Writers of Research Papers*, 7th edition.

EXERCISE 27 Choose and Limit a Topic

If you have not been assigned a topic and are asked to choose, the sheer number of possibilities may be intimidating. A good way to begin is by listing things you like, such as exploring caves, playing tennis, watching a certain TV show, playing a certain video game, or reading about pirates or famous dancers. You might even list foods you like to eat. You may think a topic like video games will not work, but they too have a history, one related to the history of both television and computers. You might think there is nothing to say about a particular type of frosted cereal or packaged breakfast pastry, but even breakfast cereal companies grew from somewhere, and advertising and creating products is a fascinating process. In addition to histories, there are issues and controversies surrounding almost everything you can think of.

After you have generated a long list, circle two or three topics that interest you the most. Then think of questions to ask about each. You may discover which topic is most usable simply by the types and numbers of questions you can formulate about the topic. If you do not find enough information on a specific topic right away, you may need to modify or broaden your research question. On the other hand, if you find too much information, narrow your focus to a more manageable research question and topic. This is also the time when you should set yourself some deadlines for completing each stage of your research paper in the amount of time available.

EXERCISE 28 Prewriting: Gather Information

Consider your topic and develop a specific question to guide your research: for example, "How did the attitudes of anti-suffragists prevent women from gaining the vote and help shape American history?"

Use Strategies 3–6 on pages 79–81 to begin focused research. As you gather your sources, carefully examine them, and keep your purpose in mind. Be sure to find information from multiple print and digital sources, and determine how the information from each source supports the points you are trying to make. Evaluate the strengths and limitations of each source, and include only the most relevant information as you write your essay. Throughout the research process, keep your audience in mind. Try to provide your audience with new, interesting information, and avoid restating facts and background information that your readers already know.

EXERCISE 29 Evaluate Your Research

After you have prepared notes from a number of sources, determine whether you can begin to draft. Here are three common problems that occur at the research stage and some advice for solving them:

- **Too few main ideas** You will need at least three or four. If you don't have enough, you will need to do more research.

- **Not enough supporting information** You may find you need more information to support your points and help your audience understand your topic. If so, explore new sources. Take more notes.

- **Too much information.** Remember to include only the most relevant and useful information. Keep your audience and purpose in mind, and omit any ideas or details that are repetitive or unnecessary.

EXERCISE 30 Make an Outline or Other Organizer

Begin to shape your ideas by creating a rough or informal outline—or by representing them visually in some other way, such as in a cluster or flowchart. Use any method that works for you. Many writers need a well-developed outline to write a successful draft. Others find their structure comes together as they write. Use your own experience as a writer as your guide.

Parts of a Research Paper

- cover (optional)
- title page or heading
- introduction
- body of paper
- conclusion
- visual aids (optional)
- Works Cited list

EXERCISE 31 Write a First Draft with Documentation

Start drafting at least three weeks before your paper is due so that you will have plenty of time to revise. Apply Strategies 7–8 from page 82. Keep the following advice in mind as well.

- **Create interest.** Although this is a research paper and your tone should be serious and your style formal, engage your audience by creating interest in your introduction and by giving your paper a compelling title. Keep your reader's attention level in mind in every paragraph, and end the paper with a memorable conclusion.

- **Use your own words.** Using effective quotations will make your paper sparkle, but most of your work should be in your own words, reflecting your ideas or findings. Don't use too many quotations one after another.

- **Include parenthetical documentation as you write.** Include your sources and in-text citations as you draft, and check quotations for complete accuracy.

EXERCISE **32** Revise Your Draft

Read through your draft many times, focusing on something different each
time: ideas and unity, organization and coherence, sentence variety, and word
choice. Check to see that you've arranged your ideas in the most logical order.
Be sure that all your topic sentences relate in some way to your thesis, or claim.
Also look for places where you might have gone off track. Eliminate weak support,
and strengthen "empty" paragraphs by adding more support, more details, and
more facts. Read your paper aloud to make sure the sentences sound smooth. Add
transitions; clear up cloudy relationships or connections by replacing vague words
with specific ones or by rewriting sentences. Do the best revising job you can, and
then ask for feedback from writing partners.

EXERCISE **33** Edit Your Draft

In addition to checking spelling, capitalization, and punctuation, make sure
that you have accurately introduced, copied, and punctuated all quotations.
Check all of your parenthetical citations and your Works Cited list against
the conventions of the style of documentation your teacher requires.

EXERCISE **34** Prepare the Final Copy and Publish

Double space your entire paper, including the Works Cited page. Read the final
paper one more time before turning it in. If you find any last-minute mistakes,
correct them.

Practical Writing: Workplace Writing

The workplace demands a broad range of writing, which can vary from memos to employee reviews to sales reports. No matter what kind of company you work for, however, you're likely to do some kind of on-the-job writing. In some forms of writing, you represent your company to others outside it, including the public and representatives of other companies. In other forms of writing, you represent yourself and your ideas to other members of your own company.

Workplace writing most commonly takes the form of e-mail, memos, reports, and proposals. Its purpose is often to give directions to colleagues and staff. The most common type of formal business writing is probably the business letter.

Before you actually enter the workplace, you can—and probably will—get a lot of practice in sending e-mail and writing business letters. There are three main types of business letters: letters of request, letters of verification or transmittal (cover letters), and letters of application. A request letter usually asks for information, although it may also place an order, register a complaint, or demand some type of correction. The business letter on page 87 is a letter of request. As you read it, think about what elements distinguish it from a friendly letter.

Heading	125 Milestone Road Philadelphia, PA 19119 March 7, 2012
Inside address	Bob Laird, Director Undergraduate Admission and Relations with Schools University of California at Berkeley 110 Sproul Hall, #5800 Berkeley, CA 94720-5800
Salutation	Dear Mr. Laird:
Clear, direct writing	I am a high school junior. During this coming summer, I will be visiting several colleges to which I plan to apply in the fall. The University of California at Berkeley will be one of my stops.
Clear statement of request	Before I arrive on campus, I would like to read everything I can about your school. Will you please send me informational materials for prospective undergraduates at U.C. Berkeley? I would like to see a course catalog, samples of student publications, and materials on admissions and student life.
Additional requests	In addition, I will need a campus map. Finally, please inform me of the procedures for obtaining a campus tour and attending a general information session. Once I know the exact date of my visit, I would like to schedule these. Thank you.
Thank you (or other closing courtesy)	
Complimentary close	Sincerely,
Signature	*Kelsey Scheier* Kelsey Scheier

Critical Thinking   After you read the business letter, answer the questions below.

1. What is the writer's purpose? Who is her audience?

2. This letter is written in the first person, yet it is not overly personal. How would you describe the tone of the letter?

3. Although this is a business letter rather than a friendly letter, it is courteous. In what way is that so?

4. The paragraphs are short. Why do you think the writer makes this choice?

5. Do you think the writer will get the response she has asked for? Why? What elements of this letter help ensure success or failure?

Writing Strategies The purpose of a business letter might be to request information, to register a complaint, or to demand some type of correction. The following strategies apply to all types of business letters.

1. **Use the correct form.** Like all business letters, this one has six parts; look back at the annotations to identify them.

   • Note that the **heading** consists of the writer's street address—city, state, and zip code—and the date of the letter. Notice that the only acceptable abbreviations in a business letter are the postal codes for states; the titles of individuals, such as *Dr.* or *Mrs.*; and, in the case of companies, designations such as *Co., Ltd.,* and *Inc.*

   • The **inside address** includes the name of the person to whom the letter is addressed and his or her title. If you don't know the person's title, address the letter to a specific department, such as Merchandise Returns. The inside address also includes the company name; the street address; and the city, state, and zip code.

   • Note that a colon follows the **salutation**, or greeting. Appropriate greetings include *Dear Ms. (Name), Dear Sir or Madam,* and *To Whom It May Concern.*

   • The **body** is written in paragraph form. The use of bulleted or numbered text may also be appropriate.

   • A comma follows the **closing**. Appropriate closings for business letters are limited by convention to *Sincerely, Sincerely yours,* and *Yours truly.* When correspondence is extremely formal, you might use *Respectfully.*

   • The **signature** appears twice: first handwritten and then, directly underneath, typed.

2. **Use correct style.** The letter on page 87 follows the full block style: Everything starts at the left, and there are no paragraph indents. In a modified block style, the heading, closing, and signature begin at the center point or just to its right. Paragraphs may or may not indent, according to the writer's choice.

   In both styles, spacing is a key part of the form. Use generous margins and an additional line of space between paragraphs and all main parts of the letter. Two or more additional lines separate the heading from the inside address.

3. Be clear, brief, and complete. A business letter should convey its point concisely. You don't need an introduction or a conclusion; instead, just say what you have to say—and then conclude. In the last line of a business letter, however, it is general practice to thank someone for his or her assistance or attention. Short paragraphs are effective in all kinds of business writing. They give the letter an easy-to-read appearance, and they convey the information in manageable units.

Although being brief is important, no business letter will succeed if it is not complete. For example, if you are asking for a product refund or replacement but do not include a heading, where should the company send a check or further correspondence? If you want your account credited but do not supply an account number, you cannot be sure your purpose will be achieved. You must provide the recipient with whatever information is needed to achieve your purpose.

Finally, a business letter must be "letter perfect." Use a spell checker, keeping in mind that it misses homophones and words correctly spelled but used in the wrong context. Print the letter out and then, after some time has passed, proofread it carefully. A letter with spelling, punctuation, or grammatical errors is an embarrassment to you and to any company you may represent.

EXERCISE 35 Choose a Topic

What kind of request do you need to make? Perhaps you, too, will soon make a campus visit. Perhaps you need to order a product or straighten out some business with an online retailer. Maybe you would like either a map of the bike path that begins in a nearby town or next season's schedule at a local stadium or performing arts center. Think of something you truly would like to request.

EXERCISE 36 Prewriting: Gather Information

The first stumbling block in writing a business letter is often obtaining the correct address as well as the name of the person to whom to send your request. If you have already had some correspondence with this recipient (such as a local club), use the address the recipient has provided. Otherwise, a telephone directory or the Internet may be your guide. A reference librarian can also help you track down this type of information. Be sure to gather information you need for the body of your letter, which may include a credit card or check number, the date of a previous request, or some information about a product. Enclose photocopies of relevant documents, such as canceled checks, a credit card statement, and receipts. Do not send originals.

EXERCISE 37 Write Your Draft

Draft all six parts of your business letter: the heading, the inside address, the salutation, the body, the closing, and the signature. As you draft the body, keep these hints in mind:

• Get to the point quickly.

• Be as brief as possible while including all of the information your reader needs in order to respond.

• Be courteous.

Remember that short paragraphs are effective in business writing. As necessary, you may even use one-sentence paragraphs.

EXERCISE 38 Revise and Edit Your Letter

Read through your draft. One step at a time, revise for ideas and unity, organization and coherence, word choice, and form.

• Be sure that you have included all necessary information and that all the information is accurate.

• Ask yourself whether you have used the best, most practical order for your information. Make sure you have broken your request into manageable paragraphs.

• Be sure you have been formal, polite, and to the point. Eliminate informal usage, contractions, fragments, and run-on sentences.

• Check the position and spacing of each text block to be sure you have used the proper business-letter form.

EXERCISE 39 Send Your Letter

Read your final copy more than once. Send a perfect copy, printing your letter out again as needed. Remember to sign your letter using, preferably, black ink. On the envelope, use the same inside address you used in the business letter, and include your complete return address just as you have stated it in the heading. Then fold your letter into thirds, so that it fits perfectly into a legal size envelope, and mail it. Keep a photocopy of your letter and its enclosures until the matter is resolved.

Writing a Timed Essay

Essay questions on standardized tests measure your ability to generate ideas relevant to a specific topic and to present those ideas clearly and logically in an appealing style, while applying the conventions of standard written English. You are asked to do all of this under time constraints.

On a standardized test, you will find essay topics, also called "prompts," that present an issue or question and ask you to develop a thoughtful written response.

Although you will be given a limited amount of time to plan and write your essay, you will be expected to develop your ideas thoroughly. The goal of a timed essay is to produce in a short time frame clear and coherent writing that follows a well-organized structure and formal style.

Most standardized tests allot 25–30 minutes for timed writing. During that time, you should organize your ideas with an outline or cluster diagram, write your essay, and use any remaining time to revise what you have written. Edit your finished essay and check that you have used the conventions of standard English, including capitalization, punctuation, and spelling.

The writing prompt below is similar to one you might encounter on a standardized test. After the prompt, you will find one writer's essay in response to it.

TEST-TAKING TIP

Most standardized test essays are scored from 6 (highest) to 1 (lowest).

Consider the following issue. Then write an essay as directed.

George Santayana wrote, "Those who cannot remember the past are condemned to repeat it." On the other hand, Michel de Montaigne advised, "Rejoice in the things that are present; all else is beyond thee."

Assignment: When does memory have value? Consider a nonfiction text, such as an essay, you have read that addresses this topic. Write an essay that discusses how the author develops his or her analysis, including the order in which points are organized and the connections made among them.

Memory has value as a key to the past and as a motivator for the future. In his speech "Hope, Despair, and Memory," Elie Wiesel discusses memory as a way to honor the sacrifices victims made during the Holocaust and as a method through which to protect humanity as a whole. He claims that memory can inspire hope for a future without injustice, and if spread worldwide, it will lead to a global effort to work toward peace.

Introduces the topic in a thesis statement, or claim

Uses vocabulary specific to the subject matter

Wiesel begins by relating his ideas about memory to his own experiences as a Holocaust survivor and as a member of the Jewish faith. He explains that he yearned to forget the traumatic experience of the Holocaust, but doing so would contradict his faith. Explaining that *Rosh Hashanah*, the Jewish New Year celebration, is also known as the day of memory, Weisel argues that remembering is a necessary part of Judaism.

Develops the topic with concrete details

Next, Wiesel explains that survivors believed that their acts of remembrance would be enough to shield themselves and others from further trauma. For example, he says that they shared poems written by children in the Jewish ghettos so that no other child would have to endure the same trials. Survivors told their stories so that the world would remember them, learn from them, and commit to a more peaceful future because of them.

Includes transitions to clarify the relationship between ideas

Wiesel's speech, however, demonstrates that the global community did not learn from these memories of the Holocaust. On the contrary, prejudices have continued to negatively affect racial and cultural groups worldwide. Specifically, Wiesel draws a connection between the Holocaust and other large-scale intolerance, such as apartheid.

Provides a concluding section that supports the information presented

Wiesel concludes by asking the audience to remember the victims of the Holocaust and other groups who have faced injustice. He says that, even though remembering such suffering causes him to despair, the act of memory fills him with hope for a better future. Memory motivates him to work toward turning this hope into reality, and he believes that, on a large-scale, it can inspire the world to change for the better.

Critical Thinking   After you read the essay on pages 91–92, answer the following questions.

1. In the introduction, how does the writer address the topic as discussed in the prompt? Review the thesis statement, or claim, and determine how it relates to the prompt.

2. What text evidence does the writer give in the response? Briefly outline the evidence, examples, and details that appear in the essay.

3. Using the scoring suggestion in the Test-Taking Tip on page 91, how would you score this essay? What suggestions, if any, might you make to improve it?

Writing Strategies   Use the following strategies as you write a timed essay.

1. Read the prompt carefully. Make sure you understand precisely what you are asked to do. For example, is the purpose to inform or persuade? Then identify (underline or circle) key ideas as you read the prompt again.

2. **Prewrite: Narrow your focus.** Remember that you will have a limited amount of time and space in which to write your essay. Know how many minutes and how many lines you will have, and plan accordingly. You will not be able to write all you know about a topic, so limit your response to a clear and manageable focus. Use only your best ideas.

3. **Prewrite: Gather and organize ideas.** You might use an outline or a cluster diagram to generate and group ideas. Spend no more than two or three minutes jotting down ideas, key words, and supporting details. Order the ideas in the sequence you plan to use them.

4. **Write the main idea in a thesis statement, or claim.** Remember that this sentence usually appears at or near the beginning of your essay.

5. **Start writing and stick to the point.** Begin with an introductory paragraph that grabs the reader's attention and includes your thesis statement. Use details that support your ideas in the clearest, most logical way possible. Use topic sentences and transitions to organize your writing. End with a strong concluding paragraph.

6. **Consider word choice and sentence variety.** Clarity is your goal, so avoid vague words and confusing phrases and sentences. Strive for vocabulary and sentence variety that fits your writing purpose.

7. **Proofread your essay.** Save two or three minutes to read over your essay and neatly correct any errors in spelling, punctuation, or usage.

EXERCISE 40 Read the Prompt Carefully

Choose one of the prompts below, and refer to that prompt as you complete Exercises 41–44.

An autobiography is a nonfictional account told from the author's perspective that reveals personal insights about his or her life. Readers can use autobiographical texts as a source of information about a historical event or time period. Such an eyewitness account can show what it is like to live through something that readers may have never experienced themselves.

Assignment: How do autobiographies teach history? Consider an autobiography or autobiographical essay you have read. Write an essay in which you determine the author's purpose and discuss how he or she uses persuasive techniques to express a particular perspective on a historical event or time period.

The most effective writers always keep their intended audience in mind. For example, informal writing conventions, such as the use of slang or text-messaging shorthand, are unacceptable in professional writing.

Assignment: How does audience affect writing? Consider a persuasive text you have read that makes an argument for a particular audience. Write an essay in which you delineate, or identify, the author's central claim and evaluate the validity, relevance, and sufficiency of his or her supporting evidence and reasoning. Pay particular attention to the author's style and tone and how it contributes to the argument.

EXERCISE 41 Prewrite: Focus, Gather, and Organize Ideas

Consider your topic, and list the text evidence you will use as support, such as relevant facts, concrete details, quotations, and examples from the texts you chose to analyze. You might use a graphic organizer or an outline. Number your ideas in the sequence you plan to use them.

EXERCISE 42 Prewrite: Thesis, or Claim

Write your main idea in a thesis statement, or claim. Decide where you will place this sentence in your essay.

EXERCISE 43 Write Your Essay

Begin with an introductory paragraph that grabs the reader's attention and includes your thesis statement. Say everything as clearly and logically as you can, and develop your essay with relevant examples that support your main idea. Use topic sentences and transitions to organize and group your ideas. Remember to choose only words and sentences that execute your writing purpose. End with a concluding paragraph that restates your main idea, poses a new question, or provides a final thought.

EXERCISE 44 Revise and Proofread Your Essay

Save two or three minutes to reread your writing. Make sure the sentences flow smoothly and are clear and succinct. Neatly cross out anything that strays from or takes away from your main idea. Correct any errors in spelling, usage, punctuation, and capitalization.

Parts of Speech

STUDENT WRITING
Narrative Essay

Eighty-Eight Keys of Ego and Humility
by Chia-Jung Tsay
high school student, Lake Grove, New York

Any musician or performing artist knows well the sheer exhilaration after a successful concert . . . as well as the pitfalls that inevitably await. In a field that is more subjective than objective, a performer has to worry about not only interpretation but also the critic and the audience. After spending almost half my life at the piano, I succumbed to the infamous "ego" that so debilitates its victims. Naive as I was, I was unaware that I suffered from the condition . . . or rather, I chose to ignore it.

The first year in the Pre-College Division of the Juilliard School, I thought of myself as an accomplished pianist. It didn't matter that most so-called child prodigies don't succeed when they mature; in my mind, I had surpassed most musicians my age and was well on my way to becoming an international concert pianist.

Little did I know that even the smallest amount of ego outweighs accomplishment and experience. The first months at Juilliard were completely wasted as I floundered, thinking myself beyond the realm of practice. My first performance for my teacher and classmates was rapidly approaching, yet I showed no initiative when it came time to practice.

I began working on the Bach C Minor Partita just three weeks before my performance. I had too much faith in myself; I had too much confidence that, being the "genius" I was, the piece would simply come to me. I really expected to absorb the piece within days and give a performance as I always had. I did manage to memorize the piece quickly, but on stage, talent can never compensate for dedicated practice. That fateful day, I approached the eighty-eight keys without hesitation. I began smoothly and was absorbed in the voices that emerged gradually as the piece progressed. Then, the inevitable happened: I could not remember the next notes of the left-hand part!

All voices were necessary for such counterpoint typical of Bach. Without the lines in the tenor and bass voices, my right hand soon stopped. I tried starting from the beginning again, only to stop at the same spot. Over and over, I wracked my mind for the next notes, but they had disappeared. I had to skip to the next section; and when I finished, I took a bow, not in glory, but in disgrace. That was the first, single, and, I hope, last unsuccessful performance of my life. I learned to overcome my ego and practice whether I played for enjoyment or for performance. I regret that such a performance is in my memory, but I will always thank it for the lessons it taught me: humility and a new respect for those who toil in spite of experience and accomplishment.

Chia-Jung Tsay's autobiographical incident is well written because he gives background information, explains the events logically, and then explains the significance of the event.

In this chapter, you'll take a close look at the different kinds of work that words do—that is, you will learn about the parts of speech. As you do the writing exercises in this chapter, you'll apply what you learn about the parts of speech.

Nouns

What names every object, every person, every place, every emotion, and every idea? Nouns name them all.

▐▐▶ **Nouns** are words that name persons, places, things, or ideas.

PERSONS	doctor, aunt, Mr. Gomez, Indira Gandhi, golfer
PLACES	Main Street, Golden Gate Bridge, stadium, theater
THINGS	table, bagel, e-mail, pillow, puppy
IDEAS	pride, dictatorship, love, hope, determination

All nouns are abstract or concrete. **Abstract nouns** name ideas and things that you cannot touch, such as grammar. **Concrete nouns** name things you can touch, taste, see, hear, or smell.

ABSTRACT	ambition, greed, goal, thought
CONCRETE	orange, backpack, rabbit, hammer, **slogan**

▐▐▶ **Proper nouns** name particular persons, places, things, or ideas. Always capitalize proper nouns, which may contain two or more words. **Common nouns** are not capitalized, because they name people and things that are general, not particular.

COMMON	athlete, book, planet, hospital, month
PROPER	Lou Gehrig, Jupiter, County General, June

▐▐▶ **Collective nouns** name a group of people, animals, or things. They name the many groups into which people, animals, places, and things fall.

    flock, team, herd, family, senate, audience

▐▐▶ **Compound nouns** consist of two or more words. Sometimes, the words in a compound noun run together as one word, or they may be hyphenated. Sometimes, a compound noun is two separate words. Use a dictionary when you aren't sure how to write a compound noun.

    ninety-one, cookbook, sea urchin, seaweed,
    house-raising, House of Representatives

Enriching Your Vocabulary

A *slogan* was once a war cry. The word *slogan* comes from the Gaelic word *sluagh-gairm*: *Sluagh* means "host" or "army"; *gairm* means "cry." Over time, the word has come to mean "words expressing the aims of a person, group, or business," such as "just say no" or "just do it."

EXERCISE 1 Identifying Nouns

Underline all the nouns in the following passage. Look for common nouns, proper nouns, abstract nouns, concrete nouns, compound nouns, and collective nouns.

[1]Grains are the basics: fundamental foods on which diets are built. [2]Today, most Americans eat rice, wheat, and other grains, and bread is regarded as the staff of life. [3]Yet the only grain that is native to the Americas is corn—or, as it is commonly called in Central America, maize.

[4]Corn did not arise naturally. [5]Evidence found in Venezuela shows it to be the careful product of the crossbreeding of many generations of grasses.

[6]Once corn appeared, the population boomed. [7]Researchers suggest that this phenomenon first occurred along the Orinoco River. [8]There, tribes that had been more or less stable grew, over a period of several hundred years, to approximately fifteen times their original size.

[9]Later, corn traveled to Mexico. [10]Carried by Spanish explorers, it reached Europe in 1496.

EXERCISE 2 Revising a Paragraph

Working Together

Work with a partner to improve the weak paragraph below by replacing the imprecise and vague nouns with specific, concrete nouns or proper nouns. Also, feel free to add specific details and combine sentences. Compare your response with those made by other pairs of classmates.

[1]It was a day in autumn. [2]The light was fading from the sky. [3]The weather was changing. [4]The boy knew he had only so much time to make it out of the woods. [5]He glanced around. [6]He looked again at the unfamiliar trees on which no signs appeared. [7]He could have been traveling for a long time in circles. [8]He could not tell. [9]If only his dog were with him now. [10]If only he had had the sense to bring some stuff in case he got stuck in the woods. [11]As it was, he had nothing. [12]He didn't have one thing.

Pronouns

▐▐▐➤ **Pronouns** are words that take the place of a noun or another pronoun.

Sometimes, you will find pronouns in the same sentence with the word or words they replace. This word or group of words that the pronoun replaces is the pronoun's **antecedent**. Arrows point to the pronouns and their antecedents in these sentences.

> Brenda and Zeke both have dogs. **She** walks **her** dog every night, but **he** walks **his** dog in the morning. **They** sometimes walk **their** dogs
>
> together on the weekends.

All the pronouns in this example are **personal pronouns** (they refer to specific people or animals). Some of these personal pronouns are shown in their **possessive forms** (*her, his, their*).

▐▐▐➤ **Indefinite pronouns** express an amount or refer to an unspecified person or thing.
> **None** of the children wanted the party to end. **Someone** left a glove.

▐▐▐➤ **Demonstrative pronouns** point to specific people or things.
> **That** is my essay. **This** is the house that was sold last week.

▐▐▐➤ **Interrogative pronouns** begin a question.
> **What** is your name? **Who** is that man in the black coat?

▐▐▐➤ **Reflexive pronouns** end in -*self* or -*selves* and refer to an earlier noun or pronoun in the sentence. **Intensive pronouns** add emphasis.
> REFLEXIVE   I found **myself** a place to sit.
> INTENSIVE   It was up to Jack **himself** to tell the truth.

Reflexive and intensive pronouns *never* serve as the subject of a sentence.
> *I*
> Liz and ~~myself~~ went to the game.

For information about **relative pronouns** and **adjective clauses**, see Lesson 8.2.

Personal Pronouns

I	you	her
me	he	it
we	him	they
us	she	them

Possessive Pronouns

my	your	his
mine	yours	its
our	her	their
ours	hers	theirs

Some Indefinite Pronouns

all	another
any	anybody
anyone	anything
both	each
either	everybody
everyone	everything
few	many
most	neither
nobody	none
no one	one
several	some
somebody	someone

Demonstrative Pronouns

this	these
that	those

Some Interrogative Pronouns

Who?	Whom?
Whose?	What?
Which?	

Reflexive and Intensive Pronouns

myself	herself
ourselves	himself
yourself	itself
yourselves	themselves

EXERCISE 3 Revising a Paragraph

Using pronouns helps writers avoid unnecessary repetition. Replace as many nouns in this paragraph as you can with pronouns, but be sure the pronoun reference is clear. You won't be able to replace all the repeated nouns. **Hint:** All the pets in this paragraph are male.

¹Many pets have lived in the White House, and as a result, the pets have become famous. ²One of the most famous First Pets was President Franklin Roosevelt's dog Fala. ³President Roosevelt loved Fala so much that President Roosevelt took Fala almost everywhere Roosevelt went. ⁴Another famous White House pet was Old Whiskers. ⁵Old Whiskers was a goat owned by Russell Harrison, the son of President Benjamin Harrison. ⁶One day, Old Whiskers ran down Pennsylvania Avenue. ⁷President Harrison chased Old Whiskers. ⁸How undignified President Harrison must have looked! ⁹Caroline Kennedy, the daughter of President John Kennedy, had a pony named Macaroni. ¹⁰Lyndon Johnson, then Vice President, gave Macaroni to Caroline. ¹¹Macaroni roamed the White House grounds.

EXERCISE 4 Writing with Pronouns

People and their pets can be a source of humor, wonder, and delight. On a separate piece of paper, write ten complete sentences about people you know or have read about and the pets that seem to "people" their lives. Try to use each type of pronoun from page 99 at least once. Underline all the pronouns in your sentences.

CONNECTING
Writing & Grammar

Write What You Think

On a separate piece of paper, write one paragraph in response to the following position. Begin by clearly stating your opinion. Then support your opinion with reasons and examples. After you have revised your writing, edit it to be sure you have used pronouns correctly.

Refer to
Composition,
Lesson 4.2, to
find strategies
for writing
persuasively.

All dogs and other large pets should be on a leash at all times when they are on public property, including parks, conservation lands, forests, nature preserves, and beaches. At no time may any dog, horse, goat, or other large animal be permitted to run or roam free on any public land.

Verbs

Add a verb to a noun and you bring the noun to life. A verb makes a noun move, stretch, sing, or breathe.

▶ **Verbs** are words that express an action or a state of being. Every sentence has at least one action verb or one linking verb.

Some action verbs show actions you can see, such as *run, rise, erupt*. Other action verbs show actions you cannot see, such as *hope, despise, imagine*.

> Although Elena **planned** the dinner, Luke **bought** the ingredients and **prepared** each dish. The dinner guests **enjoyed** Luke's cooking.

Verbs change form to indicate time. (For more about verb tenses, see Lesson 9.4.)

> Today the crew **works**. Yesterday the crew **worked**. The crew **was working** all week.

Some action verbs take direct objects. (For more about direct objects, see Lesson 6.6.)

▶ **Linking verbs** join—or link—the subject of a sentence with a word or words that identify or describe it. (For more about subjects and predicates, see Lesson 6.2.)

> Africa **is** the second largest of the seven continents.
> Suddenly, the room **became** quiet. His face **turned** red.

Some verbs can be both linking and action verbs—but not at the same time. If the word or words following the verb identify or describe the subject, the verb is a linking verb.

> LINKING VERB Ed **feels** sick. All food **tastes** strange to him.
> ACTION VERB Ed **feels** the top of the melon. He **will taste** the melon later.

▶ A **verb phrase** contains a main verb (V) plus one or more **helping** (or **auxiliary**) **verbs** (HV).

>   HV   V
> The plumber **should have been** here by now.
>
>   HV   V
> **Has**n't anyone **called** her yet?

Not (*n't* in a contraction) is never part of the verb phrase.

**Linking Verbs:
Some Forms of *To Be***

am	is
are	should be
being	was
can be	were
have been	will be
would have been	

Some Other Linking Verbs

appear	become
feel	grow
look	remain
seem	smell
sound	stay
taste	turn

Some Helping Verbs

be (is, am, are, was, were,
  been, being)
have (has, had)
do (does, did)

can	shall
could	should
may	will
might	would
must	

WRITING HINT

For writing that says more and says it better, choose action verbs whenever possible.
>   *yawns and slumps*
> Jan ~~looks tired~~.

Exercise 5 Identifying Verbs

Underline every verb and verb phrase in the following sentences.
Hint: Two sentences have more than one verb or verb phrase.

1. In Victorian times and earlier, men performed almost all secretarial or clerical duties.

2. In the United States, the earliest known ad for female typists appeared in 1875.

3. It proclaimed, "Mere girls are now earning from $10 to $20 a week with the 'Type-Writer.'"

4. Still, at that time, mostly men, and not women, were learning typing and shorthand.

5. Even New York's famous former mayor, Fiorello LaGuardia, took shorthand classes in 1906.

6. By 1940, however, the secretarial field had changed completely.

7. By that time, 93 percent of the nation's clerical help was female.

8. Have the numbers of male secretaries been increasing in recent years?

9. Do male secretaries still earn more than female secretaries, as they did in 1986?

10. A recent ad in the *Boston Globe* advertises the rate of $10 an hour for a data entry/general office worker.

Working Together

Exercise 6 Using Vivid Verbs

Work with a partner to complete each of the following sentences with one or more vivid verbs. Add any other words you may find necessary. Compare your sentences with those of other pairs.

1. The intruder ———————————————————.

2. All the dogs in the kennel ———————————— when we entered.

3. In the hospital nursery, the newborns ———————————————.

4. The crowds ———————————— into the subway entrance.

5. The meteor showers ———————————————————.

Exercise 7 Using Concrete Nouns and Vivid Verbs

On a separate piece of paper, replace each noun or pronoun with a concrete noun and each verb with a vivid verb. Rewrite any other words as needed.

1. The man looked sad.

2. The children played.

3. No one in the auditorium remained seated.

4. The clouds are in the sky.

Adjectives

Adjectives give color, size, shape, dimension, and a host of other qualities to nouns and pronouns.

▶ **Adjectives** are modifiers. They give information about the nouns and pronouns they modify.

WHAT KIND?	**yellow** ribbon, **dirty** sidewalk, **concise** report
HOW MANY?	**ten** onions, **numerous** instances, **few** visits
HOW MUCH?	**ample** food, **more** energy, **little** produce
WHICH ONE?	**this** minute, **next** summer, **second** paragraph, **last** place

Two or more adjectives may modify the same noun.

The climbers made **three desperate** attempts.

Spot is **lively**, **intelligent**, and **affectionate**.

▶ *A*, *an*, and *the* make up a subcategory of adjectives called **articles**. *The* is the **definite article**. It is an adjective that points out a particular, or definite, noun. *A* and *an* are **indefinite articles**. They point to any one—rather than just one specific—member of a group.

| INDEFINITE | Julia made **a** fabulous catch. |
| DEFINITE | **The** ball nearly sailed over **the** fence. |

▶ **Proper adjectives**, the modifying form of proper nouns, always begin with a capital letter.

Persian rug   **Filipino** music   **European** tourists

▶ Many adjectives come right before the noun they modify, but **predicate adjectives** follow a linking verb to modify the subject of a sentence. (For more about **subjects**, see Lesson 6.2.)

Lauren is **ill** today.

The water appears **cloudy** and **menacing**.

▶ When a noun modifies another noun, it functions as an adjective.

desk drawer   **opera** house   **Gillian's** coat

▶ Sometimes, an adjective is part of a compound proper noun. Always begin these adjectives with a capital letter.

Native Americans   Northern Hemisphere   Big Dipper

WRITING HINT

Avoid dull modifiers such as *good*, *nice*, *bad*, *great*, and *fun*. Sharpen your sentences with vivid adjectives.

witty, concise
Carla wrote a ~~great~~ essay.

Enriching Your Vocabulary

The word *concise* comes from the Latin prefix *com-*, meaning "with," and the Latin word *caedere*, which means "to cut" or "to strike." When you make something *concise*, you strike out or cut out everything that isn't needed. A related word is *excision*, which is a kind of surgical cut or removal.

EXERCISE 8 Identifying Adjectives

Underline the adjectives, proper adjectives, and articles in the
following paragraph.

¹What was the Columbian Exchange? ²It was an early form of global trade.
³During the colonization of the Americas, diverse foods, plants, and animals
began to be traded with Europe, Africa, and Asia. ⁴American plants such as red
tomatoes, juicy pineapples, and colorful squashes amazed the Europeans, Asians,
and Africans who had never seen them before. ⁵Of course, the Columbian
Exchange was not a one-way operation. ⁶Americans got African yams and
bananas. ⁷They got European livestock, including horses and pigs. ⁸Unfortunately,
they also got new and horrific diseases, including the deadly smallpox and
measles that became the fearful scourge of the Native American population.

EXERCISE 9 Revising Sentences to Add Information

Revise the sentences below to give the reader more information and to create
more interesting sentences. Add or change words and make up details.
Underline all the adjectives and articles in your revised sentences. Use a
separate piece of paper if necessary.

EXAMPLE   The bloodhound sniffed the evidence.
*The well-trained and eager bloodhound sniffed the ripped, stained
scrap of fabric from the man's coat.*

1. A woman walked through the garden.

2. The sky warned us that a storm was on the way.

3. The houses looked alike.

4. The horses stopped suddenly at the edge of the field.

5. A child crouched in the corner of the shed.

Adverbs

Just as adjectives add information to nouns, adverbs describe or limit other parts of speech.

▐▐▐▶ **Adverbs** modify—or tell more about—verbs, adjectives, and other adverbs.

MODIFIES VERB	She peered **hopefully** into the distance.
MODIFIES ADJECTIVE	Calvin is **extraordinarily** bright.
MODIFIES ADVERB	He left the room **rather** abruptly.

Many adverbs can come before or after the verbs they modify.

Rapidly, we descended the stairs.
We **rapidly** descended the stairs.
We descended the stairs **rapidly**.

You may think all adverbs end with the suffix *-ly*. Many do (*truly, usually, easily,* for example). Many common adverbs, however, don't end in *-ly* (*seldom, never, always, soon, today, now, here,* for example).

▐▐▐▶ **Intensifiers** are adverbs that answer the question *to what extent?*

Is Jack **somewhat** lazy about doing his homework?
Elena was **less** startled by the news than I was.
This recipe is **too** complicated.

Some Common Adverbs That Do Not End in -ly

almost	now
already	seldom
also	soon
always	still
fast	then
here	there
just	today
late	tomorrow
more	well
much	yesterday
never	yet
not (n't)	

Some Common Intensifiers

less	rather
least	really
more	so
most	somewhat
nearly	too
only	truly
quite	very
exceptionally	
extraordinarily	

STEP BY STEP

Deciding Between Adjective and Adverb

To decide whether you need to use an adjective or an adverb, first determine the part of speech of the word you need to modify.

1. If the word is a noun or pronoun, use an adjective.

   The water tasted **bad**. [*Bad* modifies *water*.]

2. If the word is a verb, adjective, or another adverb, use an adverb.

   Dan needs good advice **badly**.
   [*Badly* modifies *needs*.]

Remember that a verb may be modified by an adverb but not by an adjective. A standardized-test item may ask you to recognize an incorrect use of a modifier. See item 9 on page 314.

EXERCISE 10 Using Adverbs

To each sentence below, add at least one adverb that provides additional information. Use a different adverb in each sentence. Use a separate piece of paper, if necessary.

1. We hiked a trail in Canyonlands National Park.

2. We had hiked six miles in that arid landscape.

3. All of us were exhausted.

4. We were also looking forward to the hike's end.

5. A rattlesnake appeared in our path.

6. It was a horrifying sight.

7. All of us stepped back.

8. Evidently, however, we were also a horrifying sight to the rattlesnake.

9. It stayed still.

10. Nevertheless, we decided never to hike again.

EXERCISE 11 Choosing the Correct Modifier

You will often hear adverbs used incorrectly in speech. In writing, however, it is important to choose the right modifier. Underline the modifier in parentheses that correctly completes each sentence.

1. Do you see a doctor (regular, regularly)?

2. Some people do not take health care (serious, seriously).

3. One of the most (common, commonly) reasons for visiting a doctor is hypertension.

4. Those experiencing the pain of a middle-ear infection are almost (equal, equally) likely to seek a doctor's advice.

5. People (frequent, frequently) seek help for upper respiratory infections.

6. People do regard the need for health care (different, differently).

7. Some can be (extreme, extremely) reluctant to see a doctor if they do not consider themselves to be (serious, seriously) ill.

8. Some (simple, simply) cannot afford the cost of care.

9. Stays in the hospital can (easy, easily) cost more than several hundred dollars a day.

10. This is one reason why some people want universal health care coverage very (bad, badly).

Prepositions

➡ **Prepositions** connect another word in a sentence to a noun or pronoun (and its modifiers, if any) to form a prepositional phrase. (For more about prepositional phrases, see Lesson 7.1.)

Major fires raged **across** the park. They burned **for** eleven days.

Some prepositions are **compound**. They are made up of two or more words.

We went to the game **in spite of** the rain.
The roads were closed **because of** the race.

Some words are both prepositions and adverbs. To tell the difference, look for a prepositional phrase. If the word is part of a prepositional phrase, it is a preposition. If not, it is an adverb.

ADVERBS   In ten minutes, we will be **through** with this job.
               "Move **along**," shouted the cattle driver.

PREPOSITIONS   I walked ***through*** *the narrow hallway.*
               The news moved ***along*** *the line* quickly.

EXERCISE 12 Expanding Sentences

Expand the sentences below with prepositional phrases. Add no more than three in a row to each sentence; more than three can make a sentence singsongy. Make the sentences interesting and vivid. To do so, add details, and change words as necessary. Underline every preposition you add.

EXAMPLE   A dark shape beckoned.
          At the end of the abandoned lane, a dark shape beckoned to us.

1. The skier races.

2. The climber dangled.

3. The pile teetered.

4. The watchdog is growling.

5. People hurried.

6. Skaters glide.

7. Few paused to look up.

8. Several hours passed.

9. It was dawn.

10. The brakes screeched.

Some Commonly Used Prepositions

about	above	along
as	at	before
below	by	down
during	except	for
from	into	like
near	of	off
on	out	over
since	to	under
until	up	upon
with	without	outside
across	inside	against
through	around	toward

but (meaning "except")

Some Common Compound Prepositions

according to	due to
along with	in front of
apart from	in place of
aside from	in spite of
as to	instead of
because of	out of
in addition to	

WRITING HINT

In formal writing, avoid ending a sentence with a preposition. In informal writing, however, ending a sentence with a preposition sometimes makes sense.

FORMAL
From whom should we seek advice?

INFORMAL
Whom should we get advice from?

EXERCISE 13 Identifying Prepositional Phrases

In the following sentences, underline each prepositional phrase.

1. The abbreviation FM stands for *frequency modulation*.
2. It was invented by Edwin Howard Armstrong.
3. Armstrong was aiming for clarity at high frequencies.
4. He wanted a clear sound with a minimum of distortion.
5. According to some sources, Armstrong's inventive genius was like Edison's.
6. Thomas Edison was the inventor of the lightbulb and of the phonograph.
7. In spite of his accomplishments, many people do not know Armstrong's name.
8. He performed the first tests of his frequency-modulation transmitter from the top of the Empire State Building.
9. In spite of the marvelous quality of the sound, large broadcasting networks did not welcome his invention.
10. They worried, instead, about the huge amounts of money they had invested in AM radio.

EXERCISE 14 Distinguishing Prepositions from Adverbs

Fill in the blank with *PREP* if the underlined word functions as a preposition in the sentence. Write *ADV* if the underlined word functions as an adverb.

_____ 1. "Don't look <u>down</u>," cautioned the rock-climbing instructor.

_____ 2. We will hike <u>down</u> the mountain later.

_____ 3. Is the light <u>off</u>?

_____ 4. That record has practically gone <u>off</u> the charts.

_____ 5. Did that car just go <u>through</u> the stop sign?

_____ 6. Clean the kitchen as soon as you are <u>through</u>.

_____ 7. We walked <u>out</u> after the first act.

_____ 8. Did Will go <u>out</u> the same exit?

_____ 9. That group is operating <u>outside</u> the law.

_____10. The children played <u>outside</u> all day.

Conjunctions and Interjections

The word *conjunction* comes from two Latin sources: the prefix *con-*, meaning "together," and the root *junction*, meaning "to join."

▶ **Conjunctions** join words or groups of words.

▶ **Coordinating conjunctions** join words or groups of words that are equal in importance.

> *Dan* **and** *Derone* are twins. *They look alike,* **but** *they don't think alike.*

▶ **Correlative conjunctions** are always used in pairs.

> **Either** *Joan* **or** *I* will win the scholarship.
> **Both** *Tim* **and** *Enrique* are studying medicine.

The words or phrases joined by a pair of correlative conjunctions should be parallel.

> INCORRECT **Neither** *my mother* **nor** *father* can play the piano.
> CORRECT **Neither** *my mother* **nor** *my father* can play the piano.

▶ **Subordinating conjunctions** connect adverb clauses to main clauses. (For more about adverb clauses and a list of subordinating conjunctions, see Lesson 8.3.)

> **Even though** it is raining, we will still hold the reunion.
> We chose that site **because** María loves the view.

▶ **Interjections** express mild or strong emotion.

Interjections are the loneliest part of speech. They do not have a grammatical connection to any other part of a sentence. Set them off with a comma or an exclamation point.

> **My**, what a sad story.   **Hey**! Come back here this minute!

Coordinating Conjunctions

and	but
nor	or
so	yet

Some Correlative Conjunctions

both . . . and
either . . . or
just as . . . so (too)
neither . . . nor
not only . . . but also
whether . . . or

Some Common Interjections

ah	oh no
aha	oops
alas	ouch
bravo	sh
eureka	ugh
good grief	well
hey	wow
hooray	yo

TEST-TAKING TIP

It's important to remember that the subordinating conjunctions *because* and *although* express different meanings. On a standardized test, you may be asked to recognize which of the two correctly serves the sense of a sentence. See the Example on page 306.

EXERCISE 15 Adding Interjections to Sentences

Rewrite these sentences, adding interjections at the beginning or wherever they seem natural. Be sure to use the correct punctuation.

1. Don't lean over the edge.

2. It was a very sad day.

3. I've found it.

4. What an exciting way to spend a day.

5. You won the game.

EXERCISE 16 Identifying Conjunctions

Underline every conjunction in the paragraph below.

[1]Millions of American high school students study French, but some people question why. [2]Their question is not whether one should or should not study a foreign language. [3]Instead, they wonder if students should study French or another language. [4]They admit that French was once the language of diplomacy, and it remains important in the study of literature, art, and culture. [5]Nevertheless, French is neither an extremely widely spoken language nor a key language in business and commerce. [6]The two most frequently spoken languages are Mandarin (spoken by 17.3% of the world's population) and English (spoken by 8.4%). [7]Behind them are, in order, Hindi, Spanish, and Russian. [8]In addition, not only Arabic but also Bengali, Portuguese, and Malay-Indonesian are more frequently spoken than French is; yet 22.3% of all middle and high school students who study a foreign language study French (spoken by 2.2% of the world's population). [9]In fact, both Spanish and French students account for 87% of all the students in middle and high school language classes across the United States.

CONNECTING
Writing & Grammar

Write What You Think

On a separate piece of paper, write a paragraph giving your opinion on one of the statements below. Be sure to explain the reasons for your opinion, providing facts and examples to support it. After you have revised your writing, edit it to be sure that you have used conjunctions correctly.

Refer to **Composition**, Lesson 4.2, to find strategies for writing persuasively.

• Students in American high schools should not study a foreign language.

• Students in American high schools should study Mandarin, Hindi, Spanish, or Russian.

• Students in American high schools should study Spanish or French.

Determining a Word's Part of Speech

You already know that prepositions can also be adverbs, depending on the context. Many other words can also function as more than one part of speech. For example, *top* can be a noun, verb, adjective, or adverb.

▶ How a word is used in a sentence determines its part of speech.

NOUN	Did you hike to the **top**?
VERB	No one could **top** Logan's record.
ADJECTIVE	Roberto Clemente was a **top** performer on the baseball diamond.
ADVERB	I read about the **top** ten qualifying results.

EXERCISE 17 Identifying Parts of Speech

Identify the part of speech of each underlined word as it is used in the sentence. Use these abbreviations:

N = noun   ADJ = adjective   CONJ = conjunction
P = pronoun   ADV = adverb   INT = interjection
V = verb   PREP = preposition

_____ 1. How does the world commonly view <u>scientists</u>?

_____ 2. Some people see them as <u>evil</u> villains.

_____ 3. For <u>some</u>, scientists are intent on learning more and more, no matter what the cost.

_____ 4. For others, scientists <u>are</u> heroes, driven by their desire to do good.

_____ 5. Many scientists see themselves as <u>neither</u> heroes <u>nor</u> villains.

_____ 6. They regard themselves <u>as</u> people with a job to do.

_____ 7. In that sense, they are <u>like</u> most other people.

_____ 8. Hollywood, however, <u>seems</u> to delight in creating a different picture.

_____ 9. In films, the mad scientist is as common as, <u>well</u>, the bumbling idiot.

_____ 10. Scientists hope the day is coming <u>soon</u> when Hollywood will reconsider who they are and what they do.

Enriching Your Vocabulary

The Latin prefixes *re-* and *retro-* both mean "back." For example, to *reconsider* is to look back and consider again, and a *recrimination* is a counteraccusation, or a way of getting back at someone. A *retrospective* looks back at an entire career or other phenomena of the past; and if a raise is *retroactive*, it not only makes the future look better, but it pays you back for time you already worked at a lower rate of pay.

Revising and Editing Worksheet

Improve the following draft by revising for ideas, organization, word choice, and sentence variety. After revising, edit the draft for errors in spelling, capitalization, punctuation, and usage. Write your revised and edited version on a separate piece of paper. Compare your changes with those of a writing partner.

[1]What is best for health? [2]You should eat fruits. [3]You should eat vegetables. [4]You should exercise. [5]Perhaps most important of all, you should not smoke.

[6]Everyone knows that there is no one diet that can prevent disease. [7]Yet experts recommend certain ways of eating. [8]They recommend these same things again and again. [9]First, people have to cut down on fat. [10]People really need less saturated fat in their diets. [11]People also need less simple sugars. [12]Simple sugars are found in foods such as cookies. [13]They are found in crackers. [14]They are found in foods made from refined sugar and refined grains. [15]Some doctors also recommend a diet that is low in red meat. [16]Some doctors recommend a diet that is moderate in red meat. [17]A lot of red meat is definitely out.

[18]What is in? [19]Fruits and vegetables are in. [20]A recent finding was made by the american institute for cancer research and the world cancer research fund. [21]This finding resulted in the suggestion that eating more fruits and vegetables can eliminate some cancers, like maybe about 20 percent of them.

[22]The best fruits and vegetables are yellow. [23]They are dark green. [24]They are orange. [25]They are rich in carotenoids. [26]They are rich in vitamin C. [27]Examples are tomatoes, oranges, strawberries, grapes, broccoli, and carrots. [28]Garlic and onions are also great.

Chapter Review

EXERCISE A Identifying Parts of Speech

Identify the part of speech of each underlined word as it is used in the sentence.
Use these abbreviations:

N = noun	ADJ = adjective	CONJ = conjunction
P = pronoun	ADV = adverb	INT = interjection
V = verb	PREP = preposition	

_____ 1. <u>What</u> is teen culture?

_____ 2. Some pop history books call <u>1956</u> the first "Year of the Teenager."

_____ 3. Teenagers were beginning to arrive on the scene as an important subset <u>of</u> mainstream culture.

_____ 4. There was even a pop group that called <u>itself</u> Frankie Lymon and the Teenagers.

_____ 5. <u>Simultaneously</u>, superstar Elvis Presley was defining and mobilizing an entire generation.

_____ 6. His film counterpart, James Dean, <u>became</u> a symbol of teenage alienation in the movie *Rebel Without a Cause*.

_____ 7. <u>New</u> trends in teenage style also emerged.

_____ 8. Slicked-back hair, pedal pushers, <u>and</u> ponytails all helped teens identify themselves as a separate group.

_____ 9. No longer was <u>everyone</u> considered a child until adulthood.

_____10. <u>Oh no!</u> Now there was someone and something halfway between childhood and adulthood.

EXERCISE B Adding Adjectives and Adverbs to Sentences

Add information to the following sentences. Replace vague or general
nouns and verbs, and add adjectives and adverbs.

1. The school bell rang.

2. I saw the accident.

3. I waited for almost one hour.

4. We moved the doghouse.

5. I heard footsteps behind me.

Exercise C Revising a Report

Revise the following portion of a report on the changing status of women during Tudor times in England. Combine sentences, replace imprecise words, and add details. Correct any errors that you may find in the use of parts of speech.

[1]Tudor times are an interesting period in the history of women. [2]Tudor times are roughly the sixteenth century. [3]England had finally left the Middle Ages behind.

[4]The role of a woman before the Tudor age was limited. [5]Mostly, she stayed at home. [6]Men had all the political power. [7]They ran the show. [8]Women who did try to take power were suspect. [9]It was considered real unnatural. [10]Women usually did not go to school. [11]Most women did not learn to read. [12]Some women joined convents. [13]Women in convents got some education. [14]Women in convents had to know how to read sermons.

[15]Then, suddenly, everything changed. [16]The highest rulers in England were women. [17]The highest leaders in Scotland were women. [18]The highest leader in France was a woman. [19]In England, Mary Tudor took the throne. [20]She was followed by Elizabeth I. [21]Elizabeth I was a great queen. [22]She was powerful. [23]She ruled for forty-five years. [24]Scotland was led by Mary of Lorraine. [25]Then it was led by Mary, Queen of Scots. [26]France was led by Catherine de Médicis. [27]She was real important in France for almost half a century.

Write What You Think

CONNECTING Writing & Grammar

Write one paragraph in response to the following essay question. Begin by stating your opinion. Then support your opinion with reasons and examples. After you have revised your writing, edit it to be sure you have used adjectives, adverbs, and pronouns correctly.

How would the election of a woman as President of the United States influence the nation?

Hint: Choose a type of influence, such as political, diplomatic, cultural, or economic influence, and then discuss it.

Parts of a Sentence

STUDENT WRITING
Expository Essay

Why Pi?
by Mike Gradziel
high school student, Adams, Massachusetts

It's one of those mysterious numbers that fascinates number freaks and confuses everyone else. It really is an interesting number. The ratio of the radius of a circle to its circumference has been studied by man for thousands of years. Two simple, perfect shapes—the circle and the square—are related only by the infinitely complex number pi. It seems that we, with our great numerical intelligence, could find a geometric relationship between these two basic shapes, but we are unable to do so, and pi remains as mysterious and unknown as ever.

The Babylonians and Egyptians used values of pi three thousand years ago that were very close to the current accepted value. In Asia, Europe, and the Middle East, mathematicians had calculated pi to thirty decimal places by the 1500s. Calculations were made up to about eight hundred decimal places by the 1940s; and in 1949, ENIAC, the Electronic Numerical Integrator Computer, was used to calculate the first 2,037 digits. By 1997, the latest calculations had reached fifty-one billion digits. To visualize this, understand that one billion digits, printed in ordinary type, would extend over 1,200 miles. That's the distance you would drive from New York to Nebraska.

The letter pi, the sixteenth letter of the Greek alphabet, has only been used to represent the number for the past 250 years. Before that, various other symbols were used. . . .

Most people know pi as 3.14, but some people have memorized thousands of digits. Hiroyuki Goto set a new record in 1995 by reciting 42,000 places from memory. The number has been encoded in music and literature in many languages for the purpose of memorization. For example, if the number of letters in each word in a sentence were to correspond with a digit of pi, then the sentence "How I wish I could calculate pi" would give you 3.141592. . . .

Hundreds of digits have been encoded in this way even though the most digits of pi that anyone could ever need is probably ten or twenty.

Mike Gradziel contemplates the significance and mystery of the number pi. The essay is informative and interesting because he gives background information, a definition, and anecdotes about people who memorize the number.

Reread Mike's essay, and notice that his sentences vary in structure. As you work on sentences in this chapter, think about how you can manipulate them to communicate your ideas in an interesting way.

Complete Sentences

▶ A **sentence** is a grammatically complete group of words that expresses a thought. A sentence must express either an action or state of being and contain something that performs the action.

Every sentence starts with a capital letter and finishes with an end mark of punctuation—a period, question mark, or exclamation point.

▶ A **sentence fragment** is a group of words that is not grammatically complete. Avoid sentence fragments in formal writing.

Because sentence fragments start with a capital letter and end with an end mark of punctuation, they look just like sentences. But they are not.

FRAGMENT	Ended with a question. [What ended with a question?]
FRAGMENT	The letter to the editor. [What did the letter say or do?]
SENTENCE	The letter to the editor ended with a question.
FRAGMENT	Although the letter to the editor ended with a question. [The word *although* sets up a new expectation for information; it turns the sentence into an incomplete thought.]
SENTENCE	Although the letter to the editor ended with a question, its message was clear.

▶ Every sentence has one of four purposes:

1. **Declarative sentences** make a statement. They end with a period.
   Ancient villages lay hidden for centuries.

2. **Imperative sentences** make a command or a request. They end with either a period or (if the command shows strong feeling) an exclamation point.
   Read about the exciting discovery of the Mayan city of Copán.
   Don't procrastinate!

3. **Interrogative sentences** ask a question. They end with a question mark.
   When was the first Mayan city discovered?

4. **Exclamatory sentences** express strong feeling. They end with an exclamation point.
   What a great discovery that was!

WRITING HINT

Don't use sentence fragments in formal writing, but if you're writing dialogue, fragments can make your writing sound natural.

"What about the money?"

"Not now, Nick. Not ever."

Enriching Your Vocabulary

The root of the word *procrastinate* is the Latin word *cras,* which means "tomorrow." A *procrastinator* postpones the things he or she has to do until a future time, such as tomorrow.

EXERCISE 1 Identifying Sentence Fragments

For each numbered item, circle the letter before the words that form a complete sentence.

1. a. A trip to the dentist's office, which many people fear.
   b. A trip to the dentist's office, which many people fear, is rapidly becoming less dreadful.

2. a. Technological advances are resulting in safer, more accurate, and less painful methods of treating teeth.
   b. Technological advances for safer, more accurate, and less painful methods of treating teeth.

3. a. Dentists cut through teeth, which are the body's hardest surfaces.
   b. Because dentists cut through teeth, the body's hardest surfaces.

4. a. The use of laser light as a new method for repairing teeth.
   b. The use of laser light is a new method for repairing teeth.

5. a. New, computerized X-rays mean less radiation and more safety for patients.
   b. New, computerized X-rays less radiation and more safety for patients.

Working Together

EXERCISE 2 Writing Complete Sentences

On a separate piece of paper, rewrite the following notes, which are sentence fragments, as a paragraph made up of complete sentences. Work with a partner or small group. Be sure to begin each sentence with a capital letter and end with an appropriate end punctuation mark.

Squid

A mollusk; large head, fairly large brain

Common squid, 12–18"; giant squid, 60' or more—largest invertebrate giant squid found in ocean—1,000–2,000' deep

Has two fins; has arms near mouth; has tentacles; grabs prey with tentacles, holds prey with arms

A cephalopod—in same class as nautilus and octopus

Swims faster than any other invertebrate—forces water out of a tube—water going in one direction causes squid to move quickly in opposite direction—like a jet

Deep-sea squid shoots out ink—when chased

Subject and Predicate

Every sentence has two parts: a subject and a predicate.

▌▌▌➤ The **subject** is the part of the sentence that names the person, place, thing, or idea that the sentence is about. The **predicate** is the part of the sentence that tells what the subject does, what it is, or what happens to it. Both a subject and a predicate may be either a single word or a group of words.

SUBJECT	PREDICATE
Archimedes	exclaimed, "Eureka!"

▌▌▌➤ The **simple subject** is the key word or words in the subject. It may be more than one word when it is a compound noun (high school) or a proper noun (North America). The complete subject is made up of the simple subject and all of its modifiers.

▌▌▌➤ The **simple predicate** is always the verb or verb phrase that tells something about the subject. The complete predicate contains the verb and all of its modifiers, objects, and complements. Remember that *not* (*n't* in a contraction) is never part of a verb phrase.

You'll review objects and complements in Lessons 6.6 and 6.7.

Throughout this book, the term *subject* refers to the simple subject. The terms *verb* and *predicate* refer to the simple predicate. In the following examples, the simple subject and the simple predicate appear in boldface.

COMPLETE SUBJECT	COMPLETE PREDICATE
A **mathematician** of ancient Greece	**discovered** important principles.
Archimedes' Principle	**relates** to the behavior of solids in liquids.
The **formula** for the area of a circle	**is** one of Archimedes' achievements.
Stories about Archimedes	**have been** frequently **told** throughout the ages.
Archimedes and **Pythagoras**	**are** among the most famous Greek mathematicians.

> ## WRITING HINT
>
> The verb doesn't always come after the subject. In a question, the verb often comes first.
>
> Did you call? [*You* is the subject; *did call* is the verb.]
>
> In addition, placing the verb before the subject varies the sentence structure and can create dramatic effects. Never will I get on that ride again!

P.S. Why should you learn about subjects and predicates? After all, no one outside school will ever ask you about them. However, it is important to recognize them in order to help you avoid fragments and subject-verb agreement problems when you write.

EXERCISE 3 Identifying Subjects and Verbs

In each sentence, underline the simple subject once and the simple predicate twice. **Remember:** When the subject is a proper noun, underline the entire noun.

EXAMPLE   A famous experiment involved density.

1. King Heiron II of Syracuse was suspicious of his crown.

2. Was it made of solid gold?

3. Nobody at the time knew the answer.

4. Archimedes eventually solved the problem.

5. You could solve it, too.

6. A lump of gold of the same weight as the crown is needed for the experiment.

7. It should displace the same amount of water as the crown in question.

8. All metals have different densities.

9. Only gold will displace the same amount of water as another piece of gold of equal weight.

10. By the way, King Heiron's crown consisted only partly of gold.

Working Together

EXERCISE 4 Writing Complete Sentences

On a separate piece of paper, rewrite the following notes, which are sentence fragments, as a paragraph made up of complete sentences. Work with a partner or small group. Be sure to begin each sentence with a capital letter and end with an appropriate end punctuation mark. Compare your paragraphs with those of other pairs or groups.

Heart

Pump—needs energy to start up, keep going

Electricity—causes the heart's muscles to contract

Sparks from nerve cells—cause regular contractions

Mechanical energy—muscles squeeze & push blood valves open & shut

Heart—pumps blood to all parts of the body

Correcting Sentence Fragments

Use these strategies to correct sentence fragments.

1. **Attach it.** Join the fragment to a complete sentence before or after it.

   FRAGMENT   If you want something done. Ask a busy person.

   REVISED   If you want something done, ask a busy person.

2. **Add some words.** Add the words needed to make the group of words grammatically complete. Often, the missing word is a subject or verb, although this is not always the case.

   FRAGMENT   Uses up the time available for it.

   REVISED   Work uses up the time available for it.

3. **Drop some words.** Drop the subordinating conjunction that creates a fragment.

   FRAGMENT   Because deadlines can actually make you more efficient.

   REVISED   Deadlines can actually make you more efficient.

EXERCISE 5 Editing Sentence Fragments

On a separate piece of paper, edit each numbered item to correct all sentence fragments. Use the three strategies just presented.

1. I address and stamp the envelopes. As I watch television.

2. Even though it's not easy to do two things at once.

3. Makes me go faster.

4. C. Northcote Parkinson is the author of this theory. About being busy.

5. Parkinson's Law, about work filling the time available for it, since 1955.

STEP BY STEP

The Sentence Test
To determine whether a group of words is a sentence, ask these three questions:

1. Does it have a subject?

2. Does it have a verb?

3. Does it express a complete thought?

If you can't answer *yes* to all three questions, you have a sentence fragment. Fix it.

Enriching Your Vocabulary

The word *destitute*, used in Exercise 6, comes from the Latin root *statuere*, meaning "set or place," and the Latin prefix *de-*, meaning "down." When combined, the resulting word can be used to simply mean "lacking," but the word is more often used to mean "poverty-stricken."

EXERCISE 6 Editing Sentence Fragments

Read the paragraph below carefully. If the numbered group is not a sentence, add words or omit words to make it a sentence. Use the three strategies in this lesson, and write your corrected paragraph on a separate piece of paper.

[1]Finished *When I Was Puerto Rican* last night. [2]A great book about the childhood of the author, Esmeralda Santiago. [3]Was born in the countryside of Puerto Rico. [4]Grew up in various places in Puerto Rico. [5]Came from a large family. [6]Although the family was destitute. [7]Santiago experienced much love and tenderness. [8]During her childhood, many experiences in the countryside. [9]Learned how to eat a *guayaba*, or guava, a local fruit, and learned how to identify the song of the *coquí*, a native frog. [10]At the age of fourteen arrived in New York City. [11]Where her life changed completely. [12]She was still Puerto Rican, of course, but she was also now something else. [13]A hybrid living in an entirely new and different world. [14]A new culture, a great challenge. [15]On top of that, a new language. [16]Which made Santiago feel different and isolated from her new life. [17]In the end, however, both cultures enriched her. [18]She is now, she says, something more. [19]This book, just part of the story of that change and growth. [20]Don't miss it!

CONNECTING
Writing & Grammar

Write What You Think

On a separate piece of paper, write what you think about the following statement. State your opinion clearly, and support it with reasons and specific details. After you have revised your writing, edit it to be sure you have used complete sentences.

Although people who move from one country to another face many challenges, their lives are enriched by the moves they make. The gains of making the move outweigh the losses.

Refer to **Composition,** Lesson 4.2, to find strategies for writing persuasively.

Finding the Subject

"there" is never a subject (handwritten)

Finding the subject of a sentence is not always easy or automatic. In some sentences, less common sentence constructions or word orders may seem to bury or camouflage the subject.

▐▌▶ In an **inverted sentence**, the verb (V) comes before the subject (S).

    V   S
Down came the **rain**.

         V   S   S
Across the hall are the **offices** and **labs**.

▐▌▶ The words *here* and *there* are never the subject of a sentence. In a sentence beginning with *here* or *there*, look for the subject after the verb.

    V   S
Here is a great **hat**.

    V   S
There are several more **hats** on the rack.

▐▌▶ The subject of a sentence is never part of a prepositional phrase.

   S   V
The **name** of the book is *Beloved*. [The subject is not *book* because *of the book* is a prepositional phrase modifying *name*, the subject.]

   S   V
Several **novels** by Toni Morrison have won literary awards.

▐▌▶ To find the subject of a question, turn the question into a statement that would begin to answer the question.

   V   S
Who is **Toni Morrison**? [Toni Morrison is _____.]

In a command or request (an imperative sentence), the subject is always *you* (the person being spoken to).

The word *you* is called the *understood subject* because it does not appear in the sentence.

   S   V   V
[You] Call the doctor and ask for her advice. [*You* is the understood subject of the verbs *call* and *ask*.]

Even in direct address—which includes the name of the person being spoken to—the subject is still *you*.

      S   V   V
Caitlin, **[you]** call the doctor and ask for her advice.

STEP BY STEP

Finding the Subject

1. Find the verb or verb phrase.

2. Ask *Who* or *What* before the verb.
   The girl in the red shirt won the match.

   VERB   won

   WHO WON?   girl

3. **Remember:** *There* and *here* are never subjects, and prepositional phrases never contain the subject.

EXERCISE 7 Identifying Subjects and Verbs

In each sentence, underline the simple subject once and the verb twice.
If the subject is understood to be *you*, write the word *You* after the sentence.
Remember: When the subject is a proper noun, underline the entire proper noun.

1. Mike, look at this article about the Mississippi River.

2. Runoff water from thirty-one states and two provinces in Canada is carried by the Mississippi River.

3. Where does all that water go?

4. Forty-one percent of the runoff in the United States flows into the Gulf of Mexico.

5. Today, levees protect the land and people along the Mississippi River from floods.

6. Ms. Jorgensen, please tell us about those levees.

7. The United States Congress made flood control a federal responsibility in 1928.

8. Along the river are miles and miles of levees that the Army Corps of Engineers built.

9. Many of the levees are still considered to be too low, however.

10. There are plans for raising the levees.

11. What will the Army Corps of Engineers do?

12. Millions of tons of dirt will be moved.

13. Explain the consequences of this action.

14. There is a great deal of controversy surrounding it.

15. Tons of dirt will come from nearby acres of wetlands.

16. In fact, thousands of acres of wetlands will be lost.

17. A vocal group of environmentalists favors nonintervention.

18. On the other hand, farmers all along the delta are threatened by flooding.

19. There are huge consequences on both sides of the question.

20. Can this problem ever be fairly resolved?

Correcting Run-on Sentences

▶ A **run-on sentence** is made up of two or more sentences that are incorrectly run together as a single sentence. These sentences may be separated by a comma or no punctuation mark.

Use these five strategies to correct a run-on sentence.

1. **Separate them**. Add end punctuation and a capital letter to separate the sentences.

   RUN-ON   We went to the powwow, it was a huge gathering.

   CORRECTED We went to the powwow. It was a huge gathering.

2. **Use a coordinating conjunction**. Use a word such as *and, but, or, nor, yet,* or *so* preceded by a comma.

   RUN-ON   The word *powwow* can refer to a traditional Native American ceremony, it can refer to other conferences or gatherings.

   CORRECTED The word *powwow* can refer to a traditional Native American ceremony, **or** it can refer to other conferences or gatherings.

3. **Try a semicolon**. Use a semicolon to separate the two sentences.

   RUN-ON   Today's powwows include traditional dances they may also include fun dances and dance contests.

   CORRECTED Today's powwows include traditional dances; they may also include fun dances and dance contests.

4. **Add a conjunctive adverb**. Use a semicolon together with a conjunctive adverb (*however, therefore, nevertheless, still, also, instead,* etc.). Be sure to put a comma after the conjunctive adverb.

   RUN-ON   The word *powwow* means "gathering" it comes from an Algonquian word that refers to a spiritual leader.

   CORRECTED The word *powwow* means "gathering"; **however**, it comes from an Algonquian word that refers to a spiritual leader.

5. **Create a clause**. Turn one of the sentences into a subordinate clause. (See Chapter 8 for more on subordinate clauses.)

   RUN-ON   English settlers correctly understood that a powwow was important, they thought the word referred to a gathering instead of a person.

   CORRECTED **Although English settlers correctly understood that a powwow was important,** they thought the word referred to a gathering instead of a person.

WRITING HINT

Conjunctive adverbs make writing sound formal. Using a conjunctive adverb to correct a run-on sentence is a more common practice in research and business writing than in informal writing.

EXERCISE 8 Editing Run-on Sentences

On a separate piece of paper, correct and rewrite the run-on sentences by adding words and punctuation marks. Use a variety of strategies.

1. Joan of Arc was a military hero she is known for defending the French city of Orléans.

2. She was a remarkable hero because she was a woman, she was very young.

3. Most military leaders at the time were men, many were older than the teenaged Joan of Arc.

4. Many people regarded Joan of Arc as a religious hero, some viewed her as a witch.

5. She claimed to hear voices, she was put to death in 1431.

6. Joan was very young, she was very inspiring to many followers.

Working Together

EXERCISE 9 Editing a Report

Work with a partner or small group to correct all the run-on sentences and fragments in this report. Use a variety of strategies. Compare your changes with those of other pairs or groups.

[1]Uncle Sam is a popular personification he represents the United States. [2]No one is certain where this personification came from, its source may have been Samuel Wilson. [3]Wilson was a meat packer, he supplied meat to the army during the War of 1812. [4]He came to be called Uncle Sam, he was a generally endearing man. [5]Wilson was also extremely patriotic this is probably why the man became associated with the nation. [6]Of course, an abbreviation for Uncle Sam might be U.S., this certainly helped too. [7]The most famous representation of Uncle Sam was created by James Montgomery Flagg, he put his idea of the man "Sam" on a poster. [8]It was used to inspire patriotism during World War I, it shows a determined-looking Sam. [9]He wears a top hat with stars, a red bow tie, and a blue jacket, he says, "I want you." [10]This poster was very popular it was also used during World War II.

Direct and Indirect Objects

Although some sentences are complete with just a subject and verb, others require an object. In this lesson, you'll learn about direct objects and indirect objects.

▶ A **direct object** (DO) is a noun or pronoun that receives the action of an action verb. A direct object answers the question *whom* or *what* following the verb.

>   DO
> Rico brought **balloons**. [Rico brought—*what*?—balloons. *Balloons* is the direct object.]

>   DO   DO
> Mrs. Goldman met **Rick** and **me** at the door. [Mrs. Goldman met—*whom*?—Rick and me. *Rick* and *me* are the direct objects.]

Not all verbs take objects. Linking verbs do not take objects. Some, but not all, action verbs do take objects. Those action verbs that take objects are called **transitive verbs**.

▶ An **indirect object** (IO) is a noun or a pronoun that follows the action verb and answers the question *to whom, for whom, to what,* or *for what,* following the action verb.

Direct objects can stand alone, but indirect objects exist only when there is a direct object. An indirect object always comes before the direct object in a sentence.

>   IO   DO
> I gave **Josh** my **present**. [*To whom* did I give the present? I gave it to *Josh. Josh* is the indirect object; *present* is the direct object.]

>   IO DO
> Mr. Goldman served **me cake**. [*To whom* did Mr. Goldman serve cake? He served it to *me. Me* is the indirect object; *cake* is the direct object.]

Like subjects, direct objects and indirect objects are never part of a prepositional phrase. Even though these next two sentences mean the same thing, only the first one has an indirect object.

>   IO   IO   DO
> Please send **Aunt Marilyn** and **Uncle Jim** a thank-you **note**.
> Please send a thank-you **note** to Aunt Marilyn and Uncle Jim. [The phrase *to Aunt Marilyn and Uncle Jim* is a prepositional phrase.]

EDITING TIP

Don't place a comma between a verb or an indirect object and its object.

ORIGINAL
I read Clayton, "The Bear."

REVISED
I read Clayton "The Bear."

STEP BY STEP

Finding Direct and Indirect Objects

To find a direct object:

1. Find the action verb.

2. Ask the question *whom* or *what* after the action verb.

To find an indirect object:

1. Find the action verb.

2. Find the direct object.

3. Ask the question *to whom, for whom, to what,* or *for what* after the action verb.

EXERCISE 10 Identifying Direct and Indirect Objects

Underline every direct object and indirect object. Label them *DO* for direct object and *IO* for indirect object.

1. John Updike has written many novels, short stories, poems, and essays.

2. Janet read me one of his short stories.

3. Mrs. Tatarian showed us Updike's list of greatest authors.

4. We gave his choices our full attention.

5. His choices included Homer, Proust, and Shakespeare.

EXERCISE 11 Identifying Direct and Indirect Objects

Underline every direct object once and every indirect object twice.

[1]Updike places William Shakespeare at the top of his list of favorite authors. [2]Many would commend him for that choice. [3]Shakespeare's genius for words changed the English language. [4]His plots captivate readers. [5]His themes include human wisdom and folly, joy and sorrow, and love and revenge. [6]Year after year, decade after decade, century after century, his characters bring readers laughter, joy, wisdom, and wonder. [7]Few writers have put more music into the language than he did. [8]Even fewer have given the audience more memorable lines or have dazzled listeners with such a range of vocabulary and wit.

Refer to **Composition,** Lesson 2.2, for advice about supporting your opinions with details and evidence.

Write What You Think

On a separate piece of paper, write a paragraph giving your opinion on the statement below. Be sure to explain your opinion by providing reasons and examples to support it. After you have revised and edited your writing, underline all the direct and indirect objects.

Shakespeare is the most important writer in the high school curriculum. All students in the tenth grade should be required to read and to demonstrate a knowledge of at least two of Shakespeare's major works.

Predicate Nominatives and Predicate Adjectives

These groups of words are punctuated as sentences. But are they sentences?

> A lemon is.
> This orange tastes.

Both sentences have a subject and a verb, yet neither expresses a complete thought. Both sentences contain linking verbs. A **linking verb** is a "sensing" or "being" verb, such as those listed in the margin.

Other Linking Verbs

appear	remain
become	seem
feel	smell
grow	sound
look	taste

➠ A linking verb (LV) needs a noun or an adjective after it in order for it to express a complete thought. That noun (N) or adjective (ADJ) is called a **subject complement**.

    LV   N   LV ADJ
A lemon is a citrus **fruit**. This orange tastes **sour**.

There are two kinds of subject complements: predicate nominatives and predicate adjectives.

➠ A **predicate nominative** (PN) is a noun or pronoun that follows a linking verb and renames or identifies the subject (S).

    S   LV   PN   PN
Mr. Chesowicz is my **teacher** and **coach**. [*Teacher* and *coach* are nouns that rename the subject, *Mr. Chesowicz*.]

        S   LV PN
The best **source** of information **is he**.
[*He* is a pronoun that identifies the subject, *source*.]

➠ A **predicate adjective** (PA) is an adjective that follows a linking verb and modifies, or describes, the subject.

       S   LV PA   PA
Their best **player is fast** and **agile**. [*Fast* and *agile* are adjectives that modify the subject, *player*.]

            S   LV   PA
Despite losses, the **team remains confident**. [*Confident* is an adjective that modifies the subject, *team*.]

      S   S   LV   PA
Co-captains **Davis** and **Chang are** especially **optimistic**. [The adjective *optimistic* modifies the subjects, *Davis* and *Chang*.]

EDITING TIP

In everyday speech, when someone asks, "Is Allan there?" Allan might reply, "It's me." In formal writing, however, the answer is, instead, "It is I" or "This is he." Why? In formal writing, pronouns used as predicate nominatives must be in the subject, not object, case. (See Lessons 11.1 and 11.2.)

EXERCISE 12 Identifying Predicate Nominatives and Predicate Adjectives

Underline every predicate nominative and predicate adjective in the sentences below. In the space provided, write *PN* for predicate nominative or *PA* for predicate adjective.

_PA_ 1. The roses smell <u>fresh</u> and <u>fragrant</u>.

_PN_ 2. Joan is a great <u>gardener</u> and landscape <u>architect</u>.

_PA_ 3. We feel <u>cheerful</u> in this well-designed space.

_PA_ 4. Two common shade plants are <u>hydrangeas</u> and <u>hostas</u>.

_PA_ 5. Fresh, edible flowers look <u>spectacular</u> on a salad or cake.

EXERCISE 13 Writing a Description

Work with a partner to write a description of your high school. Try to provide both general and specific information. You might begin with its name, location, and grades. You might then compare it with other high schools in your town or city, explaining what makes your own school unique. Also include some description of the individuals and groups who make it up. Use the notes below for more ideas. When you've finished writing, underline and label every predicate adjective and predicate nominative.

Carver High School

Biggest high school in St. Louis, Missouri—grades 9–12

Strong math curriculum, A.P. and honors classes

Good football team, great school spirit

Old, run-down building, pre-WWII—needs interior paint job and bathroom renovations

New computer lab, good library

Small "in group"; a few honors students; small group of students who make no effort

What students look like and wear—small backpacks, lots of black, short hair, tight clothes

---

Revising and Editing Worksheet 1

Improve the following draft by revising for ideas, organization, word choice, and sentence variety. After revising, edit the draft for errors in spelling, capitalization, punctuation, and usage. Write your revised and edited version on a separate piece of paper. Compare your changes with those of a writing partner.

[1]Where does the word *graham* in the term *graham cracker* come from? [2]It refers to one of America's earliest health food heroes. [3]Or fanatics, depending on your opinion. [4]Sylvester Graham. [5]He was a minister he was very much concerned with the problems of drinking in society. [6]He became well known during the first half of the nineteenth century this was a time when many reformers were concerned with drinking problems in America, they formed a temperance movement.

[7]Graham wanted people to stop drinking he wanted them to go even further he wanted them to go on to cure their bodies. [8]By eating a better diet. [9]Certain foods were definitely to be avoided. [10]Mustard and ketchup, for example. [11]Which, according to Graham, made people crazy. [12]As with many health food reformers of today, Graham also wanted people to avoid meat. [13]He advised eating a vegetarian diet instead. [14]With plenty of whole grains. [15]Such as whole wheat flour instead of white flour.

[16]Soon people were shopping at Graham food stores. [17]Much like the health food stores of today. [18]Which made butchers and bakers very angry. [19]But it all turned out to be like a lot of fads. [20]And didn't last long. [21]In the meantime, however, those who believed in Graham called their flour Graham flour. [22]Their bread Graham bread. [23]And their crackers? [24]Well. [25]You guessed it. [26]Graham crackers.

Revising and Editing Worksheet 2

Improve the following draft by revising for ideas, organization, word choice, and sentence variety. After revising, edit the draft for errors in spelling, capitalization, punctuation, and usage. Write your revised and edited version on a separate piece of paper. Compare your changes with those of a writing partner.

[1]Many people know the name of Frank Lloyd Wright. [2]Far fewer know the name of Louis Sullivan. [3]Wright was a key player in the development of American architecture. [4]Sullivan was a key player in the development of American architecture. [5]Wright worked for Sullivan. [6]When Wright first came to Chicago. [7]At that time, Sullivan was a partner in the well-known firm of Adler and Sullivan. [8]Wright was unknown. [9]In fact, *master* is the term Wright used at this time to refer to Sullivan, *apprentice* is the term Wright used for himself.

[10]When Wright entered the firm, he was just twenty years old. [11]Sullivan was his boss, he was thirty-one. [12]Not long after Sullivan hired him, he and Wright became extremely close. [13]They had lengthy conversations. [14]They spent long hours working together. [15]They collaborated on drawings. [16]This was a key time for Wright to join the firm. [17]Just as it was starting work on the famous Auditorium Building in Chicago.

[18]Soon, however, Sullivan and Wright quarreled bitterly. [19]A big spender, the young Wright often faced financial problems. [20]His solution to these problems was moonlighting. [21]He continued to work for the firm of Adler and Sullivan. [22]He took other jobs on the side. [23]Other money matters clouded the relationship with the firm. [24]Questions about a deed clouded the relationship with the firm. [25]Eventually, Sullivan became furious, he fired Wright. [26]So ended the collaboration of two of America's greatest architects.

Chapter Review

EXERCISE A Identifying Subjects and Verbs

In each sentence, underline the simple subject once and the verb twice. If the subject is understood to be *you*, write *You* following the sentence.

1. Read this paragraph about windy cities. *you*

2. At the top of the list is Great Falls, Montana.

3. Its average wind speed is listed as 13.1 miles per hour.

4. Oklahoma City, Cheyenne, Boston, and Wichita all follow it on the list.

5. Isn't the city of Chicago on the list?

6. Chicago has often been referred to as the Windy City.

7. Here is the reason for that popular name.

8. Long-winded politicians blared and blasted their messages.

9. There are no actual weather data for that claim.

10. My aunt and cousins in Chicago will never believe this one!

EXERCISE B Correcting Sentence Fragments and Run-on Sentences

On a separate piece of paper, rewrite each sentence below. Rewrite sentence fragments as complete sentences, and correct run-on sentences by adding words or punctuation marks as needed. When you finish, use your sentences (you may change them as needed) to write a paragraph.

1. Marshes, swamps, and bogs, all wetlands.

2. Marshes are wetlands filled mainly with grasses swamps are filled mainly with trees and bushes.

3. No water flows into or out of a bog, mainly moss grows there.

4. Swamps are often found along rivers Okefenokee Swamp is an example.

5. Marshes are also found next to the ocean they are saltwater marshes.

6. Trees in saltwater swamps with their roots above the water.

7. Plant matter builds up in bogs it forms peat.

8. Plant matter accumulates, it does not decompose in the bog.

9. A fen is like a bog, peat builds up there.

10. Peat, rich organic matter, a powerful, natural fertilizer.

EXERCISE C Identifying Objects and Complements

In each sentence below, identify the italicized word or words. Above each word, write *DO* (direct object), *IO* (indirect object), *PA* (predicate adjective), or *PN* (predicate nominative).

1. Many people use their *hands* in conversation.

2. At times, such gestures may seem *silly* or *unnecessary*.

3. At other times, such gestures appear *meaningful*.

4. Patrick read *me* an *article* on a recent scientific study about using hands during speech.

5. People in the study were either *blind* or *sighted*.

6. Blind children used *gestures* as often as sighted children did.

7. With equal frequency, people gestured their *ideas* to both blind and sighted listeners.

8. This study gives the *world* a new *view* of gestures.

9. Gestures may be a *form* of thought or a *way* of thinking.

10. Of course, current theories are still *hypothetical*.

Write What You Think
CONNECTING
Writing & Grammar

On a separate piece of paper, write what you think about the questions below. Support your opinions with explanations and examples from your own experience. After you have revised and edited your writing, underline all the objects and complements.

Do people actually talk—or communicate meaning—with their hands? Do these gestures serve mainly to help people speak, or do they serve mainly to help people be understood? How and why do you most effectively and commonly use gestures? Do you believe they help you think?

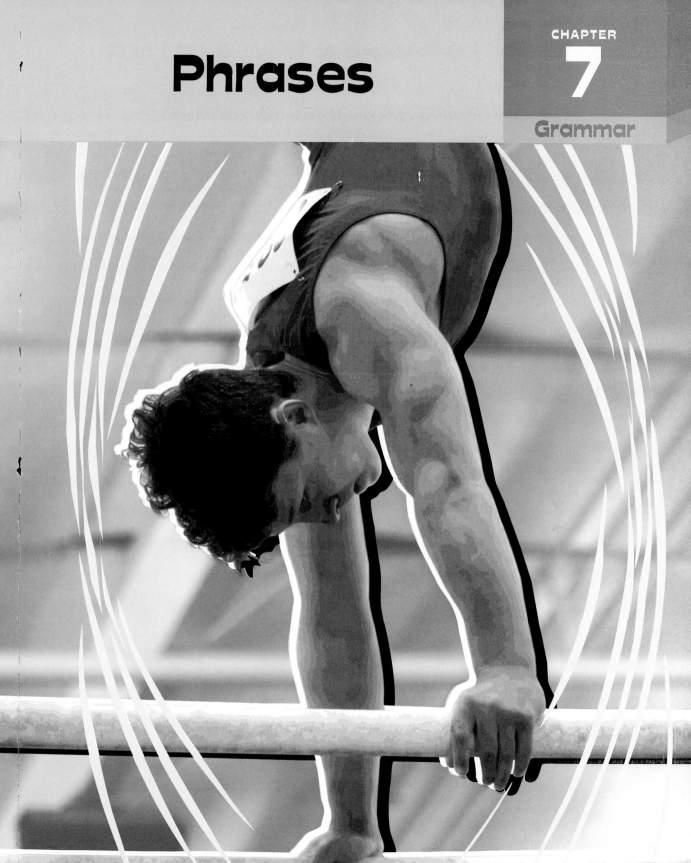

Phrases

STUDENT WRITING
Research Paper

Beyond Legend: Arthur Reconsidered
by Camilla Ann Richmond
high school student, Tampa, Florida

Written from the assumption that King Arthur did indeed exist, this paper endeavors to examine this "fictional" character's historicity, using the available resources to prove the thesis. The scope of the investigation centers on primary sources from the early medieval works of Gildas and Nennius, the definitive high medieval source Geoffrey of Monmouth, and the romances from the late Middle Ages. Secondary sources include the traditional interpretations by historians of the primary sources, interpretations that place Arthur in various locations across England. A single, more recent source supports a differing hypothesis, locating Arthur primarily in the borderlands of Scotland and northern England and creating an interesting contrast to the historical theories. The conclusion reached here suggests that the evidence against the traditional theory is much greater than that supporting it—and, therefore, that King Arthur most likely resided in Scotland. More precise conclusions focus on the location of specific castles and battles, as well as on the connection of the legends to known historical facts. The essay attempts to persuade the reader that King Arthur was real.

The paragraph above is a summary of a full-length research paper. By synthesizing her paper concisely, Camilla Ann Richmond prepares her reader for what is to come.

Part of the reason Camilla's research paper summary is effective is that she uses phrases to connect sentences and to give variety to her writing. You'll practice including phrases in the writing exercises in this chapter.

Prepositional Phrases: Adjective and Adverb Phrases

▶ A **prepositional phrase** always begins with a preposition (PREP) and ends with an object (OBJ), which is either a noun or a pronoun. A prepositional phrase may have a compound object (two or more objects). All modifiers of the object(s) are part of the prepositional phrase.

PREP	ADJ	OBJ	PREP	OBJ	OBJ	PREP	ADJ	OBJ
beyond	the high	peaks	for	you and	me	under	two	minutes

▶ A prepositional phrase adds information to a sentence by modifying another word in the sentence.

The birds flew. [Which birds? Where did they fly?]

The birds **in the aviary** flew **into the trees**.

Sometimes, a prepositional phrase modifies the object in a preceding prepositional phrase, or more than one prepositional phrase modifies a single word.

We see them fly **across our path through the woods**.
At this moment, the sparrow perches **in the oak tree**.
[Both phrases modify the verb *perches*.]

▶ An **adjective phrase** is a prepositional phrase that modifies a noun or pronoun in the sentence. Adjective phrases (like adjectives) answer the questions *which one* or *what kind*.

The bird **on the stamp** is a scarlet tanager. [The adjective phrase modifies the noun *bird*.]
This stamp is one **of several new stamps** issued last week. [The adjective phrase modifies the pronoun *one*.]

▶ An **adverb phrase** is a prepositional phrase that modifies a verb, an adjective, or another adverb.

I put the stamp **on the letter**. [The adverb phrase modifies the verb *put*.]
This is the prettiest **of all the new stamps**. [The adverb phrase modifies the adjective *prettiest*.]

▶ Some words can be either adverbs or prepositions, depending on the sentence. If the word is part of a prepositional phrase, it is a preposition. If it stands alone, it is an adverb (ADV).

ADV   PREP
When a plane flies by, we all look **up**.   We went **up** the escalator.

WRITING HINT

Prepositional phrases add information and details. They make your writing more interesting.

NO DETAILS
The woman smiled.

DETAILS
The woman **on the bench** smiled **at the puppy in a friendly way**.

EDITING TIP

Should you use a comma after a prepositional phrase at the beginning of a sentence? These example sentences will help you decide.

According to some experts, the comma is always needed for clarity.

At times the comma is omitted. This is often the case with short phrases.

With multiple phrases at the beginning of a sentence, use a comma.

In many other cases, it is fine to leave the comma out or to put it in.

EXERCISE 1 Identifying Adjective and Adverb Phrases

Underline every prepositional phrase in the sentences below, and draw an arrow to the word each phrase modifies. Label the phrase *ADJ* for an adjective phrase or *ADV* for an adverb phrase. **Hint:** Some sentences contain more than one prepositional phrase.

EXAMPLE   Adolf Hitler was born in 1889. *ADV*

1. By age sixteen, Hitler had developed an interest in politics.

2. Unfortunately, he had also developed a hatred for all non-German peoples.

3. He loved art, but an art school in Vienna rejected him.

4. For years, he lived in a state of poverty.

5. He read the works of German historians and philosophers.

6. Some of these works formed the basis of his later writings and speeches.

7. In 1913, Hitler would not fight in the Austrian Army with Jews, Slavs, and Czechs.

8. Instead, he fought for Germany in World War I.

9. After the war, the German economy was in ruins.

10. In this atmosphere of defeat and suffering, Hitler gained power.

EXERCISE 2 Revising a Description

Refer to **Composition**, Lesson 2.4, for some tips on descriptive writing.

Work with a partner or small group to revise the following draft of a description of an old, abandoned farmhouse. You may wish to research photos of old farmhouses before you write. Begin by brainstorming details about where the house is. Then make a list of sensory details (sight, smell, sound, touch, taste) that best capture this house. Write your description on a separate piece of paper. Add as many new ideas and sentences as you wish. See how many prepositional phrases you can add. When you have finished your description, compare it with those of your classmates.

[1]I approached the old farmhouse. [2]No one lived there. [3]Windows were broken.

[4]One was boarded up. [5]Paint was peeling. [6]An old car lay quietly rusting. [7]Slowly,

I opened the door.

Appositives and Appositive Phrases

▐▌▶ An **appositive** is a noun (N) or pronoun (P) that identifies or explains the noun or pronoun that precedes it.

      N   N

Our neighbor, **Mrs. Cunkelman**, is kind to us.

   P   N

Just one of the children, **Shirelle**, was absent.

▐▌▶ An **appositive phrase** is a phrase made up of an appositive and all of its modifiers.

> *Into Thin Air*, **a best-selling book**, is fascinating. [The appositive is *book*; the words *a best-selling* modify it.]

Using appositives and appositive phrases helps you to combine sentences and to avoid unnecessary repetition.

ORIGINAL   Pumpkin has a sweet temperament. Pumpkin is our
                      ten-year-old cat.

COMBINED   Pumpkin, our ten-year-old cat, has a sweet temperament.

In the combined sentence above, commas set off the appositive phrase, separating it from the rest of the sentence. The commas mark off information that is **nonessential**, or not necessary to the meaning of the sentence. Do not use commas if an appositive is **essential**, or is needed to understand the sentence.

NO COMMAS   The guitarist Manuel Barrueco performs on this CD.
                     [The appositive *Manuel Barrueco* is essential to the
                     meaning of the sentence.]

COMMAS   The guitar, a versatile instrument, has strings.
                 [The appositive *a versatile instrument* is not necessary
                 for an understanding of the meaning of the sentence.]

Enriching Your Vocabulary

The adjective *versatile* comes from the Latin verb *vertere*, which means "to turn." A *versatile* person is able to turn easily from one task or responsibility to another.

EXERCISE 3 Identifying Appositives and Appositive Phrases

Underline every appositive or appositive phrase in the sentences below. Draw an arrow to the noun or pronoun it modifies.

1. Our history teacher, Mr. Sinha, taught us about Queen Elizabeth I.

2. Her parents, Henry VIII and Anne Boleyn, are well known in English history.

3. The Elizabethan Age, a period in English history, takes its name from her reign.

4. The Elizabethan era, England's "Golden Age," spanned much of the sixteenth century.

5. The most famous literary figure of this age, William Shakespeare, was Queen Elizabeth's friend.

6. Sir Walter Raleigh, explorer and colonizer of the New World, was also one of Elizabeth's favorites.

7. The film *Elizabeth* is about her personality and her reign.

8. During her worst days, she spent time in England's most famous prison, the Tower of London.

9. She ordered the beheading of her cousin Mary.

10. The terms *ruler*, *patron of the arts*, and *trendsetter* all describe Queen Elizabeth I.

EXERCISE 4 Combining Sentences with Appositives

On a separate piece of paper, combine the sentences in each numbered item with an appositive or appositive phrase. **Remember:** Some appositives require commas; others do not.

EXAMPLE   My friend was born in Seoul. My friend is Min.
            My friend Min was born in Seoul.

1. The skeleton is 3.2 million years old. The skeleton is Lucy.

2. The treasure was found at the bottom of the sea. It was gold coins and jewels.

3. The treasure came from the *Atocha*. The *Atocha* was a large, seventeenth-century Spanish ship.

4. The pirate is legendary. He is Blackbeard.

5. Artifacts are found throughout the world. They are clues to past lives.

6. In 1947, the Dead Sea Scrolls were discovered hidden in jars. They are two-thousand-year-old religious writings.

7. The well-known paleontologist made discoveries in Africa. She is Mary Leakey.

8. The axes and spears were found by a team of scientists. They are Stone Age tools.

9. Mysteries surround Stonehenge. Stonehenge is a circle of massive stones in England.

10. In the Nile Delta, Napoleon's soldiers discovered the Rosetta Stone. It was the key to deciphering Egyptian hieroglyphics.

Participles and Participial Phrases

A **verbal** is a verb form that functions as a different part of speech. Three kinds of verbals that you will learn about in this book are participles, gerunds, and infinitives. (See Lessons 7.4 and 7.5.)

▸ A **participle** is a verb form that acts as an adjective, modifying a noun or a pronoun.

There are two kinds of participles: present and past. **Present participles** always have an *-ing* ending; **past participles** often end in *-d* or *-ed*. The past participles of irregular verbs have different endings. (See Lessons 9.2 and 9.3.)

When you use a helping verb with an *-ing* form of a verb, you create a verb phrase. When you use an *-ing* form of a verb to modify another word or phrase, you create a participle.

VERB PHRASE	Keisha **is opening** the door.
PARTICIPLE	We listened to the speaker's **opening** remarks.
VERB PHRASE	I **have written** to Jacob about our plans.
PARTICIPLE	Please submit **written** evidence of your purchase.

▸ A **participial phrase** is made up of a participle and all of its modifiers. A participial phrase may contain objects, modifiers, and prepositional phrases. The whole phrase acts as an adjective.

Waiting patiently in the line, people read or chatted.
This is the photograph **taken at our family reunion**.
The speaker, **clearing her throat**, continued her speech.

WRITING HINT

Put participial phrases next to the words they modify or as close to them as possible. If you don't, you may create something silly or senseless.

Mr. Witby hurriedly devoured his pizza running for the train.

See Lesson 12.4 for more on misplaced modifiers.

EXERCISE 5 Identifying Participles

Underline every participle and participial phrase in the sentences below. Draw an arrow to the noun or pronoun that each participle or participial phrase modifies.

EXAMPLE   I like the work of a poet  named Derek Walcott.

1. I read this book given to me by my mother.

2. These poems, composed by Derek Walcott, are some of my favorites.

3. Born a British subject on the Caribbean island of St. Lucia, Walcott now lives in the United States.

4. If you prefer, you can hear some of his recorded works on this tape.

5. Speaking without a British accent or an American accent, Walcott brings his poems to life.

EXERCISE 6 Writing Sentences with Participial Phrases

For each of the following participial phrases, write a complete sentence on a separate piece of paper. **Remember:** Use the phrase as an adjective, not as a verb.

1. imported from Mexico
2. growing in the meadow
3. waving from the driver's seat
4. riding quickly down the road
5. floating on the pond

6. shopping for new pants
7. strolling down the avenue
8. slamming her locker door
9. stolen from the museum
10. blocked by three police cars

EXERCISE 7 Identifying Participles and Participial Phrases

Underline every participle and participial phrase in the following paragraph.

[1]An article published recently by Julia Reed says that the military look is always in fashion. [2]Her article is about the style and look associated with the military. [3]Sailor suits worn by children are obvious examples. [4]Less obvious is the necktie, a look adapted by the French. [5]They originally saw Croatian soldiers in the 1600s wearing neckties. [6]Looking to the more recent past, Reed cites such fashions and accessories as khakis, the trench coat, and the Swiss Army knife. [7]She mentions jackets trimmed with gold braid and buttons. [8]In fact, she says the whole tailored look is essentially military. [9]No matter what army a commanding officer marched in, he or she always looked smart. [10]The shoulder bag, the platform shoe, and padded vests—all introduced first or invented for the military—are among the many examples of military fashion. [11]Seen first on the battlefield, even bell-bottoms are an example of military fashion that has hit the mainstream.

CONNECTING
Writing & Grammar

Refer to **Composition**, Lesson 4.2, to find strategies for writing persuasively.

Write What You Think

On a separate piece of paper, tell whether you think the military or any other influence (rock music, for example) on fashion has been mostly positive or negative. Include reasons and evidence to support your opinion, such as examples of clothing that you wear or that you have observed on other people. Be sure to revise and edit your writing.

Gerunds and Gerund Phrases

The present participle of a verb (the *-ing* form) sometimes functions as an adjective. (See Lesson 7.3.) This lesson shows what else *-ing* words can do.

▶ A **gerund** is a verb form that ends in *-ing* and acts as a noun. As these examples show, gerunds can do anything that nouns can do.

> **Jogging** is Matt's favorite exercise. [subject]
> His early morning habit is **jogging**. [predicate nominative]
> This magazine article discusses **jogging**. [direct object]
> It details the benefits and drawbacks of **jogging**. [object of the preposition]
> Some knee injuries have given **jogging** a bad name. [indirect object]

▶ A **gerund phrase** is a phrase made up of a gerund and all of its modifiers and complements. A gerund phrase's modifiers include adjectives, adverbs, and prepositional phrases. The entire phrase functions as a noun.

> **Walking the dog** is Zach's responsibility. [subject]
> Lauren's least favorite job is **walking the dog**. [predicate nominative]
> Luckily, Zach likes **taking the dog for a walk**. [direct object]
> Lauren and Zach fight about **doing jobs around the house**. [object of the preposition]

Note: Some gerunds are formed from verbs that end in *e*. See Lesson 16.3 for advice about spelling those gerunds.

Exercise 8 Identifying Gerunds and Gerund Phrases

Underline every gerund and gerund phrase in the report below. A gerund phrase may contain one or more prepositional phrases. Include these in your underlining as part of the gerund phrase. **Hint:** Some sentences have more than one gerund or gerund phrase; some sentences have none.

¹Advertising is an art, and putting a label on a can of food is more complicated than you may think. ²A journalist for the *New York Times* named Tibor Kalman took on the task of comparing the labels on seven brands of tomato sauce. ³He suggests that there is more to designing a label than first meets the eye.

TEST-TAKING TIP

Be alert to gerund phrases used as subjects in test questions, and remember the rules of subject-verb agreement: If a gerund phrase used as a subject is singular, the verb must be singular as well. See item 8 on page 314.

EDITING TIP

Use the possessive form of a noun or pronoun when you modify a gerund. Just as you would not say, "I disapprove of *him* language," you should not say, "I disapprove of *him* smoking."

their
We complimented ~~them~~ cooking.
soprano's
The ~~soprano~~ singing was unforgettable.

[4]His comparison begins with a generic, supermarket brand of sauce. [5]It has a no-nonsense look and features a picture of a very large serving of spaghetti. [6]Appealing to people's sense of economy is the goal of this label.

[7]Sending a message to the health-conscious buyer is the aim of other advertisers. [8]On their labels are such words as *organic, 100% natural, sun-dried,* and, of course, *fat-free*. [9]One label features a drawing of a huge, ripe tomato on the vine. [10]Another suggests freshness by placing two plump, perfect tomatoes side by side and surrounding them with fresh basil.

[11]Suggesting the "real" Italy is another goal of advertisers. [12]Therefore, floating in a gondola in Venice is the central visual message on one label. [13]Others go back to the "old country" by putting the phrases *di Napoli* and *Little Italy* on the jar. [14]The purpose of these labels is creating a sense of something authentic.

[15]Finally, one well-known brand has a technique all its own: displaying the handsome face of the company's founder. [16]"Selling this brand is like falling off a log," concludes Tibor Kalman.

Working Together

Exercise 9 Writing Sentences with Gerunds and Gerund Phrases

On a separate piece of paper, copy the following sentence beginnings and endings and complete them with gerunds or gerund phrases. Underline each gerund or gerund phrase you write. Exchange papers with a partner or small group to compare your answers.

1. I think the best way to teach people to read is by . . .
2. The best sports for overall fitness are . . .
3. The greatest thrill possible might be . . .
4. One thing young people sometimes overlook is . . .
5. Steps in preparing food include . . .
6. Bad habits people try to break include . . .
7. . . . are among my favorite sports.
8. . . . are long-term goals I have set for myself.
9. . . . is a good way to spend a rainy afternoon.
10. . . . are steps in making a sandwich.

Infinitives and Infinitive Phrases

▶ An **infinitive** is a verb form that is almost always preceded by the word *to*. In a sentence, an infinitive can act as a noun, an adjective, or an adverb.

> I plan **to compete**. [infinitive as noun]
> I was among the first runners **to enter**. [infinitive as adjective]
> I am eager **to win**. [infinitive as adverb]

The word *to* is part of an infinitive if a verb follows it. It is part of a prepositional phrase if an object or a phrase containing an object follows it.

> INFINITIVE   I plan **to explain** it.
> PREPOSITIONAL PHRASE   I will explain it **to the children**.

▶ An **infinitive phrase** is a phrase made up of an infinitive and all of its modifiers and complements. It may contain one or more prepositional phrases.

> **To land on the moon** was once a dream.
> We ran the race **to raise money for medical research**.

Sometimes, the word *to* that is part of an infinitive or an infinitive phrase does not appear in a sentence; it is understood.

> You need only **[to] say the word**.
> Several friends will help **[to] repair the barn**.

When you edit, you may sometimes spot a stranded infinitive phrase, as in this example.

> I was willing to do anything. **To help out during this terrible emergency**.

An infinitive phrase by itself is a sentence fragment. In this case and in similar cases, attaching it to the preceding sentence fixes the error.

> I was willing to do anything to help out during this terrible emergency.

Exercise 10 Identifying Infinitives and Infinitive Phrases

Underline every infinitive and infinitive phrase in the following report. An infinitive phrase may contain one or more prepositional phrases. Include these in your underlining as part of the infinitive phrase.
Hint: Some sentences have more than one infinitive or infinitive phrase; some sentences have none.

WRITING HINT

Is it acceptable to split an infinitive? These days, most experts say yes.

It is sometimes better to thoughtfully split an infinitive than to avoid splitting one scrupulously.

Enriching Your Vocabulary

The word *scrupulous* comes from the Latin word *scrupulosus*, which originally meant "rough or jagged." It later acquired the meaning of its English derivative: "precise or careful." The *scrupulous* housekeeper did not allow pets in the house.

[1]Would you like to learn about Dorothy West? [2]Among other things, this remarkable woman was an author, an actress, and a member of the Harlem Renaissance.

[3]West grew up in a prosperous white suburb near Boston. [4]Her father managed to run a successful business there even though he had been born into slavery. [5]Looking back, West's father commented that he never knew that "I was the wrong color to succeed. . . ."

[6]Upon reading Fyodor Dostoyevsky at the age of fourteen, West decided to become a writer. [7]Shortly after, she went on to enter a national writing contest and did well enough to be invited to the awards dinner in New York City.

[8]After that, it wasn't long before she decided to move to New York. [9]There she quickly became involved in the exciting atmosphere of the Harlem Renaissance of the 1920s.

[10]Over her lifetime, she wrote two novels. [11]In them, she strove to present her views. [12]She wanted to make life better for future generations. [13]The goal of equality was to be met by working through the establishment.

[14]West said that she never wanted "to be the last leaf on the tree," but that turned out to be the case for her. [15]She was the last of all the Harlem Renaissance members to survive. [16]She died at the age of ninety-one in 1998.

EXERCISE 11 Writing Sentences with Infinitives and Infinitive Phrases

It's New Year's Day, and you are going to make ten resolutions for the coming year. On a separate piece of paper, write ten sentences about what you plan to do, using an infinitive or infinitive phrase in each sentence.

Working Together

EXERCISE 12 Create Your Own Exercise

On a separate piece of paper, work with a partner or small group to write ten interesting sentences with infinitives and infinitive phrases. When you are finished, exchange papers and have the other pairs or groups identify the infinitives and infinitive phrases by underlining them.

Revising and Editing Worksheet 1

Improve the following draft by revising for ideas, organization, word choice, and sentence variety. After revising, edit the draft for errors in spelling, capitalization, punctuation, and usage. Write your revised and edited version on a separate piece of paper. Compare your changes with those of a writing partner.

[1]As everyone knows, even doctors make mistakes. [2]At least from time to time. [3]This is an estimate. [4]Made by doctors themselves. [5]One in every four orthopedic surgeons will operate on the wrong organ. [6]This will occur once in a thirty-year career. [7]In truth, that's not a lot of mistakes over such a long period of time. [8]Still, it's one mistake too many.

[9]One of the most famous mistakes was a foot surgery. [10]This mistake was made in Florida. [11]Amputation of the wrong foot. [12]It demonstrates the seriousness and tragedy of a single error in the operating room. [13]Doctors have also committed other serious errors. [14]For example, removing the wrong kidney and cutting into the wrong side of the body.

[15]Doctors are now taking a surprisingly simple step. [16]To stop this problem. [17]What they call "wrong-site surgery." [18]Doctors use a pen that costs about $1.50. [19]They mark the spot that needs to be cut. [20]By signing their names or writing their initials. [21]This is a reminder right on a patient's body. [22]A definitely low-tech, low-cost solution to a potentially huge problem.

[23]Doctors in hospitals across the nation are now doing this. [24]Trying to stop extremely costly malpractice suits. [25]Hoping to save patients from the suffering of unnecessary or repeated surgery. [26]Seeking to keep their own consciences free from guilt and worry. [27]For the possibility always exists. [28]Of that one priceless moment when attention or concentration may stray.

Revising and Editing Worksheet 2

Improve the following draft by revising for ideas, organization, word choice, and sentence variety. After revising, edit the draft for errors in spelling, capitalization, punctuation, and usage. Write your revised and edited version on a separate piece of paper. Compare your changes with those of a writing partner. **Hint:** Use the fact box to help you add a variety of prepositional, appositive, participial, gerund, and infinitive phrases.

Kangaroo Fact Box	
Order of mammal: Marsupial	**Types of kangaroos**
Size: Ranges from the size of rat to a body length of about 5 ft, not including tail; tail of giant kangaroo may be up to 5 ft long	**Large:** Giant, or Great Gray, Kangaroo; Red, or Woolly, Kangaroo; Wallaroo (stouter than the Giant or Great Gray)
Habitat: Australia and neighboring islands	**Smaller:** Wallabies; Potoroos, or rat kangaroos
Young: Called joey	**Physical features of large kangaroos:** Sheeplike head, large ears, heavy hind quarters; muscular tail used as a support for sitting or walking
Development: Born just under 1 in. long; crawls without help up to 12 in. to its mother's pouch. Stays in pouch until 5 to 9 months of age. Emerges from pouch and stays near mother, continuing to drink her milk, until 12 to 18 months of age	
	Distinguishing physical abilities: Large kangaroos can jump 30 feet in a single leap
Issues: Grazes vegetation over large areas; depletes and damages grazing lands	

¹The kangaroo is a special type of mammal. ²Its young are born before they are fully developed. ³They crawl into their mother's pouch. ⁴There, they feed on the mother's milk and continue to develop further. ⁵The baby joey lives in its mother's pouch for a while. ⁶The head of the joey can be seen sticking out of its mother's pouch. ⁷Eventually, the joey lives outside its pouch but still near its mother. ⁸Then it leaves.

⁹Kangaroos have short front legs. ¹⁰They have powerful hind legs. ¹¹The kangaroo has a long, muscular tail.

¹²There are several types of kangaroos. ¹³The best-known kangaroos are the large kangaroos. ¹⁴They are the Giant Kangaroo and Red Kangaroo. ¹⁵Another large species is the Wallaroo.

¹⁶Among smaller kangaroos, there are several varieties of wallabies. ¹⁷Some are the size of rabbits, and some even look like rabbits. ¹⁸A few kangaroos are as small as rats.

Chapter Review

EXERCISE A Identifying Appositives and Verbals

Identify each underlined word. Use these abbreviations.

APP = appositive   GER = gerund
PART = participle   INF = infinitive

_____ 1. My friend <u>Amina</u> told me about her favorite pastime.

_____ 2. <u>Bicycling</u> is the way she most prefers to spend her free time.

_____ 3. She wants to buy a fancy <u>racing</u> bike.

_____ 4. For now, she helps <u>keep</u> the house clean to earn money.

_____ 5. She will work hard until she has the <u>required</u> sum.

_____ 6. I enjoy a much cheaper hobby, <u>birdwatching</u>.

_____ 7. My brother <u>Leo</u> gave me the binoculars I needed.

_____ 8. We have made several <u>sightings</u> together.

_____ 9. A <u>chirping</u> sound is music to our ears.

_____10. The sight of <u>fluttering</u> wings is even more welcome.

EXERCISE B Identifying Phrases

Identify each underlined phrase. Use these abbreviations.

PREP = prepositional phrase   GER = gerund phrase
APP = appositive phrase   INF = infinitive phrase
PART = participial phrase

_____ 1. Vincent van Gogh, <u>the Dutch Impressionist painter</u>, was the subject
of the show.

_____ 2. People waited in long lines <u>to get tickets</u>.

_____ 3. <u>Painting peasant life</u> was one of van Gogh's early ambitions.

_____ 4. His famous painting *The Potato Eaters* reflects this ambition.

_____ 5. He is most famous, however, <u>for recording nature</u>.

_____ 6. <u>Filling canvases with thick brushstrokes of color</u>, van Gogh
re-created fields and meadows.

———— 7. He presented a new way of <u>looking at the land, the cypress trees, and the flowers</u>.

———— 8. Some of his most famous paintings are <u>of the springtime in Provence</u>.

———— 9. I had a chance <u>to see his haunting painting</u> *Wheatfield with Crows*.

————10. This work, <u>painted during the last months of his life</u>, is a masterpiece of bold color.

EXERCISE C Writing Sentences with Phrases

For each of the following phrases, write a complete sentence on a separate piece of paper. **Hint:** There are infinitive phrases, prepositional phrases, gerund phrases, and participial phrases.

1. to walk my dog

2. learning a new language

3. for a good cause

4. understood by no one

5. to exercise daily

6. given to young children

7. at the time

8. in the middle

9. hiking through the woods

10. acquired by my aunt

Clauses

STUDENT WRITING
Narrative Essay

Thanksgiving at the Soup Kitchen
by Katie Baker
high school student, Lawrenceville, New Jersey

Thanksgiving: What images does the mention of that holiday evoke in you? You most likely think of food: perfectly cooked turkey with fluffy stuffing and gravy, delectable cranberry sauce, light and creamy mashed potatoes—a regular feast. Complaints such as "I couldn't eat another bite!" and "I think I just gained ten pounds in one sitting!" are commonly heard after Thanksgiving meals. For the homeless people of inner-city Trenton, however, such "misfortunes" would be a welcome change. Some of those people go days, even weeks, without a real meal, while some of them eat solely from local fast-food joints—not exactly the source of the most desirable or nutritious meals.

The Trenton Area Soup Kitchen (TASK) attempts to aid such people by serving them nutritious, home-cooked meals in a safe atmosphere. TASK relies solely on generous contributions by the people of Mercer County, especially church and school groups. TASK is open each Wednesday evening for a cafeteria-style meal and for a breakfast/brunch on the last two Saturdays of each month. Ever since I was a first-grader, I've helped TASK by serving the people, helping to cook meals, and packing brown-bag lunches that are distributed to the public.

Most recently, I worked at TASK to serve the people Thanksgiving dinner. I was somewhat sad, however, because while my own mother was at home baking a large turkey with all the delicious side dishes for our family, these people did not have a home or, in some cases, a family to turn to during the holiday season. They were, however, extremely grateful and good-natured, making many jokes and putting a perpetual smile on my face because of their genuine kindness and appreciation.

My tasks were extended when I was asked to serve coffee to the people waiting outside the soup kitchen, which seats roughly ninety people at one time. The Trentonians who were waiting outside in the cold were not melancholy but were exactly the opposite: They thanked me sincerely for the hot drinks I was bringing. While I do not think that any of the people remember me personally, I have no doubt that they look forward to the caring service they receive at the soup kitchen each time they visit it. Likewise, I will never forget my time there. My Thanksgiving at home with my family was great. It was full of hot food, smiling relatives, and fun; but the looks on the faces of the people I was serving that morning—looks of sincere gratitude and appreciation—made my Thanksgiving a unique and special one.

> As you reread Katie Baker's narrative essay above, pay attention to the transition words she uses to connect the events. Words such as most *recently*, *however*, and *likewise* help connect sentences and eliminate choppy paragraphs.
>
> In addition to transition words, Katie uses clauses to connect her ideas and sentences. In this chapter, you'll practice including clauses in your own writing.

Four Types of Sentence Structures

One way to vary your writing and to make it better suit your purposes is by varying your sentence structure. There are four basic ways to structure, or build, a sentence.

▶ A **simple sentence** has one independent clause and no subordinate clauses.

A simple sentence doesn't have to be short. It may have a compound subject (s), a compound verb (v), compound objects, and many different kinds of phrases.

>   s v
> An eye has a pupil to let in light, a lens to focus the light, and a retina for changing light images into nerve signals.

▶ A **compound sentence** has two or more independent clauses and no subordinate clauses.

>   s   v   s   v
> Images on the retina are upside down, but nerve signals to the brain flip them.

▶ A **complex sentence** has one independent clause and at least one subordinate clause.

>   s v   s v
> When I read about the human eye, I learned about the optic nerve.

▶ A **compound-complex sentence** has two or more independent clauses and at least one subordinate clause.

>   s   v   s v
> The outside layer of the eye is the sclera, which is a protective coating;
> s   v
> it covers about five-sixths of the surface of the eye.

You may be asked on a standardized test to repair a run-on sentence by turning it into a compound sentence. Remember to use a comma and a suitable conjunction. See item 2 on page 312.

EXERCISE 11 Identifying Sentence Structure

Identify each type of sentence structure. Use these abbreviations.

S = simple   CX = complex
CD = compound   CD-CX = compound-complex

_____ 1. What changes in school policies could bring about better behavior in schools?

_____ 2. The Educational Testing Service recently studied the influence of five types of policies.

_____ 3. Its study, which spanned four years, noted the effects of different policies on the numbers of drug offenses, nonserious offenses, and serious offenses.

_____ 4. Serious offenses include physical violence, and nonserious offenses include cheating on tests.

_____ 5. For example, the Educational Testing Service studied the changes that occurred when schools placed a ban on gangs.

_____ 6. This policy actually resulted in an eighteen percent increase in nonserious offenses among the entire student body, and it did not change the numbers of drug offenses or serious offenses.

_____ 7. Tight security produced no change in the number of drug offenses, nor did it affect the number of serious offenses; it did, however, bring a marked drop in nonserious offenses.

_____ 8. Making students wear uniforms produced no changes whatsoever, but a small school size decreased the number of nonserious offenses by a whopping fifty-eight percent.

_____ 9. The best change in policy appears to be strict punishment, which decreased nonserious and serious offenses by eighteen percent; it also brought about a nineteen percent decrease in drug offenses.

_____ 10. It appears that strict punishments for offenses may be the answer to some behavioral problems.

CONNECTING
Writing & Grammar

Write What You Think

Refer to **Composition,** Lesson 4.2, to find strategies for writing persuasively.

On a separate piece of paper, write a paragraph proposing one change in policy at your school that you believe will decrease the incidence of violence, vandalism, aggression, drug use, or any other unwanted behavior. Address your proposal to the school board, and make it as persuasive as you can. Support your proposal with reasons and evidence. Be sure to revise and edit your writing.

Effective Sentences:
Parallel Structure

Parallel sentence structures use the same part of speech or grammatical structure to convey equal or related ideas.

▐▌▌▶ A series of equal or related ideas should be expressed in **parallel structure**, or in the same grammatical form.

1. Sentence parts linked by coordinating conjunctions (such as *and, but,* and *or*) should be parallel.

FAULTY   Time of day, amount of light, and how far you are from the subject are all factors in taking photographs. [The three items in the complete subject are not parallel; the first two consist of a noun and a prepositional phrase; the third is a noun clause.]

PARALLEL   Time of day, amount of light, and distance from the subject are all factors in taking photographs. [All three parts of the complete subject consist of a noun followed by a prepositional phrase.]

2. Sentence parts linked by correlative conjunctions (such as *either . . . or, whether . . . or, both . . . and, just as . . . so [too], not only . . . but also*) should be parallel.

FAULTY   He is not only our leader, but he is also responsible for our food. [In the first independent clause, a predicate nominative follows the verb. In the second independent clause, a predicate adjective and a phrase follow the verb.]

PARALLEL   He is **not only** our leader **but also** our cook. [A possessive pronoun and a predicate nominative follow each part of the correlative conjunction. Do not include a comma.]

PARALLEL   He is responsible **not only** for leading us **but also** for feeding us. [A prepositional phrase follows each part of the correlative conjunction. Do not include a comma.]

3. Sentence parts that compare or contrast should be parallel.

FAULTY   I was more interested in the exhibit than in what Martha said. [A prepositional phrase precedes *than*; a noun clause follows the preposition after *than*.]

PARALLEL   I was more interested in what the exhibit showed than in what Martha said. [Noun clauses both precede and follow *than*.]

PARALLEL   I was more interested in the exhibit than in Martha's comments. [Prepositional phrases both precede and follow *than*.]

Examples of faulty parallel structure appear often and in many forms on standardized tests. Make sure that the items in a series are in the same grammatical form. See item 12 on page 308.

EXERCISE 12 Identifying Parallel Structure

Decide whether each sentence below contains parallel structure. If it does, write *P* in the blank that precedes the sentence. If it is not parallel, or if it is faulty, write *F*. On a separate piece of paper, rewrite any sentence that is faulty.

_____ 1. Not only lighting a match but also twigs and mirrors can be used to start a fire.

_____ 2. We learned about uses and effects of fire in both science class and geography class.

_____ 3. Wood is more flammable than burning plastic.

_____ 4. In a steam engine, fire is used to heat water and for creating pressure.

_____ 5. Steam-powered machinery helped people spin cotton and helped with grinding flour.

_____ 6. Using steam power was more efficient than to do the work by hand.

_____ 7. Was the invention of the steam engine as important as inventing the computer?

_____ 8. It is important to know what the most common fire hazards are and some safety tips.

_____ 9. In the woods, never light a fire near dead trees or where there is a pile of brush nearby.

_____ 10. Kyle didn't know whether to throw water on the fire or if he should smother it.

CONNECTING
Writing & Grammar

Write What You Think

Write one paragraph comparing and contrasting building a fire at home for lighting, heating, or cooking with flipping an electric switch to perform the same functions. Consider the following questions.

• What are the advantages and disadvantages of each?
• What are the hazards and benefits?

After you revise your paragraph, edit it to be sure that you have used parallel structure where it is needed.

Revising and Editing Worksheet 1

Improve the following draft by revising for ideas, organization, word choice, and sentence variety. After revising, edit the draft for errors in spelling, capitalization, punctuation, and usage. Write your revised and edited version on a separate piece of paper. Compare your changes with those of a writing partner.

¹We'd lost track of the time. ²We had been riding for days. ³It was some time during the morning. ⁴After a not-so-great sunrise. ⁵That looked just like the two other sunrises we'd seen while riding this bus. ⁶We were almost in Miles City now. ⁷We would arrive in another six hours or so.

⁸Before we got on this bus. ⁹Neither Mei nor I had ever been out of Concord New Hampshire. ¹⁰That was pretty much the case, anyway. ¹¹Mei had been to the ocean once in Maine. ¹²When the Rios family took her. ¹³We had both been to visit reletives in Lowell, Massachusetts. ¹⁴I'd gone on a class trip to New York City once. ¹⁵But going west was something else. ¹⁶Something that neither one of us ever imagined. ¹⁷Even though our dad had moved there eight years ago. ¹⁸To settle on the Double V Ranch. ¹⁹Where Uncle Lee had been working and living for years.

²⁰So here we were. ²¹On our way to a place we couldn't even imagine. ²²A place not too far from Miles City, Montana. ²³To start a new life. ²⁴We couldn't bring ourselfs to think about why. ²⁵That whole, long bus ride, we never talked about it. ²⁶We just sat. ²⁷We were tired and cramped. ²⁸We looked out the window and breathed that stale bus air. ²⁹We were tired of talking about it. ³⁰We couldn't think of anything else for days after the fire. ³¹But now a kind of numbness had set in. ³²Maybe it would help us leave our old lifes behind.

Revising and Editing Worksheet 2

Improve the following draft by revising for ideas, organization, word choice, and sentence variety. After revising, edit the draft for errors in spelling, capitalization, punctuation, and usage. Write your revised and edited version on a separate piece of paper. Compare your changes with those of a writing partner.

¹Emily Dickinson's poem "I dwell in possibility" is about writing poetry. ²Which was, probably, the most important activity of Dickinson's life. ³The speaker of the poem says she "dwells in possibility." ⁴That means she lives in it. ⁵It is her home. ⁶The place she is most comfortable.

⁷She says that possibility is poetry. ⁸This is clear because Dickinson compares it to prose. ⁹She does this in the second line of the poem. ¹⁰She says it is a "fairer house than prose." ¹¹She says that poetry offers more than prose does. ¹²She says poetry is "more numerous of windows. ¹³Meaning theirs more ways to let ideas in. ¹⁴She adds that poetry is "superior—for doors." ¹⁵Also saying that poetry is better then prose for letting in new thoughts and images. ¹⁶For the speaker, poetry is a "fairer house" or a better place to live, then prose is.

¹⁷She says poetry is like possibility. ¹⁸It isn't always easy to see or for understanding. ¹⁹Because it can be "impregnable." ²⁰She also suggests the meaning in poetry can be as everlasting as the sky. ²¹The meaning is infinite. ²²It has no roof overhead to keep it inside or trap it.

²³She ends by saying thats her job. ²⁴Writing poetry. ²⁵Because it is the "fairest" or best occupation. ²⁶She doesn't need anything else or to see anyone. ²⁷Her visitors are ideas. ²⁸And when she writes a poem. ²⁹She says she is able to "gather paradise." ³⁰That's eternity again, or what is infinite possibility.

I dwell in Possibility—
A fairer House than Prose—
More numerous of Windows—
Superior—for Doors—

Of Chambers as the Cedars—
Impregnable of Eye—
And for an Everlasting Roof
The Gambrels of the Sky—

Of Visitors—the fairest—
For Occupation—This—
The spreading wide my
    narrow Hands
To gather Paradise—

Emily Dickinson

Chapter Review

EXERCISE A Identifying Independent and Subordinate Clauses

On the blank before each numbered item, write *I* for an independent clause or *S* for a subordinate clause. On a separate piece of paper, use the information in this exercise to write a paragraph.

_____ 1. Chief Joseph was the leader of the Nez Percé people.

_____ 2. Who lived by fishing, hunting, and gathering food.

_____ 3. Although they had lived in the Pacific Northwest for centuries.

_____ 4. Chief Joseph refused to move or to have his people move.

_____ 5. When the Nez Percé were ordered to a reservation.

_____ 6. Which occurred in 1877.

_____ 7. Chief Joseph and all his people fled together.

_____ 8. While they wandered for months through Oregon, Idaho, and Montana.

_____ 9. As long as the federal army hunted them.

_____ 10. Until they were outnumbered, starving, and dying.

EXERCISE B Identifying Types of Clauses

On the blank before each numbered item, identify the underlined clause in each sentence by writing *ADJ* for an adjective clause, *ADV* for an adverb clause, or *N* for a noun clause.

_____ 1. The suburbs is <u>where I live</u>.

_____ 2. There was a great movement to the suburbs <u>after World War II ended</u>.

_____ 3. <u>Because a baby boom occurred then</u>, more and more housing was needed.

_____ 4. My grandparents, <u>who were married just after the war</u>, moved to the suburbs in the late 1940s.

_____ 5. The suburbs, <u>which were often sprawling subdivisions</u>, offered space and newness.

_____ 6. <u>Whoever wanted to do so</u> could begin a new life there.

_____ 7. <u>Although the suburbs were part of the American dream</u>, they were also criticized.

_____ 8. Some people like the uniformity, <u>although many do not</u>.

EXERCISE C Identifying Sentence Structure

Underline every subordinate clause in the sentences below. Then on the blank before each numbered item, identify the sentence structure by writing *S* for simple, *CD* for compound, *CX* for complex, and *CD-CX* for compound-complex.

———————— 1. After World War II, William J. Levitt changed acres of countryside into acres of suburbia.

———————— 2. Levitt's idea was to build affordable homes that could be mass-produced.

———————— 3. Levitt's first venture, which took place on Long Island, New York, resulted in the first "Levittown."

———————— 4. It was begun in 1948; and, by 1951, it contained almost 20,000 houses.

———————— 5. Soon, there was also a Levittown, Pennsylvania, where veterans could buy houses without a down payment and where everyone else could secure a house for a deposit of just $100.

———————— 6. Levitt did not put the garage in the back of the house, as builders had done before; instead, Levitt placed the garage next to the front door, which demonstrated its new importance.

———————— 7. He gave owners fireplaces and built-in television sets.

———————— 8. Architectural historian Robert A. M. Stern notes that many people moved to the suburbs at the same time that Lucille Ball and Desi Arnaz (of *I Love Lucy*) moved there.

———————— 9. The television, the car, and the suburban house were all part of the American dream.

————————10. If most people had not owned cars, would suburbs have survived?

Write What You Think

CONNECTING
Writing & Grammar

On a separate piece of paper, write one paragraph telling what you think about the following statement. Do you agree or disagree? State your opinion clearly, and then support it with reasons and specific details. Be sure to revise and edit your writing.

Suburban communities remain the best choice in housing for families.

Cumulative Review

EXERCISE A Identifying Parts of Speech

Identify the part of speech of each underlined word as it is used in each quotation below from Mark Twain. Use these abbreviations.

N = noun   ADJ = adjective   CONJ = conjunction
PRON = pronoun   ADV = adverb   INTER = interjection
V = verb   PREP = preposition

_____1. Few things are harder to put up with than the annoyance <u>of</u> a good example.

_____2. If you tell the truth, you don't have to remember <u>anything</u>.

_____3. Virtue has <u>never</u> been as respectable as money.

_____4. Get your <u>facts</u> first, and then you can distort them as much as you please.

_____5. Wit is the <u>sudden</u> marriage of ideas that before their union were not perceived to have any relation.

EXERCISE B Identifying Phrases

On the blank before each numbered item, identify each underlined phrase by writing one of these abbreviations in the space provided.

PREP = prepositional phrase   APP = appositive phrase
PART = participial phrase   GER = gerund phrase
INF = infinitive phrase

_____1. What would you like <u>to learn about diamonds</u>?

_____2. They are <u>among the most precious</u> of all stones.

_____3. Diamonds, <u>the jewels of romance</u>, are also important in industry.

_____4. As one of the hardest substances <u>known on Earth</u>, diamonds are very useful.

_____5. An industrial diamond's uses include grinding tools and <u>polishing a variety of substances</u>.

_____6. Bort, <u>the world's cheapest industrial diamond</u>, is used for grinding.

_____7. <u>Drilling rock</u> is one use of carbonado, or black, diamonds.

_____8. <u>Used in activities as varied as dental surgery and engraving</u>, diamonds are versatile.

EXERCISE C Identifying Clauses

Underline every subordinate clause in the sentences below. Then, in the space before each sentence, identify each clause by writing *ADJ* for an adjective clause, *ADV* for an adverb clause, or *N* for a noun clause.

———————1. James Audubon, who was a naturalist, is famous for his paintings of birds.

———————2. When he had enough paintings, he looked for a publisher.

———————3. He had to look outside the country because no American publisher was interested.

———————4. What he needed was an audience to appreciate his highly detailed, accurate work.

———————5. He found such an audience in England, where his exhibitions were successful.

———————6. He went on to create *The Birds of America*, which is his masterpiece.

———————7. When people say *Audubon* today, they are usually referring to the society of bird-watchers.

———————9. A central concern of the Audubon Society is how people can protect birds and their habitats.

EXERCISE D Writing Complete Sentences

On a separate piece of paper, revise and edit the following paragraph to correct sentence fragments and run-on sentences and to eliminate wordiness.

¹The Sahara Desert in Africa. ²The world's greatest hot, dry stretch of land. ³Its average annual rainfall is usually less than ten inches, this is the amount of rainfall that defines a desert. ⁴So little water. ⁵Makes it almost impossible for anything to grow. ⁶Winds prevent growth too, they act like a sandblasting machine. ⁷Winds form giant dunes of swirling sand, these dunes are always changing shape. ⁸The wind also wears down any rock, it carries away pebbles. ⁹Creating sand and more sand, blowing endlessly. ¹⁰Across the Sahara's more than three and one-half million square miles of land.

Using Verbs

STUDENT WRITING
Expository Essay
The Greatest Athlete of All Time
by Tammy Scherer
high school student, Jim Thorpe, Pennsylvania

His athletic abilities far surpass those of any athlete of the past or present. He accomplished what no other athlete has ever done, and he stands alone as perhaps the greatest athlete of the century. James Francis Thorpe, a Sac and Fox Indian, was a football and Olympic star. Named "the greatest athlete in the world" by King Gustav V of Sweden, Jim Thorpe has accomplishments to which few others can even begin to compare.

Thorpe excelled in every athletic event he attempted. His athletic career began in 1904 at Carlisle Indian School in Carlisle, Pennsylvania. There he met Glenn "Pop" Warner, who served as both the football and track coach for the school. Thorpe began to participate and soon became one of the best athletes on both teams. That summer, Thorpe tried his hand at baseball. He played for a North Carolina team and earned approximately sixty dollars.

The 1912 Olympic Games were held in Stockholm, Sweden. These Games were a defining moment in his life. After he was awarded gold medals in both the pentathlon and the decathlon, Thorpe was considered to be the greatest athlete in the world.

Thorpe was confronted with many accusations after the Games because of the brief time he played professional baseball. The Amateur Athletic Association reclaimed Thorpe's medals and removed his name from the record books. Playing for teams during the summer was common among collegiate athletes at the time, and Thorpe was quoted as saying, "I was doing what I knew several other college athletes had done."

His athletic career continued despite this setback. Thorpe played professional baseball for the New York Giants, Cincinnati Reds, and Boston Braves. Thorpe made the transition to football in 1915 when he played for the Canton Bulldogs. He was named President of the American Professional Football Association, which would later be known as the National Football League.

After numerous attempts by his daughter, Grace, to overturn the Amateur Athletic Association's decision, Thorpe's medals were returned in 1982 after the International Olympic Committee's president, Juan Antonio Samaranch, proposed that Thorpe's amateur athlete status be reinstated.

In 1950, the Associated Press named Thorpe the greatest athlete of the first half of the twentieth century. Since 1996, Grace Thorpe has been working to have her father named Athlete of the Century.

Because Tammy Scherer's essay focuses on the athlete who is her town's namesake, she can be sure her audience is familiar with her topic. Her writing style is informative, yet it doesn't bog the reader down with too much detail.

Knowing your audience is not the only important part of writing effectively. Using verbs and verb tenses correctly makes your writing powerful. You'll focus on verbs in the writing exercises in this chapter.

Regular Verbs

▐▐▐▶ All verbs have four basic forms, or **principal parts**. They are the present, the present participle, the past, and the past participle.

Verbs are classified as regular or irregular, depending on how they form the past and past participle.

▐▐▐▶ Regular verbs add -*d* or -*ed* to the present tense to form the past and past participle.

Principal Parts of Regular Verbs			
PRESENT	**PRESENT PARTICIPLE** (Use with *am, is, are, was, were.*)	**PAST**	**PAST PARTICIPLE** (Use with *has, had, have.*)
need wish look	(is) needing (is) wishing (is) looking	needed wished looked	(had) needed (had) wished (had) looked

The **present participle** of regular verbs ends with -*ing*. It works with a helping verb, a form of the verb *be* (*am, is, are, was,* or *were*), to make a verb phrase.

> I **am watching** this movie. My cousin **was watching** it earlier.

The **past participle** of regular verbs ends in -*d* or -*ed*. It works with a helping verb, a form of the verb *have* (*has, have,* or *had*), to make a verb phrase.

> I **have stopped** here frequently.
> Jim **had stopped** here yesterday.

When you add -*ing* and -*(e)d* to the present form of a verb, the spelling sometimes changes. For example, you may need to drop the final -*e*, change a final -*y* to *i*, or double the final consonant.

> like + -*ed* = lik**ed**   worry + -*ed* = worr**ied**   hop + -*ed* = ho**pped**

(For more about spelling rules, see Chapter 16.)

A few regular verbs have alternate forms. Both are correct, although the -*ed* form is more common and tends to sound less formal.

> I **dreamed** about the ocean last night. I **dreamt** about the ocean last night.
> Who had **lighted** all those candles? Who had **lit** all those candles?

Enriching Your Vocabulary

The verb *precipitate* stems from the Latin word *praeceps*, meaning "head first." In Exercise 2, it is used in the case where one event brings on another. Drastic air pressure changes *precipitate* a violent thunderstorm.

EDITING TIP

A participle cannot do the job of a verb alone. It needs a helping verb.
                is
Mary ∧ hoping for some snow tomorrow.

Exercise 1 Using Principal Parts of Regular Verbs

Complete each sentence by writing the correct past form or past participle form of the verb in parentheses. Some sentences have more than one verb in parentheses.

EXAMPLE   When Martha (open) *opened* the present, she (smile) *smiled*.

1. We (hike) ———— to the same location where Eliza had (camp) ————.

2. I have (learn) ———— a great deal about this state.

3. Jeb had (marry) ———— his childhood sweetheart.

4. We (shop) ———— until the stores (close) ————.

5. That group has (organize) ———— the recycling campaign in town.

6. Bad weather (delay) ———— the opening of the new site.

7. They (pack) ————, (load) ————, and (carry) ———— all their own equipment.

8. Has anyone (admit) ———— to taking the last clean towel?

9. I have (wash) ———— and (dry) ———— the dishes every night this week.

10. When we (reach) ———— the meeting place, we (sigh) ———— with relief.

Exercise 2 Editing a Report

On a separate piece of paper, edit the following portion of a history report so that it more accurately outlines events that took place in the past. Use the past form or past participle form of each italicized verb. Change words or phrases, as needed, to accommodate the changes in tense.

¹The Aztec empire *reaches* its height in the 1400s. ²By that time, the Aztecs *gain* control over a huge trading network. ³Because of this vast trading network, wealth *flows* into the fabulous cities of the empire.

⁴By the early 1500s, however, even the mighty Aztec empire *weakens*. ⁵Problems that *exist* for a long time *start* to become far more serious. ⁶For one thing, in the past, the empire always *collects* tribute from the people it *conquers*. ⁷Perhaps even more significant, the empire always *demands* sacrifice from these same people. ⁸As the empire *increases* in size, these demands *accelerate*. ⁹This development *precipitates* more and more unrest in the empire. ¹⁰Soon, people *revolt*. ¹¹The leader at the time, Montezuma II, *grants* a few, but not enough, concessions. ¹²Then the Spanish *arrive*.

Irregular Verbs 1

Like all languages, English has irregular verbs. **Irregular verbs** form the past tense and past participle in unpredictable ways. The most common irregular verb is *to be*. Its forms are listed at the right.

▐▐▌➡ Use the principal parts of these common irregular verbs correctly when you write and speak.

Forms of *to be*

Present

I am	we are
you are	you are
he, she, it is	they are

Past

I was	we were
you were	you were
he, she, it was	they were

Principal Parts of Common Irregular Verbs			
PRESENT	PRESENT PARTICIPLE (Use with *am, is, are, was, were*.)	PAST	PAST PARTICIPLE (Use with *has, had, have*.)
[be] is, are	(is) being	was, were	(had) been
begin	(is) beginning	began	(had) begun
blow	(is) blowing	blew	(had) blown
break	(is) breaking	broke	(had) broken
bring	(is) bringing	brought	(had) brought
build	(is) building	built	(had) built
burst	(is) bursting	burst	(had) burst
catch	(is) catching	caught	(had) caught
choose	(is) choosing	chose	(had) chosen
come	(is) coming	came	(had) come
cost	(is) costing	cost	(had) cost
dive	(is) diving	dived; dove	(had) dived; dove
do	(is) doing	did	(had) done
draw	(is) drawing	drew	(had) drawn
drink	(is) drinking	drank	(had) drunk
drive	(is) driving	drove	(had) driven
eat	(is) eating	ate	(had) eaten
fall	(is) falling	fell	(had) fallen
feel	(is) feeling	felt	(had) felt
find	(is) finding	found	(had) found
freeze	(is) freezing	froze	(had) frozen
get	(is) getting	got	(had) got; gotten
give	(is) giving	gave	(had) given
go	(is) going	went	(had) gone
grow	(is) growing	grew	(had) grown
hurt	(is) hurting	hurt	(had) hurt
know	(is) knowing	knew	(had) known
lay (to put or place)	(is) laying	laid	(had) laid
lead	(is) leading	led	(had) led

WRITING HINT

When you are required to speak and write standard English, as you are in school or at work, make sure you use the verb *be* correctly.

She *is* at work now.

She *will* be home later.

P.S. When you aren't sure about a verb form, look the verb up in a dictionary. The entry word is the present form. All dictionaries list the principal parts of irregular verbs, usually after the pronunciation.

   eat (ēt), **ate**, **eaten**, **eating**

If no verb forms follow the entry word, the verb is regular.

EXERCISE 3 Using Irregular Verbs

On a separate piece of paper, rewrite each sentence using the past form or the past participle form of the verb in parentheses. **Remember:** With a form of the helping verb *have*, use the past participle.

EXAMPLE   The ground had (freeze) early that winter.
The ground had frozen early that winter.

1. We have (find) the best place to watch birds.

2. Have you (bring) your binoculars with you today?

3. We (eat) and (drink) a lot after the long, tiring hike.

4. I (feel) bad when I (get) a low grade.

5. Sylvia has (be) absent quite often this term.

6. Mick (give) up only shortly after he (begin) the race.

7. Jenna (break) the record for number of catches in one season when

   she (catch) that ball.

8. When we saw the water, we (know) the dam had (burst).

9. His car had (cost) quite a bit less than his house.

10. Pete had (drive) for several hours in the rain.

11. If he had not (fall), he would not have (hurt) himself.

12. Jan (lay) her drawings on the table.

13. Francisco (lead) me to the place where Mindy had (go) before me.

14. Several new plants (grow) in the garden.

15. I do not know who (build) this house.

16. The high winds had (blow) down some power lines.

17. I would have (come) earlier if I had (know) when the party started.

18. What have you (do) to your hair?

19. We watched as Peter (dive) gracefully from the high board.

20. I had (choose) this gift long before your birthday.

Irregular Verbs 2

English has many irregular verbs. This lesson and the previous one list the most frequently used irregular verbs.

▐▶ Use the principal parts of these common irregular verbs correctly when you write and speak.

Principal Parts of Common Irregular Verbs			
PRESENT	PRESENT PARTICIPLE (Use with *am, is, are, was, were.*)	PAST	PAST PARTICIPLE (Use with *has, had, have.*)
lend	(is) lending	lent	(had) lent
lie (to rest or recline)	(is) lying	lay	(had) lain
lose	(is) losing	lost	(had) lost
make	(is) making	made	(had) made
meet	(is) meeting	met	(had) met
put	(is) putting	put	(had) put
ride	(is) riding	rode	(had) ridden
ring	(is) ringing	rang	(had) rung
rise	(is) rising	rose	(had) risen
run	(is) running	ran	(had) run
say	(is) saying	said	(had) said
see	(is) seeing	saw	(had) seen
sell	(is) selling	sold	(had) sold
send	(is) sending	sent	(had) sent
set	(is) setting	set	(had) set
shrink	(is) shrinking	shrank; shrunk	(had) shrunk; shrunken
sing	(is) singing	sang	(had) sung
sink	(is) sinking	sank; sunk	(had) sunk
sit	(is) sitting	sat	(had) sat
speak	(is) speaking	spoke	(had) spoken
stand	(is) standing	stood	(had) stood
steal	(is) stealing	stole	(had) stolen
swim	(is) swimming	swam	(had) swum
swing	(is) swinging	swung	(had) swung
take	(is) taking	took	(had) taken
teach	(is) teaching	taught	(had) taught
tell	(is) telling	told	(had) told
throw	(is) throwing	threw	(had) thrown
wear	(is) wearing	wore	(had) worn
win	(is) winning	won	(had) won
write	(is) writing	wrote	(had) written

WRITING HINT

Lay and *lie*, *sit* and *set*, and *raise* and *rise* are often confused. With few exceptions, *lay*, *raise*, and *set* take objects; *lie*, *rise*, and *sit* don't. If you can't remember, or get a *handle* on, which is which, remember the word *hands*. *Lay*, *raise*, and *set* can take *hands* as an object, as in *lay hands* (on), *set hands* (on), and *raise hands*. On the other hand, it is not possible to "lie hands," "sit hands," or "rise hands."

EXERCISE 4 Using Irregular Verbs

On a separate piece of paper, rewrite each sentence using the correct past form or past participle form of the verb in parentheses.

1. I (see) the emotion in her eyes as she (speak).

2. Had Julio (run) faster than Eva had (throw) the ball to first base?

3. After Eliot (swing) and missed, we knew we had (win) the game.

4. The letter had (lie) unread on the table all day.

5. We (sit) for so long that our legs hurt when we finally (stand) up.

EXERCISE 5 Editing a Paragraph

In the following paragraph, cross out each incorrect verb, and write the correct verb above it. You may need to correct spelling as well as verb forms.

   ¹I have meet and speaked with many teachers, students, and school board members about the exorbitant amount of time we have sank into standardized tests in our schools. ²Many of us are seen some negative effects of these tests. ³Too much emphasis has been putted on testing. ⁴For example, in English class, we are sometimes teached how to take the writing test instead of how to write. ⁵We have took the big picture out of history by concentrating on isolated facts that might be tested. ⁶We have throwed out parts of our math curriculum in order to emphasize those parts that are on state competency tests. ⁷Not enough has been sayed and writed on this subject, though much has been losed as a result of too much testing.

Write What You Think

On a separate piece of paper, write a paragraph giving your opinion on one of the statements below. State your opinion clearly at the outset, and support your opinion with reasons and examples. When you finish revising your paragraph, edit it to be sure you have used verb forms correctly.

• Standardized tests are a necessary part of the educational system.

• We should eliminate all standardized tests except those that are used for college entrance examinations.

• We need standardized tests to establish minimum levels of competence for graduation.

Verb Tense

IIII➤ A **verb tense** expresses the time an action was performed.

Every English verb has three **simple tenses** (present, past, and future) and three **perfect tenses** (present perfect, past perfect, and future perfect).

The Six Verb Tenses		
TENSE	**WHAT IT SHOWS**	**EXAMPLE**
Present	action happening in the present; action that happens repeatedly	I **win**. Julie **wins** again and again.
Past	action completed in the past	I **won**.
Future	action that will happen in the future	You and he **will win**. We **shall win**.
Present perfect	action completed recently or in the indefinite past	I **have won**. She **has won**.
Past perfect	action that happened before another action	I **had** already **won** before the game ended.
Future perfect	action that will happen before a future action or time	In another minute, our team **will have won**.

Each tense also has a **progressive form**, which is made up of a helping verb and the present participle (the *-ing* form). The progressive forms show ongoing action.

The Progressive Forms of the Six Tenses	
PROGRESSIVE FORM	**EXAMPLE**
Present progressive	(**am**, **is**, **are**) **winning**
Past progressive	(**was**, **were**) **winning**
Future progressive	**will be winning**
Present perfect progressive	(**has**, **have**) **been winning**
Past perfect progressive	**had been winning**
Future perfect progressive	**will have been winning**

IIII➤ In most cases, use the same tense in the same sentence or sequence of ideas.

ORIGINAL   Kari **opens** her eyes and **checked** out the room. Where **was** she, she **wonders**.

REVISED   Kari **opened** her eyes and **checked** out the room. Where **was** she, she **wondered**.

IIII➤ Sometimes, it is necessary to change, or shift, tenses because the meaning of the sentence or the context requires it. In this case, use verb tenses that make sense.

Kari **arrived** yesterday. She **is** on vacation, and she **will go** home next week.

WRITING HINT

There is yet another verb form that's helpful for showing emphasis in writing—the **emphatic form**.

We **do ride** the train to school.

He **did ride** the train last week.

She **does ride** the train for an hour.

TEST-TAKING TIP

A test item may contain an incorrect tense shift, an error in which a verb does not properly express the frame of reference represented in a sentence. See item 15 on page 316.

EXERCISE 6 Writing Sentences Using Varied Verb Tenses

On a separate piece of paper, write a complete sentence using the italicized verb and the intended meaning.

1. *turn*—action that happens repeatedly
2. *finish*—action that will happen before a future action
3. *regret*—action happening in the present
4. *eat*—action completed recently
5. *arrive*—action that happened before another action
6. *become*—action completed in the past
7. *write*—action completed in the indefinite past
8. *rent*—action that will happen before a future time
9. *decide*—action that will happen in the future
10. *jump*—action that happened before another action

EXERCISE 7 Making Verb Tenses Consistent

On a separate piece of paper, revise each of the following sentences in which you find unnecessary shifts in verb tense. If a sentence doesn't need revising, write *C* for *correct*. **Hint:** Most of the sentences that need revising can be fixed in more than one way.

1. Moira opened the window and looks out.
2. By the time it is noon, I will finish this book.
3. I have played in every round of the tournament, and I won each time.
4. Mrs. McDonagh beeps the horn when she picked us up.
5. Tomorrow is the surprise party, so we are there early.
6. We had already drawn the winning ticket when you add yours to the hat.
7. Because it was so cold, we all wore extra layers.
8. As the earth turns on its axis, day became night.
9. I have written six pages before Irene even begins.
10. Tomás has run six races this year, and he won five of them.

Using the Active Voice

▐▐▶ When a verb is in the **active voice**, the subject of the sentence performs an action. When a verb is in the **passive voice**, the subject receives an action.

You can recognize the passive voice by finding a form of the helping verb *be* and a past participle.

ACTIVE	Isabel **repaired** the broken tile.
PASSIVE	The broken tile **was repaired** by Isabel.
ACTIVE	Mr. Sung **has reported** the accident on Trent Road.
PASSIVE	The accident on Trent Road **has been reported** by Mr. Sung.

▐▐▶ Use the active voice whenever possible. It is more direct and forceful than the passive voice.

Sometimes, however, you must use the passive voice. The passive voice is acceptable under two circumstances: when you do not know the performer of the action and when the performer of the action is not important.

> A sweater **had been removed** from the coatroom. [If you do not know who performed the action, you must use the passive voice.]
> The bridge **was completed** in 1889. [If it is not important to know who performed the action, the passive voice is a good choice.]

Enriching Your Vocabulary

The word *wanes*, used in Exercise 8, comes from the Old English word *wanian*, which means "to decrease." A *waning* moon is one that gets smaller after a full moon.

EXERCISE 8 Identifying Passive Voice and Active Voice

Read each sentence below. Write *A* if the verb is in the active voice. Write *P* if the verb is in the passive voice.

_____ 1. Last week, a tornado was reported in Greenville County.

_____ 2. A tornado starts out as a whirl of dust.

_____ 3. Suddenly, the dust rises from the ground.

_____ 4. Right before your eyes, a funnel is formed.

_____ 5. The funnel is filled with debris, dirt, and moisture.

_____ 6. Usually, the funnel is more narrow near the ground than at the top.

_____ 7. Anything on the ground can be caught in the spiral of a tornado.

_____ 8. Even a car can be carried away by its powerful force.

_____ 9. Suddenly, the spiral shrinks and begins to tilt.

_____10. As this tornado wanes, another may form.

EXERCISE 9 Using the Active Voice

Each sentence below is written in the passive voice. On a separate piece of paper, either explain why the passive voice is appropriate, or rewrite the sentence using the active voice.

EXAMPLE   Many American novels have been made into films.
           Keep the passive voice. The performer of the action is unknown.

1. American literature from the second half of the nineteenth century is being studied by our class.

2. _The Adventures of Huckleberry Finn_ and other works by Mark Twain have been read by us.

3. _Sister Carrie_, a story of a young woman in the city, was included in our reading list.

4. _Sister Carrie_ was written by Theodore Dreiser.

5. The poem "We Wear the Mask" was assigned to us by Ms. Monto.

6. The poem was composed in 1896.

7. This poem by Paul Laurence Dunbar is considered by many to be a groundbreaking work on the topic of race.

8. Since Dunbar's time, many moving works on this theme have been written.

9. We also studied Edith Wharton's _The Age of Innocence_, which was made into a film by Martin Scorsese.

10. For the most part, this movie was praised by critics, but it was ignored or criticized by many moviegoers.

Revising and Editing Worksheet 1

Improve the following draft by revising for ideas, organization, word choice, and sentence variety. After revising, edit the draft for errors in spelling, capitalization, punctuation, and usage. Write your revised and edited version on a separate piece of paper. Compare your changes with those of a writing partner.

[1]If you had visited a web site lately, you know it can be a great place to find information. [2]At the same time, it often offered something good to look at or listen to.

[3]Web page design had not always been this good. [4]As many people knew, scientists in Geneva have created the World Wide Web around 1988. [5]They want to exchange information, and, at first, that's all they done. [6]Theirs is a world of gray screens and print without a single audio reminder or video clip. [7]Then outsiders discover the web, and nothing be the same since.

[8]Although Web pages are around for less than three decades, designers transform them in a short period. [9]Soon, gray and dull was out, and glitzy is in. [10]Anyone who had wanted high-interest graphics now had had them.

[11]The problem is, however, that these early web pages designed to appeal to the masses are challenging to use. [12]After clicking on a link, users sometimes be losed forever in cyberspace. [13]Designs fail to make it clear what the user should done next.

[14]Still, in the brief history of the Web, it isn't long before designers have realized that getting information from the site was more important than the fanciest possible graphics. [15]Such designers revise their sites, making them easier to use. [16]Some pages given up some of their visual appeal, but that is part of the tradeoff.

[17]Today, web pages usually mixed appealing graphics with clarity. [18]Designers have leaved the confusing designs behind without sacrificing the look of the page. [19]People today sometimes admire these pages just for their art.

Revising and Editing Worksheet 2

Improve the following draft by revising for ideas, organization, word choice, and sentence variety. After revising, edit the draft for errors in spelling, capitalization, punctuation, and usage. Write your revised and edited version on a separate piece of paper. Compare your changes with those of a writing partner.

[1]One of most admired musicians of our times is Wynton Marsalis. [2]He was widely known as a jazz trumpet player, but he had also gained a considerable reputation as a composer. [3]He had also been holded in high regard by some people as a composer of classical works.

[4]Marsalis growed up in New Orleans. [5]Where he was surrounded by jazz. [6]A love of music was communicated to him by his father, a professional jazz musician and teacher. [7]In such an atmosphere, it wasn't long before the young Wynton achieved success. [8]Although he did not begun to play trumpet until the age of twelve. [9]By the age of twenty, his first album as a jazz bandleader had been released by him.

[10]When Marsalis composes, jazz and classical elements are often combined by him. [11]That is, the line between jazz and classical music is blurred by his music. [12]In fact, for Marsalis, as for other musicians, jazz in some ways *is* America's classical music. [13]It is regarded by many musicians as having a similar intellectual content. [14]And as requiring the same technical virtuosity.

[15]Marsalis, a spokesperson for the importance of jazz, has identified some of the artists and albums that most inspired him. [16]In a list of his top ten albums are included works by Louis Armstrong, Count Basie, Ornette Coleman, John Coltrane, and Charlie Parker. [17]Also listed by Marsalis are Thelonious Monk, Jelly Roll Morton, and Duke Ellington.

Chapter Review

EXERCISE A Using Irregular Verbs

On a separate piece of paper, write the past form or past participle form of the verb in parentheses that correctly completes each sentence. In some cases, there may be more than one correct answer.

1. I have (wear) out my old sneakers, and I need new ones.

2. How long have you (know) Michael?

3. Dirty clothes (lie) all over the floor.

4. My grandmother (rise) at five o'clock this morning.

5. The builder (set) stakes in the ground to mark the lot.

6. Marcus (choose) several items from the new catalog.

7. I could not watch when Justin (dive) from the high board.

8. Mr. Alpers has (take) Erica to the doctor.

9. My grandmother has (see) that movie several times.

10. I had no idea where all that money (go).

11. My mother (teach) me how to prune a shrub.

12. Have you (begin) your history paper yet?

13. The other team put up a good fight, but we (win).

14. Gil has (say) nothing to me about the trip.

15. Right after my birthday, I (send) out ten thank-you notes.

16. Jade has not always (feel) entirely welcome here.

17. Those unkind words have (hurt) our relationship.

18. They (get) my e-mail address from an online directory.

EXERCISE B Using Verb Tenses

Change the italicized verbs to fit the meaning specified in parentheses.

1. Great art always *attract* visitors. (action that happens repeatedly)

2. It *be* a source of pleasure throughout the centuries. (action completed in the indefinite past)

3. I remember when I *see* my first painting by Picasso, *The Old Guitarist*. (action completed in the past)

4. It *hang* in the Art Institute of Chicago. (ongoing action in the past)

5. I *look* at pictures of it before I saw the real thing. (action that happened before another action)

EXERCISE C Identifying Voice

On the line before each sentence, write *A* if the sentence is in the active voice. Write *P-A* if the sentence is in the passive voice and the use of the passive voice is appropriate. Write *P-I* if the sentence is in the passive voice and the use of the passive voice is inappropriate.

_____ 1. That the core of the earth is solid has been believed by scientists for a long time.

_____ 2. No direct evidence had been found to support this theory until recently.

_____ 3. Now a paper has been authored by Emile Okal.

_____ 4. It confirms what scientists have long suspected.

_____ 5. The earth is composed of a rocky mantle floating on a liquid core of molten iron.

_____ 6. Okal based his study on an analysis of seismic waves.

_____ 7. Seismic waves change as they pass through the center of the earth.

_____ 8. A layering of solid and liquid was theorized and confirmed by the study.

EXERCISE D Editing a Report

On a separate piece of paper, edit the report below for the correct use of verbs. Use the correct forms of verbs, make verb tenses consistent, and correct any inappropriate uses of the passive voice. Make any other edits that you think will improve the paragraphs.

¹What be the most widely distributed meat-eating mammal on Earth? ²It was the red fox. ³This beautiful creature has been a member of the dog family, although it was in some ways more like a cat. ⁴That it hunts alone like a cat, pounces like a cat, is agile like a cat, and even has had catlike whiskers has been noted by scientists.

⁵Scientists will also have been observing that the red fox is a survivor. ⁶In days when other species disappear, the red fox survives and it multiplied. ⁷Today, the red fox is finded throughout most of the Northern Hemisphere and in Australia. ⁸What has enable it to survive? ⁹Two adaptations are often mentioned by scientists. ¹⁰Both had helped the red fox hunt at night. ¹¹One is its eyes, which have a light-enhancing membrane for night vision. ¹²A second is its hind legs. ¹³These given it power to lunge and pounce quickly and from great distances. ¹⁴In fact, red foxes will have been observed leaping as far as seventeen feet over level ground.

Subject-Verb Agreement

CHAPTER

10

Usage

STUDENT WRITING
Persuasive Essay

Community Service Requirement Can Benefit Students
by Lauren Keane
high school student, San Francisco, California

Which is the more productive way to spend one hundred hours: sprawled on the couch watching TV or volunteering? What if those hours were distributed over four years—on a project of your choice—and were required for graduation? Chances are you might consider rearranging your schedule.

Spending time working in our communities shouldn't be just encouraged; it should be required. Our school teaches us about the academic side of life, but it often falls short by not teaching us enough about the *living* side of life.

Community service benefits us as it does the people we help. "Part of being a citizen is being involved and being part of a community," said social studies teacher Kristen Lubenow, who requires students to complete fifteen hours of volunteer work to pass her class. "Community service teaches students the costs and benefits of their actions, and it shows them how their input to an organization or a community can make a difference."

Many of Lubenow's students spend time in fields that they are considering as career choices. "It's a good way to find out whether you really want to be a doctor, for example," Lubenow said, "and if that's not the right choice for you, you'd rather find that out in high school than in med school."

Some people would argue that schools should not require community service because such service is too removed from the school environment and is inconsistent with academic graduation requirements. But community service requirements don't crowd us into classrooms with our noses buried in textbooks that tell us about how other people have changed the world. Instead, they turn us out into that world and let us make our own changes. Maybe that isn't traditional "learning," but it is infinitely more useful in life.

As principal Paul Cheng states in the school's Student Handbook, "[Our] high school's mission is to encourage the individuals who attend to contribute their skills, creativity, and intellect in a way that benefits both themselves and the wider community of which they are a part." Without a service requirement, the school's wholly academic curriculum cannot realistically meet this goal.

So, time to turn off the TV. Your four and a half minutes a day will benefit you just as much as it will help others, and you may find an area that sparks your interest as a possible career. Schools should require us to give back to our community the assistance that it has given us. "If all 2,800 students were out there volunteering," Lubenow said, "imagine what an impact we could have."

Lauren Keane's opinion statement appears in the first sentence of the second paragraph. She supports her opinion with reasons and quotations. She addresses the arguments against her opinion, and she ends with a call to action.

Making verbs agree with subjects is second nature to most native English speakers. However, certain subjects make agreement tricky. You'll learn about those situations in this chapter.

Agreement in Person and Number

We use the term **person** when we discuss the subject of a sentence. The pronoun subjects *I* and *we* are **first-person pronouns**. The subject *you* is a **second-person pronoun**. *He, she, it,* and *they* are **third-person pronouns**. Any noun subject is also third person.

Along with person, we use the term **number** when we discuss the subject of a sentence. A subject that names one person, place, or thing is **singular**. A subject that names more than one person, place, or thing is **plural**.

IIII➤ A third-person **singular subject** takes a **singular verb**. A third-person **plural subject** takes a **plural verb**. The chart below shows how the verbs *wash* and *dry* change their forms only when they follow a third-person singular subject.

Subject-Verb Agreement in the Present Tense		
PERSON	**SINGULAR SUBJECT**	**PLURAL SUBJECT**
First	I **wash** and **dry** the dishes.	We **wash** and **dry** the dishes.
Second	You **wash** and **dry** the dishes.	You **wash** and **dry** the dishes.
Third	He **washes** and **dries** the dishes. Maria **washes** and **dries** the dishes.	They **wash** and **dry** the dishes. The men **wash** and **dry** the dishes.

The verb *be* has three forms to match person and number in the present tense. (See the side column.)

IIII➤ In a verb phrase, the helping verb (HV) must agree with the subject (S).

$\overset{\text{S}}{\quad}\overset{\text{HV}}{\quad}$

Matt and I **have** been looking for you all day.

$\overset{\text{S}}{\quad}\overset{\text{HV}}{\quad}$

Katrina **does**n't know about the surprise party.

EXERCISE 1 Editing a Report

Cross out each verb below that does not agree with its subject. Write the correct form of the verb above it.

¹The subject is a quiet eight-year-old. ²Her attitude reflect low self-esteem. ³Her behavior show she is reluctant to communicate with others. ⁴She have an urge to retreat, which characterizes her social interactions. ⁵In the classroom, she reveal her sense of being different from others.

Present Tense Forms of *Be*

Singular
I **am** here.
You **are** here.
He **is** here.

Plural
We **are** here.
You **are** here.
They **are** here.

> **EDITING TIP**
>
> *Doesn't* is singular; *don't* is plural.
> doesn't
> Eliza ~~don't~~ ever want to leave early.

⁶She also feel inferior to them. ⁷Her poor reading skills is contributing factors to her feelings of inferiority. ⁸At this time, however, her special-needs teacher recommend more work on building self-esteem than on reading skills. ⁹Such action have proven to be the best way to help children with similar problems.

¹⁰Self-esteem are basic to every discussion about personality. ¹¹Yet what is self-esteem, exactly? ¹²Most experts agrees that self-esteem is how people regard themselves. ¹³It is commonly perceived that high self-esteem result in feeling good about oneself based on one's achievements. ¹⁴Indeed, self-esteem are more critical to the emotional stability of every individual than intelligence, power, or money.

¹⁵In the late 1960s, studies on the topic of self-esteem was at their height. ¹⁶Most studies reported the positive effects on personalities. ¹⁷Since then, some studies has challenged the positive ideas. ¹⁸For example, researchers shows that criminals has high self-esteem. ¹⁹In fact, they scores alongside traditional overachievers on self-esteem indicator tests. ²⁰For this reason, researchers recognizes that building high self-esteem in children, such as the eight-year-old subject above, must be only one part of a plan to help them achieve success at school.

CONNECTING
Writing & Grammar

See
Composition,
Lesson 4.2, to
find strategies
for writing
persuasively.

Write What You Think

On a separate piece of paper, write one paragraph about the following statement. State your opinion clearly at the beginning of the paragraph, and then support it with reasons, details, and explanations. Be sure to revise and edit your writing and to check for subject-verb agreement.

Educators in elementary, middle, and high schools should devote at least as much time and effort to self-esteem issues as to subject-area instruction.

Agreement with Intervening Phrases and Inverted Subjects

Sometimes, the subject of a sentence is not easy to find.

▐▐▐▶ A prepositional phrase that comes between the subject and verb is called an **intervening phrase**.

Sometimes, a word in the intervening phrase may appear to be the subject of the sentence. This is often the case when it is next to the verb. When you write, make sure the verb (v) agrees with the subject (s)—no matter how far away it is from the verb—and not with the object of a preposition in the intervening phrase.

> S   V
> **One** of the band members **is** ill today. [*Of the band members* is a prepositional phrase. *One* is the subject, not *members*.]
>
> S   V
> **Most** of the students in our class **do** volunteer work. [*Do* agrees with *most*, not *students* or *class*.]

▐▐▐▶ A verb must agree with the subject even when a negative word (such as *not*, *no*, or *never*) follows it.

> S   V
> The **truth**, not more stories, **is** what I want to hear.

▐▐▐▶ A verb must agree with the subject even when the subject follows the verb.

> V   S
> In the town square **stands** a stone **monument**.
>
> V   S
> There **goes** the finest **car** on the road today.
>
> V   S
> What **is** the **source** of the data in this chart?

▐▐▐▶ A verb agrees with the subject, not with the predicate nominative (PN). Don't be confused by a predicate nominative following a linking verb. Find the subject, and then make the verb agree.

> S   V   PN
> Enrique's **hobby is** tropical fish.
>
> S   V   PN   PN
> This **report is** all facts and figures.

Enriching Your Vocabulary

The word *diligence* comes from the Latin verb *diligere*, meaning "to esteem highly or select." It is used, as in Exercise 2, to mean "careful effort or perseverance." A student's *diligence* at grammar will earn him or her high marks on writing tests.

EXERCISE 2 Choosing the Correct Verb

Underline the subject of each sentence and the verb in parentheses that agrees with the subject.

1. What (is, are) the reasons for attending college for four years?

2. What (make, makes) this amount of time just right?

3. History, not logic, (seem, seems) to have determined this length of time.

4. At the time of Harvard's opening, students in Cambridge, England, (was, were) attending college for four years.

5. Today, some students, though by no means all, (earn, earns) their degrees in four years.

6. Sixty-four percent of all college students in 1991 (was, were) five-year students.

7. In support of this trend (is, are) several factors.

8. The soaring cost of a higher education (is, are) one of them.

9. Among those in search of a higher education (is, are) students on a budget.

10. Hundreds, if not thousands, of today's students (take, takes) time out to work.

11. The end result of the education—not just its cost—also (motivate, motivates) students.

12. In the minds of some students (is, are) a dual degree, a kind of insurance policy for their future.

13. The requirements for professional degrees (has, have) also changed.

14. A degree in some fields (require, requires) an internship or other practical experience.

15. These experiences, not lack of diligence, (add, adds) time to a college education.

16. On the other hand, some students in college today (graduate, graduates) in just three years.

17. In these cases, the cost of a college education (go, goes) down.

18. Colleges with a three-year program (defend, defends) their efficiency and professionalism.

19. In these programs (is, are) only the most highly motivated students.

20. At the heart of every decision about the length of a college education (lie, lies) individual choice.

Agreement with Indefinite Pronouns

▐▐▐▶ An **indefinite pronoun** expresses an amount or refers to an unspecified person or thing. Some indefinite pronouns are always singular and take singular verbs. Others are always plural and take plural verbs.

SINGULAR	**Everybody** on my soccer team **shows** up for practice every day.
SINGULAR	**No one** ever **misses** a single practice or meet.
PLURAL	**Several** of us **meet** for additional drills and exercises.

Always Singular

anybody	neither
anyone	nobody
each	no one
either	one
everybody	somebody
everyone	someone

Always Plural

both	many
few	several

▐▐▐▶ The indefinite pronouns *all*, *any*, *most*, and *some* can be either singular or plural. Depending on the word they refer to, these pronouns take either a singular or plural verb.

Use a singular verb (v) when the indefinite pronouns *all*, *any*, *most*, and *some* refer to a singular word. Use a plural verb when these pronouns refer to a plural word.

SINGULAR	S V **All** of the water **has** run out of the tub.
PLURAL	S V **All** of the runners **have** been training for months.
SINGULAR	S V Which one may I take? **Any is** fine.
PLURAL	S Where may I sit? **Any** of the seats in that section V **are** open.
SINGULAR	S V **Most** of her writing **is** illegible.
PLURAL	S V **Most** of the letters **are** illegible.
SINGULAR	S V **Some** of the woodwork **was** refinished.
PLURAL	S V **Some** of the rooms **were** renovated.

EDITING TIP

The pronoun *none* is especially tricky. Use a singular verb only when you can think of the subject as "none of it." Use a plural verb when you can substitute "none of them."

None of the bread **was** left this morning. [None of *it* was left this morning.]

None of the stories **contain** a flashback. [None of *them* contain a flashback.]

EXERCISE 3 Choosing the Correct Verb

Underline the subject of each sentence and the verb in parentheses that agrees in number with the subject.

1. Everyone (know, knows) about the importance of flossing.

2. One of the benefits (is, are) clean teeth.

3. Many of us (realize, realizes) the effects of not flossing.

4. Some of the effects (include, includes) red, swollen, or tender gums.

5. Everybody in my class (is, are) also aware of the possibility of gum disease.

6. No one (underestimate, underestimates) the problems of gingivitis, a gum disease.

7. Anyone, at any age, (need, needs) to floss.

8. Of all adults age sixty and over, some (have, has) lost all their teeth.

9. Some—and perhaps as many as half—of all high school students (has, have) gingivitis.

10. Almost nobody at our age (think, thinks) about this problem much.

11. Still, somebody in my homeroom (receive, receives) treatment for gum disease.

12. Do any of those with the disease (understand, understands) all the possible side effects?

13. Some of the serious consequences (is, are) complications related to heart disease, diabetes, and pneumonia.

14. Several of these complications (is, are) linked to the oral bacteria from gum disease that show up in the bloodstream.

15. Each of these conditions (get, gets) worse with oral infections.

16. Both of our doctors (recommend, recommends) preventive measures.

17. A few of these recommendations (is, are) getting plenty of calcium to maximize bone development before age thirty, flossing and brushing daily, and going to the dentist regularly.

18. None of this information (is, are) reassuring!

19. Nobody with health concerns (hear, hears) it without asking questions.

20. Some of us (visit, visits) *www.perio.org* for answers to our questions.

Exercise 4 Writing Complete Sentences

On a separate piece of paper, write a complete sentence for each numbered item, using the group of words as the subject of the sentence.

EXAMPLE   One of my favorite books
One of my favorite books is A Yellow Raft in Blue Water.

1. Several of my relatives

2. Everybody on our soccer team

3. Few of the computers in our school

4. No one in my homeroom

5. Some of my neighbors

6. Most of my friends

7. None of the software

8. None of the Web sites

9. Anybody in this school district

10. Both of our bicycles

Agreement with Compound Subjects

A sentence has a **compound subject** when two or more subjects share the same verb. In the present tense, use the following rules to select the correct verb form.

▶ When two or more singular subjects are joined by *and*, they take a plural verb.

> Both the brittle star **and** the sea cucumber **live** deep in the sea.
> A dolphin **and** a flying fish **break** the surface of the water.

▶ When two or more singular subjects are joined by *or* or *nor*, they take a singular verb.

> A turtle **or** a shark **swims** in the sunlit zone.
> Neither Scott **nor** Samantha **is** a scuba diver.

▶ When a singular subject and a plural subject are joined by *or* or *nor*, the verb agrees with the subject closer to it.

> Neither still air **nor** high winds **are** perfect for sailing.
> Either mild breezes **or** a calm sea **is** ideal.
> **Are** the winds **or** the sea rough tonight?
> **Is** the wind **or** the waves a danger to the boat?

EXERCISE 5 Choose the Correct Verb

Underline the verb in parentheses that agrees with the subject.

1. *Weather* and *climate* (is, are) two terms that are frequently confused.

2. Neither Sally nor her parents (confuse, confuses) the two terms.

3. To some extent, either the average temperature or the amounts of rainfall (determine, determines) climate.

4. (Is, Are) an isolated instance or uncommon events part of weather or climate?

5. Storm clouds, hot and cold fronts, and other events of daily weather (is, are) always changing.

6. *Polar*, *temperate*, and *coastal* (is, are) all names of climate zones.

EDITING TIP

Some compound subjects, such as *macaroni and cheese*, name just one thing. They take a singular verb.

The **macaroni and cheese is** hot and delicious.

TEST-TAKING TIP

A standardized-test item may ask you to correct subject-verb agreement in items in which compound subjects are linked by *nor*. See item 4 on page 313.

7. Neither a tropical climate nor a subtropical climate typically (has, have) dry days.

8. In a subtropical climate, (is, are) high humidity or showers more likely to occur?

9. A hot, dry summer and a cool, wet winter (is, are) part of the Mediterranean climate.

10. Neither snowy winters nor dry winters (occur, occurs) there.

11. Snowfalls or a rainy summer sometimes (happen, happens).

12. Either normal variations in temperature or global warming (cause, causes) the greenhouse effect.

13. (Is, Are) greenhouse gases or some other cause changing our climate?

14. Neither scientists nor the government (know, knows) for sure.

15. (Is, Are) carbon monoxide or methane the more serious greenhouse gas?

EXERCISE 6 Create Your Own Exercise

With a partner or a group, make up five sentences like the ones in Exercise 5. You may write about any topic, and each sentence may be on a different topic. Use compound subjects. Exchange sentences with another pair or group of classmates, and see if you agree on the correct answers.

EXERCISE 7 Writing a Paragraph

Write a paragraph based on the following notes. Then get together in a small group to read your paragraphs aloud and to check subject-verb agreement.

Arid Climates

Extremes of hot & cold; remarkable changes between day & night temps

Major changes between summer & winter temps

Sahara, Mojave, Arabian, and Thar Deserts—all arid

Dangerous sandstorms, high winds

Dunes, worn-down rock, oceans of sand, vast areas

Inland areas of intense dryness; in high-pressure zones—dry, warm air evaporates any water

Has neither winds from the ocean to bring rain nor low-pressure areas for rain clouds to form

---

Other Problems in Agreement

�……▶ **Collective nouns** name a group of people or things. The list on the right gives examples of collective nouns.

Use a singular verb when you think that the collective noun is acting as one single unit. Use a plural verb when you think of the collective noun as multiple members acting independently of one another.

> The **committee is** holding its weekly meeting.
> [*Committee* refers to a single unit and takes a singular verb.]
> The **committee have** many different ideas for the event.
> [*Committee* refers to multiple members and takes a plural verb.]

It's not always obvious whether a collective noun is acting as a single unit or as multiple members. If you're not sure, use the verb form (singular or plural) that you think sounds better.

▭……▶ Some nouns ending in *-s* function as singular subjects and take a singular verb. Some function as plural subjects and take a plural verb. A few may be either singular or plural.

The nouns that are always plural are usually a pair of something or an object made up of parts working together. See the examples on the right.

> The **scissors need** to be sharpened.
> These **eyeglasses are** badly scratched.
> Those **pants drag** on the floor.

▭……▶ The title of a work of art (painting, literature, or music) is always a singular subject and takes a singular verb.

> *Sunflowers* **is** one of van Gogh's most famous paintings.
> *The Nick Adams Stories* **is** my favorite work by Hemingway.

▭……▶ Use a singular verb with a third-person subject that names a single amount or time. Use a plural verb with a third-person subject that refers to multiple items.

> **Two pennies is** not much money. [a single amount]
> The **two pennies are** both dated 1950. [multiple pennies]
> **Ten days is** not a long time. [a single time period]
> These **ten days are** like ten years. [multiple items]

▭……▶ Use a singular verb when *many a(n)*, *every*, or *each* comes before a compound subject.

> **Many a** boy and girl **aspires** to be on the stage.
> **Every** gardener and farmer **enjoys** the rain.
> **Each** appetizer and entrée on the menu **is** delicious.

Some Collective Nouns

audience	group
class	herd
club	(the) media
committee	(the) press
crowd	(the) public
family	team
flock	

Singular

mathematics	news
measles	physics
mumps	

Plural

binoculars	scissors
eyeglasses	slacks
pants	stairs

Singular or Plural

acoustics	statistics
politics	

EXERCISE 8 Choosing the Correct Verb

Underline the verb in parentheses that agrees with the subject.

1. Measles (is, are) a common childhood disease.

2. Physics (is, are) the science of matter and energy.

3. Cézanne's *Apples and Oranges* (is, are) my favorite still life painting.

4. The public (demand, demands) varying degrees of accountability from politicians.

5. Five dollars (is, are) too much for one of those sandwiches.

6. These binoculars (has, have) excellent lenses.

7. Politics (is, are) Olivia's major.

8. One by one, the audience (leave, leaves) the theater.

9. The crowd (go, goes) wild after each touchdown.

10. The group (decide, decides) what to do next.

EXERCISE 9 Editing a Press Release

Find each error in subject-verb agreement below. Cross out the incorrect verb, and write the correct verb above it.

¹The Duluth Audubon Club are meeting in Remis Auditorium on Saturday, October 3, at 9:00 A.M. ²The public are welcome.

³Come learn about birds in the greater Duluth area. ⁴At each Saturday meeting, a committee presents a slide show on local birds and habitats. ⁵Afterwards, the audience asks questions. ⁶Birding walks in the local area is also announced.

⁷Should you join us on our next walk, long pants is recommended, as we go through grassy areas. ⁸Binoculars is also important. ⁹Sorry, but neither very young children nor a favorite pet are welcome.

¹⁰Statistics shows decreasing bird populations in the Duluth area. ¹¹Many a committed birder and activist are needed to help restore habitats and to raise awareness. ¹²Please join us next Saturday.

Revising and Editing Worksheet 1

Improve the following draft by revising for ideas, organization, word choice, and sentence variety. After revising, edit the draft for errors in spelling, capitalization, punctuation, and usage. Write your revised and edited version on a separate piece of paper. Compare your changes with those of a writing partner.

[1]Yin and yang are a well-known symbol. [2]Two halfes makes up the yin-yang symbol. [3]These two halfes is forces, elements, and opposites. [4]On the femenine, passive side are yin, darkness, cold, and wetness is all associated with this side. [5]Some of its other associations is earth, departure, weakness, sorrow and death. [6]Yang is its masculin side. [7]Light, heat, and driness. [8]Among its other associations is heaven, summer, mountain, arrival. [9]Also joy and life. [10]Neither yin nor yang exist alone. [11]Together they produces everything that comes into existance. [12]Order, not chaos, result from their regular interaction.

[13]Every man, woman, and child in China understand this symbol. [14]It is an ancient symbol. [15]Perhaps three thousand years has passed since the idea first came into being. [16]Over time, many of the Chinese schools of thought and religious ideas has incorporated this concept. [17]One of them are Taoism. [18]The balance of natural forces are a central concept in this belief system.

[19]According to Chinese beliefs, the good health of a person and of the whole world depend on yin and yang. [20]Is it a surprise that all of the foods is classifyed accordingly. [21]Yin foods are "cooling" foods, yang foods are "heating" foods. [22]There are a middle group of foods, too, [23]This group balance the yin and yang. [24]It includes foods such as rice and bread.

[25]Yin and yang—and the ideas associated with it—are everywhere in China. [26]Everyone in China recognize this symbol, many of them wear it. [27]Some of the people plan their meals according to it. [28]Its presence on buildings and in artwork are taken for granted. [29]Even Chinese politics incorporate ideas associated with this principal.

Revising and Editing Worksheet 2

Improve the following draft by revising for ideas, organization, word choice, and sentence variety. After revising, edit the draft for errors in spelling, capitalization, punctuation, and usage. Write your revised and edited version on a separate piece of paper. Compare your changes with those of a writing partner.

[1]Among the books on that shelf, is nonfiction works. [2]One of the books is Diane Ackerman's book about the five senses. [3]*A Natural History of the Senses* are my favorite book on this topic. [4]Anyone in the world could learn something from this book. [5]It's intended audience are people who are curious and enjoys poetic and imaginative writing.

[6]Smell, touch, taste, hearing, vision, and synesthesia (the combination of senses) is the major divisions of the book. [7]In each division is several short essays and reflections. [8]For example, the section on smell includes explorations of topics they range from noses and roses to the science of smelling and sneezing. [9]Niether the topics of perfumes nor sweat is left out. [10]Under the heading of hearing is topics ranging from deafness to the violin. [11]Acoustics are explored, so is whale songs.

[12]Either "A Famous Nose" or "How to Watch the Sky" are my favorite essays. [13]In "A Famous Nose," Ackerman describes a "professional nose" who works for a perfume company. [14]Niether the sutleties of rose varieties nor the cent of a cleanser ever escape her. [15]In "How to Watch the Sky," the various moods and movements of the sky is discussed and celebrated.

[16]Many a reader and book club member have enjoyed this book. [17]Several of them has commented favorably on Ackerman's use of poetic language. [18]Although someone in an online interview claims the writing is not scientific. [19]None of the facts for this claim is given. [20]Furthermore, the professional press have almost universally praised the book.

Chapter Review

EXERCISE A Choosing the Correct Verb

Underline the verb in parentheses that agrees with the subject of
each sentence.

1. At our food club meeting, Elena, Rob, and I (discuss, discusses) herbs.

2. One of America's favorite herbs (is, are) parsley.

3. Either parsley or chives (is, are) often used as a garnish.

4. Neither celery flakes nor chervil (appear, appears) frequently on
   dinner tables.

5. Everybody in the Friendly Gourmets (love, loves) basil.

6. Either California basil or French varieties (is, are) often used in our recipes.

7. The club also (enjoy, enjoys) cilantro, sometimes called Chinese parsley.

8. Nobody in the club (has, have) an unkind word for that delicious herb.

9. Three tablespoons of fresh cilantro in a stew (is, are) not too much.

10. (Is, Are) lemongrass or some other Thai herbs used?

11. Most of us (put, puts) lemongrass in soups.

12. Several of us (is, are) also wild about bay leaves.

13. Bay leaves and dill weed (is, are) perfect for spaghetti sauce.

14. Many a Greek salad or Turkish kebob (contain, contains) oregano.

15. Every cook or would-be cook (love, loves) it.

EXERCISE B Editing a Paragraph

Find each mistake in subject-verb agreement in the following paragraph. Cross
out the incorrect verb, and write the correct verb above it.

¹Research on the subject of air quality at indoor skating rinks have

recently been conducted, and the news are bad. ²Anybody on a hockey team

or on other teams face possible risks. ³In fact, everyone at certain rinks

breathes in unhealthy air. ⁴Many a hockey player and recreational skater

have already reported trouble breathing after skating in some rinks. ⁵Some

of the ice-resurfacing machines has been shown to give off dangerous levels

of nitrogen dioxide. ⁶Indoor rinks with poor ventilation often has dangerously high levels of this gas. [7]Propane-powered ice-resurfacing machines give off large amounts of this gas. [8]Neither propane machines nor a gasoline-powered machine are considered safe. [9]One hundred thousand dollars are the estimated cost of an electric-powered machine. [10]Statistics suggests this money may be well spent.

EXERCISE C Writing Complete Sentences

On a separate piece of paper, write a complete sentence for each numbered item. Begin your sentences with the given word or group of words. If the verb is not given, use present-tense verbs, and check your sentences for correct subject-verb agreement.

1. Many a . . .
2. Statistics . . .
3. Those black pants . . .
4. None of my teachers . . .
5. The student council . . .
6. In the front yard is . . .
7. Neither Eliot nor his classmates . . .
8. The books on this desk . . .
9. The space-station crew . . .
10. Two bones in her hand . . .
11. Sixteen dollars . . .
12. Either Dubuque or Cedar Rapids . . .
13. Most of the beach . . .
14. All of the roast . . .
15. Rock 'n' roll . . .
16. Either the flutes or the piccolo . . .
17. *Great Expectations* . . .
18. Happiness, not material possessions, . . .
19. Both Jenna and her parents . . .
20. What . . . ?

EXERCISE D Writing a Comparison

Think of two musical instruments, two singers, or two groups or bands that you like a great deal. Using present-tense verbs and a variety of compound subjects, write a paragraph comparing and contrasting them. Include as many specific details as possible.

CHAPTER REVIEW

Using Pronouns

STUDENT WRITING
Expository Essay

by Jana Zabkova
high school student, Lakewood, Ohio

Seeing kids wander Lakewood streets at night one too many times, Reverend Paula Maeder Connor was thrilled when Lakewood Youth Services asked her to host a garage band concert at her church.

"We thought we should give the kids someplace to go," Connor, minister of Trinity Lutheran Church, said.

Junior Dave Taha's band, Comfort in Misery, and another local youth band, Cryptonym, headlined the show. "We had a good time. It was sort of a hoopla of people just running around," Taha said.

Ron Colucci, clinical supervisor of Lakewood Youth Services, called Connor to arrange the concert. He said a group of local agencies and businesses, including the Beck Center, Riverside Music Academy, and the Lakewood Music Settlement, would join together to allow youths an opportunity to perform musically. The group sent flyers around town asking young musicians to contact Youth Services if interested in participating in a concert.

Two concerts have occurred so far, one at Trinity this spring and one at the Beck Center in January. The group plans one for this summer. Connor said the concert was a cross-generational affair, mixing teenagers who came to listen to the music with parents who came to help things run smoothly. "People brought their moms, some of whom have never seen anything like this," Connor said.

Kids in fishnets and combat boots seemed strange to some adults, Connor explained, "but we probably looked just as strange to them in our jeans and sweat-shirts."

The church council, which votes on what takes place in Trinity Church, agreed that a youth concert would be a great idea. . . .

Colucci and the organizers are looking for all types of teen musicians. Although mostly rock bands have signed up in the past, they're hoping to appeal to musicians of all varieties.

Jana Zabkova's report of a community event includes quotations from those involved.

Reread the essay, and pay particular attention to the author's pronouns. You'll get many opportunities to practice using pronouns in the writing exercises in this chapter.

Using Subject Pronouns

Subject Pronouns	
SINGULAR	**PLURAL**
I, you, he, she, it	we, you, they

▐▐▐▶ Use a **subject pronoun** when the pronoun functions as the subject (s) of a sentence or a clause.

      S   S
Roosevelt and **I** find information on the Internet.

    S
We often visit *.edu* and *.gov* sites.

                  S
The information that **we** find on the Internet is quite intriguing.

▐▐▐▶ Use a subject pronoun when the pronoun functions as the predicate nominative of a sentence or a clause.

Remember: A **predicate nominative** (PN) is a noun or pronoun that follows a form of *be* and renames or identifies the subject. (See Lesson 6.7.)

                                       PN   PN
The most frequent Internet users in our class are Roosevelt and **I**.

                          PN   PN
Other frequent users of the Internet are Tarik and **she**.

                 PN   PN
Still other users, who are Mrs. Jacobs and **he**, visit the Internet less frequently.

EXERCISE 1 Choosing the Correct Pronoun

Underline the pronoun in parentheses that correctly completes each sentence.

    EXAMPLE   The visitors to this Web site are (<u>we</u>, us).

1. Larry, Tanya, and (I, me) read about today's college freshmen.

2. (We, Us) are interested in their plans and attitudes.

3. Among students who will soon attend college are Tanya and (I, me).

4. (She and I, Her and me) will be freshmen in less than three years.

WRITING HINT

When someone on the phone asks for you, do you reply, "It is I" or "This is she"? Those are the grammatically correct answers in formal writing and speaking. Informally, however, most people say "It's me."

STEP BY STEP

Which pronoun would you use in this sentence?

Gabe and (I, me) already saw that video.

1. Say the sentence with just the pronoun as the subject.

    Me already saw that video.
    [sounds wrong]

    I already saw that video.
    [sounds right]

2. Use the pronoun that sounds right in the compound subject.

    Gabe and I already saw that video.

5. Larry is already a college freshman; in some ways, the subject of this article is (he, him).

6. Its subject is other freshmen across the nation and (he, him).

7. The subject of an annual survey are (they, them).

8. Among the readers of the survey are educators, college students, and (we, us).

9. I read parts of it to Ms. Wong; (she, her) found it surprising.

10. She showed it to our principal; she and (he, him) both studied it carefully.

EXERCISE 2 Editing Paragraphs

Edit the following paragraph to correct all errors in pronoun usage.

¹Luke, Vikram, and me found a report on our nation's college freshmen on the Internet. ²Linda Sax and other professionals at the Higher Education Research Institute wrote it. ³She and them are at the University of California in Los Angeles.

⁴Their report shows that 39.4 percent of today's college freshmen want to earn a master's degree. ⁵This is an all-time high. ⁶Yet, them study less than older students. ⁷Survey director Linda Sax has a theory about this report. ⁸Her says this shows new freshmen attitudes; them are more motivated by credentials than by a love of learning. ⁹Is her critical of freshmen? ¹⁰No, Luke and me think that her is just reporting a fact. ¹¹The most critical people are, perhaps, the readers of this survey. ¹²They may even be us!

Write What You Think

On a separate piece of paper, write one paragraph responding to one of the following statements. State your opinion clearly at the beginning of the paragraph, and then support it with reasons, details, and explanations. After you revise your writing, edit your paragraph for correct pronoun usage.

Refer to **Composition**, Lesson 4.2, to find strategies for writing persuasively.

• Earning more money is the least important reason for getting an education.

• Every student should be required to stay in school until he or she graduates from college.

Using Object Pronouns

Object Pronouns	
SINGULAR	**PLURAL**
me, you, him, her, it	us, you, them

▐▐▐➤ Use an **object pronoun** when the pronoun functions as the direct object (**DO**) or indirect object (**IO**) of a sentence or a clause.

      DO   **DO**
Dad took Liam and **me** to Kitty Hawk.

      IO   **DO**
He showed **us** the site of the first flight.

▐▐▐➤ Use an object pronoun when the pronoun functions as the object of a preposition (**OP**) in a sentence.

                            OP   **OP**
Dad told the story of the first flight to Liam and **me**.

   OP   **OP**
For Dad and **us**, this was an interesting day.

With a compound object, use the same Step-by-Step approach you learned for subject pronouns. (See page 205.) Test each pronoun alone, and say the sentence aloud to yourself. Your ear will tell you which pronoun to use.

EDITING TIP

Be sure to use an object pronoun when the pronoun functions as the object of a preposition. Avoid these common errors:

WRONG
between you and I

RIGHT
between you and **me**

WRONG
for Ben and she

RIGHT
for Ben and **her**

EXERCISE 3 Editing Sentences

Edit the following sentences for the use of subject and object pronouns. Cross out a pronoun that is used incorrectly, and write the correct one above it. If a sentence is correct, write *C* after it. **Hint:** First, check to see what function the pronoun performs in the sentence.

1. Brian and me read about the brothers Wilbur and Orville Wright.

2. The world credits they with the invention of the first practical airplane.

3. Orville Wright is especially interesting to Brian and I.

4. Ms. Alzein read us an article about him.

5. She also showed Brian and I photos of the first flight.

6. To Brian and she, the photos seemed a bit unreal.

7. Even Kitty Hawk did not look real to Ms. Alzein and we.

8. Ms. Alzein told Brian and I that this first flight took place in 1903.

9. Orville was the pilot, and the credit for the flight goes to he.

10. Both of them helped build the plane, of course.

11. Because of our interest in Orville, Brian and me both researched him.

12. Between Brian and I, we uncovered more than one hundred good sources.

13. The long list of works about Orville amazed Brian and I.

14. He became president of the American Wright Company.

15. Brian and me also learned that, after Wilbur died in 1912, Orville lived thirty-six more years.

EXERCISE 4 Choosing the Correct Pronoun

Underline the pronoun in parentheses that correctly completes each sentence. You may wish to review the rules in Lesson 11.1.

EXAMPLE   The visitors to this Web site are (<u>we</u>, us).

1. Neither Augie nor (I, me) know much about this museum.

2. Sara gave Augie and (I, me) a pamphlet about it.

3. It took (Augie and me, Augie and I) a while to read it.

4. (Augie and I, Augie and we) learned that the Wright brothers' *Kitty Hawk Flyer* is at the museum.

5. This plane took (they, them) on their first flights.

6. A trip to the museum would be worth it for Augie and (I, me) just to see that one plane.

7. Waiting for (we, us) there are other great aircraft, too.

8. For example, it would thrill Augie and (I, me) to see the replica of *Sputnik I.*

9. Mr. Hochberg told Sara and (I, me) all about this satellite.

10. Mr. Hochberg and (she, her) said it started the space race.

11. The Russians launched *Sputnik I*; it was made by (they, them).

12. For (they, them), the launching of this satellite meant beating the United States into space.

13. Mr. Hochberg explained to (we, us) that the real *Sputnik I* burned up in the atmosphere.

14. The space museum is fascinating to Mr. Hochberg and (she, her).

15. When we think about the century of air and space travel, Mr. Hochberg, Augie, and (I, me) are inspired.

Who or Whom?

||||➡ Use the subject pronoun *who* when the pronoun functions as a subject in a sentence or in a clause.

> **Who** was named as the best author? [*Who* is the subject of the sentence.]
>
> Eudora Welty, **who was named the class favorite**, wrote "A Worn Path." [*Who* is the subject of the adjective clause.]

You can check your choice of pronoun by replacing *who/whom* with *he/him* or *she/her*. If *he/she* sounds right in the sentence, use the subject pronoun *who*. If *him/her* sounds right, choose the object pronoun *whom*. Follow these steps.

1. State the sentence, inserting your options.

> (Who, whom) should we contact?

2. Change the question into a statement.

> We should contact (who, whom).

3. Substitute *he* or *she* for *who* and *him* or *her* for *whom*.

> We should contact **he**.   or   We should contact **him**.

4. Decide which pronoun sounds right. [In this case, *him* sounds right.]

5. If *he* or *she* (the subject pronoun) sounds right, substitute *who*. If *him* or *her* (the object pronoun) sounds right, substitute *whom*.

> **Whom** should we contact? [*Whom* is the object pronoun.]

||||➡ Use the object pronoun *whom* when the pronoun functions as a direct object, an indirect object, or the object of a preposition in a sentence or in a clause.

> This is the doctor **whom** *Jeffrey saw*. [*Whom* is the direct object of the adjective clause *Jeffrey saw whom*.]
>
> This book should be returned to **whom**? [*Whom* is the object of the preposition *to*.]

When you are choosing between *who* or *whom*, ignore expressions such as *I think* and *I hope* that interrupt a subordinate clause.

> Those are the skaters **who**, I believe, won the championship. [*Who* is the subject of the clause *who won the championship*.]

P.S. Most people don't use *whom* in everyday speech. When they do— as in the expression "To whom am I speaking?"—it sometimes sounds pretentious. Nevertheless, in formal writing and speaking, *whom* is still required whenever it functions as an object.

Subject Form
who

Object Form
whom

EDITING TIP

Use *who* or *whom* with people, but use *that* or *which* with animals or things.

>   *whom*
> She is the person ~~that~~ I spoke with.
>
>   *that*
> Ruffles is the cutest cat ~~whom~~ I ever met.

Enriching Your Vocabulary

The verb *encroaching*, as used in Exercise 5, comes from the old French word *encrochier*, which means "to seize upon." In English, it is used to mean "trespass." A male elephant that *encroaches* on the territory of another male will find an angry challenger.

EXERCISE 5 Choosing the Correct Pronoun

Underline the pronoun in parentheses that correctly completes each sentence.

EXAMPLE   We read about women (who, whom) helped change American history.

1. (Who, Whom) did you read about?
2. Nanyehi was the first woman (who, whom) we read about.
3. (Who, Whom) was this woman?
4. She was a Cherokee woman (who, whom) was given the title of Beloved Woman.
5. She wanted peaceful relations between her people and the Europeans, (who, whom) were encroaching into the Cherokee's territory.
6. She was also one of the Cherokee (who, whom), I think, argued against giving up the Cherokee homeland.
7. Were there other women (who, whom) you studied?
8. We learned about Francisca Hinestrosa, (who, whom) disguised herself as a man on DeSoto's expedition to Florida.
9. Hinestrosa, about (who, whom) historians know very little, must have been quite brave.
10. She was a woman (who, whom), I'm certain, was ahead of her time.

EXERCISE 6 Editing a Paragraph

Edit the following paragraph to correct all errors in the use of *who* and *whom*.
Hint: Some sentences contain no errors.

¹Do you know whom [*who*] Elizabeth Blackwell was? ²She was a woman who was ahead of her time. ³Born in England in 1821, she moved to the United States as a child. ⁴She became a teacher before deciding to pursue a career in medicine. ⁵At first, she studied privately with male doctors whom [*who*] supported her cause. ⁶Geneva College accepted her in 1847, but its students, whom [*who*] were hostile to her, made her education difficult. ⁷She graduated in 1849, receiving the first medical diploma granted to a woman. ⁸Still, Blackwell, who [*whom*] professors knew to be capable, could not get hired. ⁹Then, she won the support of the Society of Friends, whom [*who*] began referring sick people to her. ¹⁰At last, the woman who [*whom*] the whole world would later respect, gained the respect of a few patients.

Appositives and Incomplete Constructions

Remember that an **appositive** identifies or renames a noun or pronoun that comes right before it.

||||▶ Pronouns can be appositives or part of appositive phrases. The form of the pronoun that is used in an appositive depends on what the pronoun refers to. Use a subject pronoun if the appositive refers to a subject or a predicate nominative. Use an object pronoun if the appositive refers to a direct object, an indirect object, or the object of a preposition.

> The co-captains, Audra and **I**, helped direct the team. [The pronoun *I* refers to *co-captains*, the subject of the sentence.]
> The leaders are the co-captains, Audra and **I**. [The pronoun *I* refers to *co-captains*, the predicate nominative of the sentence.]
> We chose the starting lineup, Lily, Fran, Nira, Bev, and **her**. [The pronoun *her* refers to *lineup*, the direct object of the sentence.]
> We rely most on our best forwards, Bev and **me**. [The pronoun *me* refers to *forwards*, the object of the preposition *on*.]
> The coach gave the forwards, Bev and **me**, good advice. [The pronoun *me* refers to *forwards*, the indirect object of the sentence.]

||||▶ When the pronoun *we* or *us* is followed by a noun appositive, choose the pronoun form you would use if the pronoun were alone in the sentence.

> **We** Spartans won the league championship. [You would say, "*We* won the league championship."]
> This victory didn't surprise **us** players. [You would say, "This victory didn't surprise *us*."]

||||▶ In an incomplete construction, choose the pronoun form you would use if the sentence were completed.

An **incomplete construction** omits some words, which are understood. Usually, an incomplete construction is a comparison. It comes at the end of a sentence and starts with the word *than* or *as*. In the following incomplete constructions, the omitted words appear in brackets.

> I exercise more frequently *than **he** [does]*.
> He is not nearly as fit *as **I** [am]*.
> Rico likes to read more *than **I** [like to read]*.

STEP BY STEP

Which pronoun would you use in this sentence?

(We, Us) Hawaiians know how to surf.

1. Say the sentence with just the pronoun and not the appositive.

   Us know how to surf. [sounds wrong]

   We know how to surf. [sounds right]

2. Use the pronoun that sounds right.

   We Hawaiians know how to surf.

WRITING HINT

The meaning of a sentence can sometimes change with the pronoun you choose, especially when your sentence construction is incomplete.

Alyssa writes to Manuel more than [she writes to] **me**.

Alyssa writes to Manuel more than **I** [write to Manuel].

EXERCISE 7 Choosing the Correct Pronoun

Underline the pronoun in parentheses that correctly completes the sentence.

1. (We, <u>Us</u>) students learn about Jupiter.

2. Jason called his friends, Arsenio and (he, <u>him</u>).

3. The soloists, Jackie, Ira, and (<u>I</u>, me), are nervous.

4. The director gave two of the actors, Tranh and (he, <u>him</u>), their parts.

5. The judges overlooked the last contestant, (I, <u>me</u>).

6. Isn't Connor a lot older than (<u>he</u>, him)?

7. The audience applauded loudly for (we, <u>us</u>) gymnasts.

8. Dr. DeLargy gave (we, <u>us</u>) team members our yearly physical.

9. The jugglers, Mei and (<u>he</u>, him), are the last performers.

10. Robyn isn't always as strong a swimmer as (<u>I</u>, me).

EXERCISE 8 Editing Sentences

Cross out the incorrect pronoun in each sentence below, and write the correct pronoun above it. If a sentence is correct, write *C* after it.

1. The information about Saturn's rings amazed we students.

2. That bookcase is a lot taller than me.

3. The torchbearers in the ceremony are the captains, Dave and him.

4. The nurses in training, Zoe and him, work hard every day.

5. The president awarded the two best riders, Sal and I, first prize.

6. By the end of the day, he was almost as exhausted as me.

7. Us runners must drink plenty of water.

8. I e-mailed the notification to both winners, Jasmine and she.

9. No two brothers in the world are as different as them. C

10. Aunt Janet sends her love to us nieces and nephews.   C

Agreement with Antecedent

A pronoun must agree with its **antecedent**, the word that the pronoun refers to.

▊▊▊➤ Use a plural pronoun to refer to two or more antecedents joined by *and*.

> Eileen, Dom, and Noel are entering **their** dogs in the show.

▊▊▊➤ Use a singular pronoun to refer to two or more singular antecedents joined by *or* or *nor*.

> Either Jill or Danielle will enter **her** poodle.

▊▊▊➤ Use a singular pronoun when the sentence has a compound subject but refers to only one person.

> That dog groomer and beagle expert is entering **his** best beagle.

▊▊▊➤ Use a singular pronoun when the antecedent is a singular indefinite pronoun. See the list in the margin.

> One of those women lost **her** dog's papers.

When a singular indefinite pronoun refers to both males and females, use *his or her*.

> Everyone has **his or her** own ideas about which dog should win.

EXERCISE 9 Choosing the Correct Pronoun

Underline the pronoun in parentheses that agrees with its antecedent.

1. My cousins Ian and Ryan tell me about (his, <u>their</u>) dog.
2. Everyone on the boys' soccer team has (<u>his</u>, their) own locker.
3. Neither Helen nor Sharon has completed (<u>her</u>, their) report.
4. Each of the girls carefully revised (her, <u>their</u>) essay.
5. The winner and two-time champion waved to (<u>his</u>, their) fans.
6. Lea, Belinda, and Gail introduced me to (her, <u>their</u>) favorite aunt.
7. No one knows what (their, <u>his or her</u>) future will bring.
8. Either Phil or Ned is on (<u>his</u>, their) way to get help.
9. Someone has left (their, <u>his or her</u>) hat on that bench.
10. My aunt and uncle give me (her, <u>their</u>) advice on everything.

Singular Indefinite Pronouns

anybody	anyone
each	either
everybody	everyone
neither	nobody
no one	one
somebody	someone

WRITING **HINT**

Sometimes, *his or her* sounds wordy or contrived. You can avoid this by making the subject plural.

Every owner has **his or her** own ideas about which dog should win.

Owners have **their** own ideas about which dog should win.

TEST-TAKING **TIP**

Standardized tests often ask you to recognize errors in pronoun and antecedent agreement. The pronouns *its* and *their* can be especially tricky. Remember: First find the correct antecedent; then determine if the pronoun agrees with it. See item 5 on page 307.

EXERCISE 10 Editing a Report

The following report contains errors in pronoun-antecedent agreement. Cross out each error, and write the correct pronoun above it.

¹Not every parent talks about their [*his or her*] expenses. ²When parents do discuss this subject, however, some will mention the costs of raising his or her children. ³Indeed, estimates of their costs are quite high. ⁴Today's average parent will spend a great part of their [*his or her*] salary on their [*his or her*] children. ⁵For each child, a parent will pay a substantial amount over the course of seventeen years. ⁶Today, does anyone think their [*his or her*] job stops there?

⁷Of course, anyone in the ranks of parenthood knows that their [*his or her*] costs involve more than just money. ⁸Each of the parents may make some of their [*his or her*] biggest choices in life based on having children. ⁹These include where to live, what job to take, and what goals to pursue. ¹⁰One mother and working woman notes that their [*his or her*] greatest gift is time. ¹¹A father of young children comments that any free time that might have been his in the past isn't there anymore. ¹²Instead, this time belongs to their [*his*] children.

CONNECTING
Writing & Grammar

Write What You Think

Refer to **Composition**, Lesson 4.2, to find strategies for writing persuasively.

On a separate piece of paper, write one paragraph about the following statement. State your opinion clearly at the beginning of the paragraph, and then support it with anecdotal evidence. That is, refer to specific parents and children you know or have heard about (though you may wish to rename them). After you finish revising your writing, edit your paragraph for pronoun-antecedent agreement.

No child fully appreciates his or her parent(s) until later in life.

Clear Pronoun Reference

▐▶ When you use a pronoun, be sure to include all of the words that are needed to complete its meaning.

UNCLEAR	Billy looks up to Mr. Carver more than **I**.
CLEAR	Billy looks up to Mr. Carver more than I look up to Mr. Carver.
CLEAR	Billy looks up to Mr. Carver more than he looks up to me.

▐▶ Avoid constructions in which pronouns can refer to more than one antecedent.

UNCLEAR	Janet discussed the project with Elaine because **she** knew all of the details. [It is ambiguous, not clear, to whom *she* refers. Maybe Elaine knew all of the details, or perhaps Janet knew all of the details.]
CLEAR	Janet discussed the project with Elaine because **Janet** knew all of the details.

▐▶ Avoid using *they*, *it*, and *you* (as well as *their*, *its*, *your*, and *yours*) to refer to an unnamed person or group.

UNCLEAR	**They** say it will be cold tomorrow. [Who are *they*?]
CLEAR	The Channel 6 meteorologist predicts cold weather tomorrow.
UNCLEAR	**It** says in the dictionary that *fulsome* means "excessive." [What does *it* refer to?]
CLEAR	The dictionary says that *fulsome* means "excessive."
UNCLEAR	Some teachers do not let **you** wear a hat in class. [Who is *you*?]
CLEAR	Some teachers do not let students wear hats in class.
UNCLEAR	In every town, **you** have **your** disagreements over the budget. [Who is *you*? What does *your* refer to?]
CLEAR	In every town, people disagree over the budget.

It is correct, however, to use *you*, stated or implied, in directions or instructions.

CLEAR	Go to the first stoplight, and take a left. Look for the sixth house on your left. It is a white house with blue trim.

P.S. In speech, pronoun usage is fairly relaxed. Not only will you often hear—and perhaps use—constructions such as "Everybody has their own opinions," but you may also make statements such as "They say too much Vitamin C is bad for you."

TEST-TAKING TIP

An item on a standardized test may contain a pronoun with an unclear or absent antecedent. Such an incomplete pronoun reference results from omitted words that would clarify the identity of the pronoun. See item 19 on page 310.

Enriching Your Vocabulary

The Latin verb *avere*, meaning "to desire," is the root of the word *avid*, which is used in Exercise 11 and can mean "greedy, or having an intense desire." *Avid* is more commonly used to mean "enthusiastic," as in an *avid* birdwatcher.

EXERCISE 11 Editing Sentences

Edit the following sentences for correct pronoun-antecedent agreement. In some sentences, you may cross out a single pronoun and write the correct pronoun above it. In other sentences, you may need to add or delete words. Some sentences may need a rewrite. If a sentence is correct, write *C* after it.

1. You have your naysayers on every issue.

2. It says in the newspaper that the vote is on Tuesday.

3. Jill took the hamster out of its cage while she washed it.

4. In the beginning pages, it tells about the Civil War.

5. Leo took the covers off the seats and cleaned them.

6. Ed shared his information with Tom because he had an avid interest in the subject.

7. Cindy told Robyn that she had made a big mistake.

8. David told Dad that Jim is as fast a runner as he.

9. They say it's too late to register for driver's education this term.

10. First, remove the plastic wrapping. Then place the package print-side down in the microwave.

11. Myrna gave Tammy a copy of *Stunt*, one of her favorite CDs.

12. In Roman times, you did not visit the dentist to get your teeth cleaned.

13. You have your student parking spaces and your faculty parking spaces.

14. Did you hear what they said about those food additives?

15. I knocked the glass into the vase and broke it.

16. Shira advised Susan not to let her dog off the leash.

17. You should do twelve repetitions of this exercise. Then take a rest.

18. It says to add the dry ingredients to the liquid mixture.

19. Dean gave his friend Nicolas the jacket, which he loved.

20. Rich is best friends with Nate even though he is four years older.

Using Modifiers

STUDENT WRITING
Expository Essay

Breaking All Boundaries, Reaching New Heights
by Nikole Mandrell Shipley, Stacey Ho, and Sarah Fox
high school students, Cincinnati, Ohio

Robin Miller never needs a second chance to make a first impression, according to most people who follow in-line skating. This talented, optimistic female in-liner serves as a role model from first introductions to grueling interviews and shared training-camp experiences, always setting an example for others. Excitement reigns as both Miller and interviewer meet each other for this interview. Conjuring up thirteen questions in a few minutes may be a harrowing journalistic experience because a mere glance at Miller's life and accomplishments will leave almost everyone in awe.

Miller started skating in 1994 on a pair of rented recreation skates. In 1995, she got her first pair of new professional skates. She said she started skating competitively just for the fun of it.

"You don't realize how big a trick it is until you look back," Miller says. Fun soon led her to participate in aggressive competitions. She trains at Camp Woodward, an extreme/gymnastics sports camp, and attributes much of her success to its staff.

"Gosh, I learned everything at Woodward," she claims. "It's the perfect place to learn." Miller also adds that Woodward has a "great atmosphere" and that the places to skate have a lot of diversity for both beginners and pros. Located in Woodward, Pennsylvania, this extreme sports training facility receives many accolades regarding Miller's training. This combination of training and inspiration has proved to be unbeatable.

Miller's biggest supporter is her mom. "My mom is very cool and very supportive," she says. Friendships have also proved to be an integral part of her success, as Miller attributes much to the people she worked with in Cincinnati.

When Miller is not skating, she spends her time in engineering school. She has received an associate degree in chemical engineering and is currently earning her bachelor's degree in mechanical engineering. However, engineering was not always Miller's dream.

"I love to write," she says. "I wanted to go to art school, but I had a scholarship to engineering school, so that is where I went."

With her positive attitude toward both life and in-line skating, Robin Miller has proved herself to be both a great person and a role model for anyone, no matter what his or her interests. Miller loves what she does and the people she works with. As demonstrated by her bright smile, she is a very optimistic person—both on and off her skates.

> The essay above was written after an interview that the authors had with Robin Miller. They have summarized the most important parts of their interview to give an accurate and lively description of their subject.
>
> As you reread the essay, pay attention to the modifiers—the adjectives and adverbs. Modifiers add color and freshness to your writing. You'll practice adding modifiers to your writing in the exercises in this chapter.

Forming the Degrees of Comparison

When you compare everything from places to actions and people to animals, you use **degrees of comparison**. The three degrees, or forms, of comparison are **positive**, **comparative**, and **superlative**.

POSITIVE   A coyote runs **fast**.

COMPARATIVE When a lion is charging, it runs **faster** than a coyote.

SUPERLATIVE   The cheetah is the **fastest** animal of all.

Irregular Degrees of Comparison

good	better	best
well	better	best
bad	worse	worst
badly	worse	worst
ill	worse	worst
many	more	most
much	more	most
little	less or lesser	least
far	farther further	farthest furthest

▶ **One-syllable modifiers** To form the comparative or superlative degrees of most one-syllable modifiers, add -er or -est. (Sometimes, it is necessary to double the final consonant or drop a final -e.)

old, old**er**, old**est**   fast, fast**er**, fast**est**

large, larg**er**, larg**est**   slim, slim**mer**, slim**mest**

▶ **Two-syllable modifiers** To form the comparative or superlative degrees of two-syllable modifiers, either add -er or -est (making any necessary spelling changes) or use more or most. If you are in doubt about what to do, use your dictionary. If -er or -est forms do not appear in the dictionary entry for the adjective or adverb, use more or most.

frisky, frisk**ier**, frisk**iest**   careful, **more** careful, **most** careful

dirty, dirt**ier**, dirt**iest**   rapid, **more** rapid, **most** rapid

EDITING TIP

Avoid double comparisons. Never add both the -er or -est form and more or most.

We went the ~~most~~ slowest of anyone there.

▶ **Two-syllable modifiers that end in -ly** To form the comparative or superlative degrees of two-syllable adverbs that end in -ly, add more or most. To form the comparative degrees of two-syllable adjectives that end in -ly, add -er or -est.

ADVERBS   slowly, **more** slowly, **most** slowly
             fully, **more** fully, **most** fully

ADJECTIVES   lovely, lovel**ier**, lovel**iest**
             ugly, ugl**ier**, ugl**iest**

▶ **Three or more syllable modifiers** To form the comparative or superlative degrees of most modifiers of three or more syllables, add more or most.

dangerous, **more** dangerous, **most** dangerous

incredible, **more** incredible, **most** incredible

STEP BY STEP

To form the comparative and superlative degree of modifiers:

1. Count the number of syllables.
2. Apply the appropriate rule or consult a dictionary.
   one syllable = -er and -est
   two syllables = listen and decide
   three or more syllables = add more or most
   -ly adverbs = more or most

▶ **Decreasing degrees** For all decreasing degrees of comparison, use less and least.

cold, **less** cold, **least** cold   inventive, **less** inventive, **least** inventive

▶ **Irregular modifiers** The modifiers in the side column form their degrees of comparison irregularly.

EXERCISE 1 Forming Degrees of Comparison

On a separate piece of paper, write the comparative and superlative forms for each modifier listed.

1. valuable
2. hopeful
3. reasonable
4. lively
5. dimly

6. poor
7. awkward
8. clean
9. quiet
10. visible

EXERCISE 2 Editing an Article

Edit the following article for the correct forms of comparison. Cross out any incorrect form, and write the correct one above it. Make any other changes that you think would improve the paragraph.

¹Is the roller coaster the most frighteningest of all the rides in amusement parks? ²Designers try their most hardest to make it that way. ³They build the highest rises and the deepest dips. ⁴They maximize speed. ⁵As a result, people will often name the roller coaster as the bestest or the most worst experience in an amusement park.

⁶Some of today's therapists are reaching out to those who say the roller coaster is the more terrifying experience—possibly in the universe. ⁷Those with the most deepest fears of the roller coaster are now given advice on making the experience lesser stressful. ⁸Researchers note that these fears come from the most likeliest sources: getting sick in the past, being put on a ride against one's will, or other, even worser experiences in childhood. ⁹The fear that is sometimes the most easiest to deal with is the fear of accidents. ¹⁰This is because riding a roller coaster is one of the most safe things anyone can do. ¹¹In fact, the odds against a fatal accident are 300 million to 1.

EXERCISE 3 Writing a Paragraph

Use transition words as you write to compare. Refer to **Composition**, Lesson 2.3, for a list.

On a separate piece of paper, write a paragraph in which you compare two or more objects, people, animals, or places. Here are some possible topics.

two video games
two pieces of music

three pet dogs
three movies

three foods
three trees or flowers

Include at least four comparative or superlative forms in your paragraph, and underline them.

Using the Degrees of Comparison

▷ Use the comparative degree to compare two things. Use the superlative degree to compare three or more things.

COMPARATIVE Lake Michigan is **larger** than Lake Erie.
SUPERLATIVE Lake Superior is the **largest** of the Great Lakes.

In conversation, you may hear people using the superlative form to compare just two things. In formal writing and speaking, however, always use the comparative for two things and the superlative for three or more.

▷ Avoid double comparisons. Use either *more* (or *most*) or *-er* (or *-est*), but never use the word *more* (or *most*) and an *-er* (or *-est*) word together.

INCORRECT Angel Falls is more higher than Yosemite Falls.
CORRECT Angel Falls is **higher** than Yosemite Falls.

INCORRECT Angel Falls is the most highest waterfall in the world.
CORRECT Angel Falls is the **highest** waterfall in the world.

▷ Some adjectives—such as *excellent, perfect, faultless, flawless, ideal, immaculate,* and *unique*—don't take comparative or superlative forms. These are **absolute adjectives**. They are already "the most" they can be. For example, if something is *flawless* ("without a flaw"), it can't be "more flawless"; if something is *unique* ("one of a kind"), it can't be "most unique."

Her description of the event was **flawless**.
She made it clear that the moment was **unique**.

EXERCISE 4 Choosing the Correct Degree of Comparison

Underline the modifier in parentheses that correctly completes each sentence.

EXAMPLE   Is the snail the (slower, <u>slowest</u>) of all animals?

1. Even the sloth moves (more quicker, more quickly) than the snail.

2. The giant tortoise is just a bit (speedier, more speedier) than the sloth.

3. Is the greyhound the (faster, fastest) of all dogs?

4. The cape hunting dog is actually (swifter, swiftest) than the greyhound.

EDITING TIP

Sometimes, writers and speakers use the word *less* when they should be using *fewer*.

This line is for ten or ~~less~~ ^fewer^ items.

I'm eating ~~less~~ ^fewer^ calories than I used to.

A child eats **less** food than an adult.

Use *fewer* before nouns that can be counted and *less* before nouns that represent the volume or mass of something.

TEST-TAKING TIP

Be alert for standardized-test items in which the word *more* or *most* is used with a modifier signifying a degree of comparison. See item 16 on page 309.

5. Of all animals, which lives the (longer, longest)?

6. The average life of an elephant is long, but that of a hippopotamus is (longer, longest).

7. Do the (larger, largest) animals live the longest?

8. Well, a squirrel lives (fewer, fewest) years than a horse.

9. A mouse has a much (short, shorter) life span than a monkey.

10. Humans have long lives but are not the (bigger, biggest) of all animals.

EXERCISE 5 Editing Sentences

Edit the following sentences for the use of degrees of comparison. Cross out any incorrect modifier, and write the correct one above it. If a sentence is correct, write *C* after it. **Hint:** A sentence may contain more than one error.

1. I can find facts more quickly in an almanac than I can on the Internet.

2. My almanac is the usefulest reference book I own.

3. For fast facts, it is more better than an encyclopedia.

4. On just one page, for example, it lists the lowest point, most deep lake, and most rainiest spot in the United States.

5. It records the high bridge in the United States, too: the Royal Gorge Bridge, in Colorado.

6. Did you know that Kalawao, Hawaii, is the most smallest county in the country?

7. The almanac even lists the deepest well, which is in Washita County, Oklahoma.

8. Buying an almanac is the bestest thing you can do.

9. An almanac gives you the larger number of facts for the fewest amount of money.

10. It's the better investment of all the books you can buy.

Write What You Think

On a separate piece of paper, write a paragraph in response to the question below. Be sure to give reasons to support your choices. After you have revised your writing, edit it to be sure you have used comparative and superlative forms of modifiers correctly.

You are being sent on a space mission that requires you to travel alone in space for six months. The space capsule has no radio, TV, or music, but you may take three books with you. What three books will you take, and why?

Illogical Comparisons and Double Negatives

▐▐▐▶ Avoid illogical comparisons. Use the word *other* or *else* to compare something with others in its group.

INCORRECT	Farouk knows more about waterfalls than anyone in our class. [Farouk is in our class. How can he know more than himself?]
CORRECT	Farouk knows more about waterfalls than anyone **else** in our class.
INCORRECT	He thinks Niagara Falls is more beautiful than any waterfall in the world. [How can it be more beautiful than itself?]
CORRECT	He thinks Niagara Falls is more beautiful than any **other** waterfall in the world.

▐▐▐▶ Avoid unclear comparisons. Add whatever words are necessary to make a comparison clear.

UNCLEAR	Farouk is more interested in waterfalls than Darlene.
CLEAR	Farouk is more interested in waterfalls than Darlene is.
CLEAR	Farouk is more interested in waterfalls than in Darlene.

▐▐▐▶ Avoid using two negative words together. Only one negative word is needed to express a negative idea. Count the contraction *-n't* (meaning "not") as a negative word.

INCORRECT	Investigators haven't never discovered what happened to Amelia Earhart.
CORRECT	Investigators have never discovered what happened to Amelia Earhart.
CORRECT	Investigators haven't ever discovered what happened to Amelia Earhart.
INCORRECT	Has nobody ever found nothing from her plane?
CORRECT	Has nothing ever been found from her plane?
CORRECT	Hasn't anybody ever found anything from her plane?
INCORRECT	No one has yet to find no debris from her plane.
CORRECT	No one has yet to find any debris from her plane.
CORRECT	No debris from her plane has yet been found.

▐▐▐▶ As the examples show, you can correct most double negatives in more than one way. Choose the wording that sounds best to you.

| CHANGE | nobody | never | no one | nothing | none |
| TO | anybody | ever | anyone | anything | any |

Words That Express a Negative Meaning

hardly	no one
never	not (*n't*)
no	nothing
nobody	scarcely
none	

WRITING HINT

In everyday speech, some people say *ain't* instead of *am not*, *isn't*, or *aren't*. In formal writing, however, *ain't* is widely considered inappropriate.

Enriching Your Vocabulary

The noun *debris* comes from the old French verb *desbrisier*, which means "to break apart." The English word refers to the broken bits or rubble after some destruction. The *debris* from Hurricane Georges left the streets impassable.

EXERCISE 6 Editing Sentences

Edit the following sentences to eliminate illogical comparisons, unclear comparisons, and double negatives. Use a separate piece of paper if necessary. If a sentence is correct, write *C* after it.

1. To me, American runner Wilma Rudolph was braver than any athlete.

2. She was also more successful than most athletes.

3. Yet her life didn't hardly begin with happiness.

4. She was born smaller than most babies.

5. At the age of four, she contracted polio, then the more dreaded disease of all.

6. After that, she didn't never walk normally for years.

7. She wasn't no way allowed to attend public school.

8. As a result, she lived a lonelier life than anyone in her large family.

9. She must have had more courage than anyone who ever lived.

10. At the age of eleven, she didn't no longer need her leg braces.

11. She became a better basketball player than anyone ever dreamed she would become.

12. She would become an even best runner than basketball player.

13. In the 1956 Olympics, Rudolph did not win no individual races.

14. But in 1960, in Rome, she did better than any American woman.

15. No woman before her had never won three track-and-field gold medals at a single Olympic Games.

16. The girl who couldn't scarcely walk as a child had run to glory.

17. Later, she became a teacher and coach, a job best suited to her background than any other job.

18. I believe Rudolph was more of an inspiration to players than any coach in the world.

19. Is there anyone who wouldn't not have respected her?

20. In the race of life, I think Rudolph was a better runner than anyone I know.

EXERCISE 7 Writing a Paragraph

Write a paragraph about someone famous or familiar. Explain what is outstanding or unusual about that person's character, accomplishments, or life's work. When you are finished, reread your paragraph to be sure you have avoided illogical and unclear comparisons. Also be sure you have used the correct forms of modifiers and have avoided double negatives.

Misplaced Modifiers

A **misplaced modifier** is a word, phrase, or clause that is in the wrong place in a sentence. Because it is misplaced, it ends up modifying one word when it should modify another word instead.

MISPLACED	Kate wrote a letter about her trip to her best friend. [Did Kate make a "trip to her best friend"? The prepositional phrase is misplaced.]
CORRECT	Kate wrote a letter to her best friend about her trip.

To correct a misplaced modifier, move it as close as possible to the word you want it to modify. You may also reword the sentence.

MISPLACED	This morning, I ate toast in my robe.
CORRECT	In my robe this morning, I ate toast.
CORRECT	While I was still in my robe this morning, I ate toast.
MISPLACED	Is that woman over there with the small child the one who gave you a dirty look? [Who gave the dirty look, the woman or the small child? The adjective clause is misplaced.]
CORRECT	Is the woman who gave you the dirty look the one over there with the small child?
MISPLACED	I saw the movie about the whale that everyone said was **mawkish**.
CORRECT	I saw the movie that everyone said was mawkish. It was about a whale.

The word *already* is often misplaced. The meaning of a sentence can depend on its correct placement.

MISPLACED	You told me that you finished your essay already. [Did you already tell me, or did you already finish the essay? The single word *already* is misplaced.]
CORRECT	You already told me that you finished your essay.
CORRECT	You told me that you already finished your essay.

WRITING HINT

The word *only* is often misplaced. In this next example, the meaning of the sentence changes depending on the placement.

I drink **only** juice in the morning.

I drink juice **only** in the morning.

In the following sentence, *only* is clearly misplaced.

I only have one more lap to run.

Enriching Your Vocabulary

Although its root is the Middle English word *mawke*, meaning "maggot," the word *mawkish* has evolved to mean "sickening in a sentimental way." *Mawkish* greeting cards make you feel disgusted with their insipid sweetness.

EXERCISE 8 Editing Sentences

On a separate piece of paper, rewrite each sentence to correct the misplaced modifiers.

1. We looked at pictures of tarantulas in Masako's living room.

2. We do not have any books about asteroids in our house.

3. The accused criminal only requested one phone call.

4. Renee is the girl in the convertible with red hair.

5. Elena sat thinking about the 10K race in her room at night.

6. The announcer made it clear that smoking is bad for you on the television.

7. We made money at the lecture on refreshments.

8. Governor Jacobsen mentioned the new stadium in his speech.

9. Erik is the tenor in the choir with a beard.

10. That company makes computers for industries with high-speed chips.

11. We send letters to various parts of the country with free return-address stickers.

12. I told Jake about the flood on the phone.

13. David wondered about the cause of earthquakes in science class.

14. The team only practices on Saturdays and Mondays.

15. We have shampoos for a variety of hair types on that shelf.

16. We listened to the songs of whales at Derek's house.

17. We have dishes for our guests with curry.

18. I saw the pictures of herds of elephants in that magazine.

19. We poured lemonade for everyone in tall glasses.

20. Jacques only paid me half of what he owed me.

Working Together

EXERCISE 9 Create Your Own Exercise

Work with a partner to create at least five sentences that contain misplaced modifiers. Try to think of sentences in which inadvertantly humorous situations are caused by misplaced modifiers. Then exchange your sentences with those written by another pair, and correct them.

Dangling Modifiers

A **dangling modifier** is a word, phrase, or clause that does not logically modify any word in the sentence. Unlike a sentence with a misplaced modifier, a sentence with a dangling modifier is often missing some important information—most commonly the subject of the sentence. Or if the subject is stated at all, it is buried in the sentence as a direct object.

▥▶ Correct a dangling modifier by rewording the sentence. Add a word or words that the phrase or clause can modify.

DANGLING   Looking out my kitchen window, two foxes ran across the yard.

CORRECT   When I looked out my kitchen window, I saw two foxes run across the yard.

DANGLING   After searching for hours, the missing letter turned up on my dresser.

CORRECT   After searching for hours, I found the missing letter on my dresser.

> **TEST-TAKING TIP**
>
> A dangling modifier is a frequently-tested sentence error. You can recognize one by asking yourself if a nonessential phrase or clause describes the noun nearest it. See item 5 on page 313.

EXERCISE 10 Editing Sentences

On a separate piece of paper, rewrite each sentence to correct dangling modifiers.

1. After agreeing to a cease-fire, the fighting began again.

2. Having crossed the finish line, the spectators watched as the exhausted skier collapsed.

3. Flapping in the breeze, I watched the towels on the clothesline.

4. After hiking in the darkness for half the night, the sun finally rose.

5. Sitting alone in the house, every noise seemed suspicious.

6. Before ending the discussion, the budget cuts came up.

7. Flying south for the winter, we saw several flocks of geese.

8. While racing for the train, the man's hat blew off his head.

9. Before leaving for the play, dinner was served.

10. After studying hard all year, a good grade was earned.

EXERCISE 11 Editing a Paragraph

Work with a partner to correct the dangling modifiers in this paragraph. Use a separate piece of paper if necessary. When you are finished, compare your revisions with those made by other pairs.

¹Facing oil embargoes in the 1970s, the national maximum speed limit was reduced to save gasoline to 55 miles per hour. ²Arguing that it also saved lives, the new speed limits were embraced by policy makers. ³Now every state except Hawaii has abandoned the speed limits of the 1970s. ⁴Traveling down the road at faster and faster speeds, accident rates are predicted to go up. ⁵However, that doesn't always happen. ⁶Expecting the automobile death rate to increase as a result, it has surprised many people to find that it has not. ⁷In fact, the death rate is actually down slightly. ⁸Nevertheless, there are some contradictions in the data. ⁹After studying accident rates on interstate highways, accident rates on rural roads must also be considered. ¹⁰These are the nation's deadliest roads: two-lane highways with sharp curves and narrow shoulders. ¹¹Not being affected by the national speed limit, people do not actually know how changing speed limits affects death rates on these dangerous back roads.

CONNECTING
Writing & Grammar

Refer to **Composition**, Lesson 4.2, to find strategies for writing persuasively.

Write What You Think

On a separate piece of paper, write a paragraph giving your opinion on the proposed new law below. State your opinion clearly at the beginning of the paragraph, and support it with reasons and examples. After you finish revising, edit to be sure you have used modifiers correctly.

A driver who receives more than two speeding tickets during a two-year period should lose his or her driver's license for at least one year.

Revising and Editing Worksheet 1

Improve the following draft by revising for ideas, organization, word choice, and sentence variety. After revising, edit the draft for errors in spelling, capitalization, punctuation, and usage. Write your revised and edited version on a separate piece of paper. Compare your changes with those of a writing partner.

[1]After using a household product, the trash can is not always the best place for it. [2]Some of these products can do serious harm to the environment. [3]Many have far more lasting affects then people realize. [4]Some people only think these products contaminate the land. [5]In fact, dangerous chemicals also make there way into our air and water.

[6]When throwing out a simple household battery, cadmium, lithium, and other dangerous elements get into the waste system. [7]Instead, batteries should be taken to the most nearest reclamation center. [8]Drain cleaners are also hazardouser than many people suspect. [9]By taking them to a hazardous waste center, potential enviromental problems are solved. [10]Furniture polish is just as deadly as drain cleaners, don't never just throw unused portions or containers into the trash can.

[11]Besides participating in hazardous waste programs, other alternatives to creating hazardous wastes exist. [12]For almost every cleanser, polish, preservative, and stain, there is an alternative. [13]For example, many people say undiluted white vinegar in a spray bottle works just as good as ammonia-based cleaners. [14]Between toilet bowl cleansers and a simple paste of lemon juice and borax. [15]Some say the paste works best. [16]To avoid toxic, flammable turpentine and thinners, as well as oil-based paints that should not no way be put in the trash, use water-based paints instead. [17]Similarly, stains and varnishes are worst for the environment than latex or water-based finishes.

Revising and Editing Worksheet 2

Improve the following draft by revising for ideas, organization, word choice, and sentence variety. After revising, edit the draft for errors in spelling, capitalization, punctuation, and usage. Write your revised and edited version on a separate piece of paper. Compare your changes with those of a writing partner.

[1]Is change occurring fastest now than in any period in history? [2]Marveling at the many computer advances of the last few years, yes is the answer many people give without hesitation. [3]Yet historians are most careful. [4]They point to another era as the time of the most greatest change: from the late 1850s to approximately 1903. [5]They say this era was truly a time of breakthroughs. [6]Our own time, by comparison, tends only to be a time of upgrades. [7]Despite everything from cloning sheep to using e-mail.

[8]What defines the second half of the nineteenth and early twentieth century as the time of extraordinariest change? [9]The Bessemer steel-making process, the automobile, the diesel engine, the airplane, the radio, the telephone. [10]And, let's not never forget, the light bulb. [11]And that's only naming some of the new inventions and products.

[12]Citing recent advances in information technology, great progress seems undeniable. [13]A more larger portion of our economy than ever is tied up in this sector. [14]Software manufacturing is now the nation's third bigger industry. [15](Only automobiles and electronics have most sales.) [16]Being invested in information technology and seeing it skyrocket, the impression is formed that things are changing quickest than ever. [17]However, more better and better chips do not equal the breakthrough of the invention of the microchip. [18]More faster and faster modems do not equal the breakthrough of the invention of the telephone.

[19]While living in the late 1800s, horse travel changed to train, car, plane, and subway travel. [20]Candles to lightbulbs. [21]Life on farms to life in cities. [22]That was the real period in American history of unbridled change.

Chapter Review

Exercise A Using Degrees of Comparison

Edit the following sentences for the correct use of modifiers. If you find an error, cross out the word or phrase, and rewrite it correctly on a separate piece of paper. If the sentence is correct, write *C* after it. **Hint:** A sentence may contain more than one error.

1. What is the more famous speech in American history?

2. Bharat and I thought about the great speeches of all time.

3. Patrick Henry's famous speech before the Virginia Convention was forceful and effective than most speeches.

4. Sojourner Truth's "Ain't I a Woman?" was perhaps the more memorable speech ever made on behalf of women's rights.

5. John F. Kennedy's inaugural address is more frequentlier quoted than many peacetime presidential addresses.

6. Nevertheless, Bharat and I chose the "I Have a Dream" speech by Dr. Martin Luther King, Jr., as the most best of all the speeches ever given.

7. We think it is the most eloquentest.

8. It speaks to the struggle for the most fundamentalest rights.

9. It is more rhythmic than music, more moving than poetry.

10. In short, it is the more stirring speech we ever heard.

Exercise B Correcting Double Negatives and Illogical Comparisons

Edit the following sentences for the correct use of negatives and comparisons. If you find an error, cross out the word or phrase, and rewrite the sentence correctly on a separate piece of paper. If the sentence is correct, write C after it.

1. Rita is more interested in Abraham Lincoln than Corinne.

2. No one couldn't forget the name Abraham Lincoln.

3. Lincoln may, in fact, be more admired than any President.

4. He had a reputation for being more honest than anyone in his era.

5. He could not scarcely be compared with today's politicians.

6. He probably appeared more homespun and plain than anyone in politics.

7. He hardly never lost his frontier accent.

8. His log cabin with its dirt floor was more humble than most presidents' birthplaces.

9. He didn't never go to college.

10. In fact, he hadn't scarcely a year of schoolhouse education.

EXERCISE C Editing a Report

Edit the following paragraphs to correct all errors in the use of modifiers. Use a separate piece of paper. **Hint:** Some sentences have more than one error. Some have no errors.

[1]Topping the list of America's health concerns, many people point to smoking. [2]Former Surgeon General C. Everett Koop, for example, regards this health threat as more great than any health threat in America. [3]At least one-third of all cancer deaths may be caused by smoking cigarettes. [4]Smoking is also one of the faster routes to heart disease.

[5]Smoking is not scarcely the only health problem, however. [6]Leaving almost fifty million people without insurance, some say the health care system itself is problem number one. [7]Living without insurance, preventive health care is often not an option.

[8]Others point to increasing obesity as one of America's importantest health problems. [9]This is a serious issue, with half of all Americans overweight. [10]As many as 300,000 people may die as a result of obesity each year. [11]Some people may think this problem only affects adults. [12]Regrettably, today, a more greater number of young Americans are classified as overweight as well as obese than twenty years ago.

Cumulative Review

EXERCISE A Using Verbs Correctly

On a separate piece of paper, correct all of the errors in verb usage in the following sentences. Look for incorrect verbs and verb forms, unnecessary shifts in verb tense, and unnecessary use of the passive voice.

1. Taos Pueblo in New Mexico was visited by us.
2. I had already learned a lot before our visit there ends.
3. The Taos Native Americans sat down roots here almost one thousand years ago.
4. They builded multistoried adobe structures.
5. These structures have standed the test of time.
6. We were told by guides that the traditions of this community has changed very little over time.
7. For example, people continue to bake their bread in outdoor domed ovens just as they done for centuries.
8. We finded a unique way of life in this community.
9. Despite both the Anglo and the Spanish presence, these people have choosed to preserve their own heritage.
10. The Taos people have keeped their own ceremonies, beliefs, and identity.

EXERCISE B Subject-Verb Agreement

Underline the verb in parentheses that agrees with the subject.

1. Everyone in our club (pay, pays) dues.
2. Most of our club members (attend, attends) all our meetings.
3. Service, not fun activities, (is, are) the focus of our club.
4. Several of us (is, are) active in community outreach.
5. None of our members (expect, expects) any payback or reward.
6. (Is, Are) only eleventh graders or the whole school eligible to join?
7. Neither ninth graders nor tenth graders (is, are) able to join.
8. This club (consist, consists) of motivated people.
9. Ten hours a week (is, are) a typical commitment of time.
10. "Helping Hearts and Hands" (is, are) our club newsletter.

EXERCISE C Using Pronouns Correctly

Underline the pronoun in parentheses that correctly completes each sentence.

1. (We, Us) students learned about Eleanor Roosevelt.

2. The stories about her made us want to know more about (who, whom) she really was.

3. (She, Her), like other First Ladies, helped change attitudes about the role of the First Lady.

4. There are few First Ladies (who, whom) have played such an active role in politics.

5. Many people, including Tammy and (me, I), admire her tireless good work.

6. Tammy and (I, me) read about her efforts on behalf of poor people.

7. She was one person (who, whom) many people turned to during the Depression.

8. The First Couple, Franklin and (she, her), became known for their compassion.

9. Everyone in our class has completed (his or her, their) report on the Roosevelts.

10. The first people to present will be Tammy and (I, me).

EXERCISE D Using Modifiers Correctly

On a separate piece of paper, rewrite each sentence to correct all errors in the use of modifiers. **Hint:** Some sentences may have more than one error.

1. Deb knows more about robots than any student in our class.

2. We only have one person in the class who knows more about them: our teacher, Mrs. Colpak.

3. From milking cows to walking inside volcanoes, just about anything can be done by robots.

4. Robots can do many tasks more better and more cheaply than humans.

5. Having both a computer and sensors, decisions are even made by some robots.

6. Robots work with more accuracy and lesser boredom than most humans.

7. Robots must be complexer, more agile, and, in many cases, more small.

239

STUDENT WRITING
Expository Essay

Students 'Sign Up' for New Class
by Jamie Hui
high school student, Potomac, Maryland

A sign language course that is being offered for the first time as a ninth-period class allows students to earn a full foreign language credit.

The approval of the sign language course as a foreign language subject this summer follows the national trend to recognize the importance of this communication skill.

The course, taught by Susan Gershowitz, is designed to teach sign language, deaf culture, and deaf awareness. Gershowitz, a deaf teacher who currently teaches at Wootton, Quince Orchard, and Churchill, is teaching sign language to hearing students for the first time after twenty-five years of teaching only deaf children. "I wanted to start something new . . . to be a pioneer," Gershowitz said.

Although the class includes only twelve students, Gershowitz is optimistic that the course's popularity will rise once students realize that school credit is being offered. "My classes at Wootton are already full with thirty-five students," Gershowitz said.

Although senior Lorraine Sensenig takes French 6 during the school day, she chose to learn sign language after school as well. "I once saw someone interpreting a song in sign language and thought it was something I wanted to do," Sensenig said. "Sign language can be applied like any other foreign language—except you don't talk."

Junior Tenley Thompson said she appreciates the unique way sign language is taught. "There is no written book," Thompson said. "I always need to pay attention to the teacher's hands and facial expressions."

Despite the common stereotype that the deaf cannot speak, Gershowitz stresses that "every deaf person can talk, but [many] choose not to use their voices—it has nothing to do with intelligence. . . . Most people think of sign language as just hand gestures and do not recognize it as another language." In fact, American Sign Language varies greatly from the English language because the two languages do not share a similar grammatical structure.

In an effort to make people more aware of sign language and the deaf, Gershowitz plans to incorporate both standardized and personal curricula into the new course. Her students will perform road shows at elementary schools and sign at the senior graduation. . . .

Part of the purpose of Jamie Hui's expository essay is to generate interest in the new sign language class. Since few students are aware of the class, Jamie uses quotations from the teacher of the class and from a student, as well as some background information about sign language to inform her audience.

Notice how Jamie punctuates her quotations, phrases, and paragraphs. You'll review many punctuation rules in the writing exercises in this chapter.

End Marks and Abbreviations

End every sentence with an appropriate end punctuation mark.

▶ Use a **period** at the end of a statement (declarative sentence).
We learned about Aesop**.**

▶ Use a **question mark** at the end of a direct question (interrogative sentence). An indirect question ends with a period.

DIRECT   Did Aesop really exist**?**
INDIRECT Some wonder whether Aesop really existed**.**

▶ Use an **exclamation point** at the end of an exclamation (exclamatory sentence).
What wonderful little stories those fables are**!**

▶ Use either a period or an exclamation point at the end of a command (imperative sentence).
Read this fable about a dog and a wolf**.**
Look at the fantastic illustrations**!**

▶ Use a period after many abbreviations.

In general, when you write a paper or report for school or work, avoid all but the most common abbreviations. Abbreviations that are acceptable in formal writing include abbreviations of time, such as *A.M.* or *P.M.* and *B.C.* or *B.C.E.*, and certain titles used before names, such as *Mr.* and *Dr.*

Abbreviations with Periods				
Initials and Titles	Alice Kang, M.D. Dr. A. O. Stein		Mr. Roberto Ramos, Sr. Rev. Felicia R. White	
Times	A.M.	P.M.	B.C.	A.D.	B.C.E.
Others	Co.	Inc.	vs.	et al.	etc.

An **acronym** is a word formed from the first letters of several words, such as *radar* (**ra**dio **d**etecting **a**nd **r**anging). Do not use periods with acronyms.

It is common to omit the period following certain abbreviations, such as *yd* (yard), and after almost all metric abbreviations, such as *km* (kilometer) and *cc* (cubic centimeter). Other common abbreviations that don't take periods include the postal abbreviations for states (*OR, VA, WI*); government and international agencies (*CIA, IRS, USAF, UNICEF, USDA*); and common terms such as *AM* and *FM, TV, CPU,* and *ASAP.*

EDITING TIP

When an abbreviation comes at the end of a sentence, use only one period.

These tales survive from the sixth century B**.**C**.**

Don't omit a comma, a question mark, or an exclamation point following an abbreviation.

What was life like in the sixth century B**.**C**.?**

If you don't know whether to use a period with an abbreviation, look it up. Do be prepared for variation, however. For example, you may find both *US* and *U.S.*, *R.S.V.P.* and *RSVP*, *M.C.* and *MC*.

EXERCISE 1 Proofreading Sentences

Proofread the following sentences to add missing punctuation marks, to change incorrect punctuation, or to delete unnecessary punctuation. **Hint:** Some sentences have more than one error.

1. I wonder whether Twyla will attend the cattle show today?

2. It will be at the Reynolds Farm at 9:00 AM.

3. Mrs Reynolds will talk to us about her prizewinning Holsteins.

4. Cattle may have been domesticated as long ago as 6,000 BC.

5. Milk from the Reynolds's farm meets U.S.D.A. standards

6. Have you ever seen the Reynolds's milking operation

7. What a huge farm it is.

8. I sure would love to be James Reynolds, Jr

9. I wonder how many people it takes to run that operation?

10. Mr and Mrs Reynolds rise at 5:00 AM and sometimes do not finish their chores until 8:00 PM

EXERCISE 2 Proofreading a Press Release

Proofread this press release to eliminate errors in the use of punctuation. **Hint:** This includes eliminating the inappropriate use of abbreviations in formal writing. Rewrite the press release on a separate piece of paper.

[1]At 5:00 PM in the Statler Aud. of Clark Univ., Dr Lindsay P Hryniewich will deliver a lecture on nutrition [2]Dr Hryniewich teaches at Yale U and has consulted with the US Dept. of Health and Human Services. [3]She will speak about the strategies for meeting daily nutritional requirements. [4]The lecture is sponsored by the Whole-Grain Cereal Co. of Milwaukee, WI. [5]Admission is free!

Commas in a Series

Sometimes, it's hard to decide whether to leave a comma out or to put one in. In most cases, however, knowing a few simple rules will help you decide whether—or where—a comma belongs.

▐▶ Use a comma to separate items in a series.

A **series** contains three or more of the same grammatical structures in a row. For example, a series might consist of three nouns, three adjectives, three prepositional phrases, three verbs, or three independent clauses.

> We are learning about the **jewelry, makeup,** and **hairstyles** of ancient Egyptians.
> We find information **in books, in atlases,** and **on the Internet**.

▐▶ Use a comma to separate two or more adjectives that precede and modify the same noun. (But see the Step-by-Step box in the margin below, which describes the exception to this rule.)

> The **hot, dry** air of Egypt preserved many objects through the centuries.

However, don't use a comma when the last adjective in a series is really part of a compound noun. You can tell if one of the adjectives belongs to the noun if you can reverse the position of the adjectives.

> We studied the ornate**,** mysterious mummy case. [*Mummy case* is a compound noun.]

See Lesson 14.2 for more on punctuating items in a series.

EXERCISE 3 Proofreading Sentences

In the following sentences, insert commas wherever they are needed. If a sentence does not need any commas, write *C* after it.

1. The names Howard Carter Lord Henry Carnarvon and King Tutankhamen often appear together.

2. Howard Carter was a famous British archaeologist.

3. Lord Carnarvon supplied Carter with money encouragement and other support.

EDITING TIP

When coordinating conjunctions (such as *and* or *or*) appear between each item in a series, do not use commas.

Mindy or Alice or Cheryl wrote those hieroglyphs.

If the items in the series are independent clauses, however, use the commas.

Mindy researched the hieroglyphs**,** and Alice helped her**,** but Cheryl wrote them.

STEP BY STEP

Follow these steps to decide whether to put a comma between two adjectives before a noun.

1. Try placing *and* between the adjectives. If *and* makes sense, use a comma.

   We learned about the legendary [and] breathtaking beauty: Queen Nefertiti.

2. If *and* doesn't make sense, don't use a comma.

   This was clearly one ~~and~~ powerful queen.

Chapter 13 • Punctuation: End Marks and Commas **243**

4. Tutankhamen was a young wealthy king of Egypt.

5. Others said there were no tombs left to be found, but Carter never gave up digging searching and hoping.

6. The discovery of a step buried in the sand mystified thrilled and stunned workers.

7. Soon, they discovered a tomb door with a seal a passageway filled with rubble and another door engraved with hieroglyphics.

8. Through the first door down the passageway and through the second door they went.

9. They worked with trembling hands beating hearts and alert minds.

10. Among many other things, they found statues chariots and furniture.

11. Scale-model boats ornate chests and game boards greeted their eyes.

12. Most objects were found in the entry chamber the burial chamber and a treasury room.

13. Awed stunned and amazed, the archaeologists uncovered vast wealth.

14. The recovered items revealed clues to Egyptian life death and afterlife.

15. This splendid rich treasure trove would amaze the world.

EXERCISE 4 Proofreading a Paragraph

Proofread the following paragraph. Add commas as needed. **Hint:** Not every sentence needs changes.

[1]Sequoyah, whose name is also spelled Sequoya, Sikwayi and Sequoia, was a Cherokee trader silversmith and leader. [2]Because his tribe had no written language, Sequoyah set about creating one unified system of writing. [3]He began this work in 1809. [4]At first, he tried using pictographs similar to the ones used by the ancient Egyptians. [5](In fact, the Maya Aztec Delaware and Chippewa all created hieroglyphic writing systems.) [6]Then he began adapting letters from English Greek and Hebrew. [7]By 1821, he had created the first Cherokee alphabet. [8]It had more than eighty characters, which represented the syllables of the Cherokee language. [9]Sequoyah's new imaginative writing system spread rapidly. [10]Soon the Cherokee were writing letters newspapers and books in their own language.

Commas with Compound Sentences and Introductory Elements

The coordinating conjunctions (*and*, *but*, *or*, *nor*, *for*, *so*, and *yet*) can join two or more independent clauses to form a compound sentence.

> For more on commas with introductory elements, see Lesson 13.5.

▶ Use a comma before the coordinating conjunction that joins two independent clauses in a compound sentence.

Planets orbit the sun, and moons orbit the planets.
What are Jupiter's moons, and when were they discovered?
Look at Saturn through this telescope, and find the planet's rings.

▶ Use a comma after an introductory participle or participial phrase.

Amazed, we viewed the Andromeda galaxy.
Amazed by what we saw, we looked at the massive galaxy.

▶ Use a comma after an introductory infinitive phrase.

To see some planets and stars, you need a powerful telescope.

▶ Use a comma after an introductory adverb clause.

Because Galileo discovered Jupiter's four largest moons, they are called Galilean moons.

▶ Use a comma after an introductory prepositional phrase or a series of introductory prepositional phrases.

Beneath a cloudy atmosphere, we find the planet Jupiter.
Beneath a cloudy atmosphere with fierce storms and lightning bolts, we find Jupiter.

When a sentence begins with a short prepositional phrase, such as "on the left," a comma isn't always necessary. Nevertheless, adding the comma ensures that your meaning is clear. Do not, however, place a comma after an introductory prepositional phrase when the subject (s) follows the verb (v).

Beyond our own limited horizons **are**(v) other **galaxies**(s).

▶ Use commas whenever they are necessary to prevent misreading.

UNCLEAR	Soon after we left the observatory.
CLEAR	Soon after, we left the observatory.
UNCLEAR	If you want to join us next time.
CLEAR	If you want to, join us next time.

EDITING TIP

Don't confuse a compound sentence with a sentence that has a compound subject or a compound verb. You don't need a comma between parts of a compound subject and a compound verb.

COMPOUND VERB
We contacted the observatory and got permission to visit.
[no comma]

COMPOUND SENTENCE
The telescopes are powerful, but the night is cloudy.
[comma]

WRITING HINT

Introductory elements are often movable. To vary your writing, try placing these elements in different positions.

At different times of the year, we see different objects in the sky.

We see, **at different times of the year,** different objects in the sky.

We see different objects in the sky **at different times of the year**.

EXERCISE 5 Editing Paragraphs

Edit the following paragraphs for the correct use of commas. Insert commas wherever they are needed.

[1]What are asteroids and where are they found? [2]In some ways asteroids are miniplanets. [3]Some are no wider than a few kilometers but the largest, Ceres, has a diameter of about 600 miles. [4]Although most asteroids are found in the asteroid belt between Mars and Jupiter some are on their own.

[5]When an asteroid plunges into Earth's atmosphere it becomes a meteor. [6]Speeding through the atmosphere these space particles begin to glow with heat. [7]Think about the shooting stars you have seen and recall the brief but exciting flash of light they produce. [8]Many of these meteors burn up in space but a few reach Earth. [9]When they do they are called meteorites.

[10]At times asteroids cross the orbit of planets. [11]To guess what happens in that case you don't need much imagination. [12]Think about a relatively small object meeting up with a very large one and visualize the result. [13]Of course such crashes are rare.

Working Together

EXERCISE 6 Revising Sentences

Work with a partner to revise each sentence so that it begins with an introductory element. Add commas where necessary.

1. You can see the Big Dipper all year long if you live north of Cairo or Miami.

2. The Big Dipper never disappears below the horizon unlike most constellations.

3. Some star patterns that can be seen all year long are called circumpolar constellations.

4. You can use the Big Dipper to find other constellations in the sky.

5. The Big Dipper seems, for example, to empty into the Little Dipper.

6. Cepheus, the King, and Cassiopeia, the Queen, can be found near the Big and Little Dippers.

7. All you need to keep track of the time of year appears before your eyes in the night sky.

Commas with Sentence Interrupters and Nonessential Elements

Interrupters are words, phrases, or clauses that interrupt the main thought of a sentence. An interrupter can usually appear almost anywhere in the sentence without changing the meaning of the sentence. If it appears at the beginning or end of the sentence, use a single comma to set it off. If it appears in the middle, use a pair of commas.

▷ Use commas to set off a noun of direct address, the name of a person being spoken to.

> **Linda**, do you know who invented the first computer?

▷ Use commas to set off nonessential appositives and appositive phrases.

> Charles Babbage**, an Englishman,** is viewed as the inventor of the computer.
> ENIAC**, the first all-electronic computer,** was built in 1945.

▷ Use commas to set off parenthetical expressions and transitional expressions that interrupt a sentence.

> ENIAC was**, by the way,** no desktop delight.
> At fifty feet in length, it was**, needless to say,** a bit large.

▷ Use commas to set off a nonessential adjective clause. Do not use commas with an essential adjective clause. An **essential adjective clause** is necessary to make the meaning of the sentence clear. Usually, it answers the question *Which one(s)*. (A clause that begins with the word *that* is usually an essential clause.) A **nonessential adjective clause**, on the other hand, adds information, but the sentence makes sense without it.

> NONESSENTIAL ENIAC**, which contained 18,000 vacuum tubes,** used a great deal of energy.
> ESSENTIAL People **who used it** were always replacing the costly tubes.
> NONESSENTIAL The transistor**, which soon replaced the vacuum tube,** was much smaller.
> ESSENTIAL Microchips **that contained transistors** were the next step in computer development.

Some Common Parenthetical and Transitional Expressions

as a result	in contrast
after all	in fact
by the way	incidentally
for example	of course
however	therefore
as a matter of fact	
consequently	
needless to say	
nevertheless	

STEP BY STEP

Follow these steps to decide whether an adjective clause should be set off with commas.

1. Try saying the sentence aloud without the adjective clause.
2. If the sentence makes sense without the adjective clause, that clause is *nonessential*. Use commas to set off the clause.
3. If the sentence doesn't make sense without the clause, that clause is *essential*. Do not use commas.

EXERCISE 7 Proofreading Sentences

Proofread the following sentences, adding commas where they are needed. Write *C* if the sentence is correct.

1. Boxing an ancient sport has been around for several thousand years.

2. A Greek mural which is dated 1520 B.C. shows fighters wearing gloves.

3. The year 688 B.C. marked the introduction of boxing as an Olympic sport.

4. Despite its glorious past, boxing is nevertheless a controversial sport.

5. The repeated blows to the head that a fighter endures damage the brain.

6. The American Medical Association which investigated boxing has called for a total and complete ban of the sport.

7. Did you know Sammy that since 1940 at least three hundred professional boxers have died of injuries from their sport?

8. Laila Ali Muhammad Ali's youngest daughter stunned many with her decision to become a professional boxer.

9. Her father who suffers from Parkinson's disease received many injuries in the ring.

10. The debilitating nature of Ali's illness Parkinson's disease has stirred debate over the negative effects of a boxing career.

Write What You Think

On a separate piece of paper, write a paragraph giving your opinion on one of the statements below. State your opinion clearly at the outset, and support your opinion with reasons and examples. When you are finished revising, edit to be sure that you have used commas correctly, especially with interrupters and nonessential elements.

Refer to **Composition,** Lesson 4.2, to find strategies for writing persuasively.

• Because of the number of injuries and deaths that result from professional boxing matches, the sport should be banned.

• Female professional boxing deserves the same serious attention that male professional boxing receives.

Other Comma Uses

▐▶ Use a comma to set off *well, yes, no, first, second,* and single-word adjectives that begin a sentence.

> **Yes,** I have visited our nation's capital.
> **Well,** it's one of the most beautiful cities I have seen and a **bastion** of American history and culture.
> **First,** we saw the Washington Monument.
> **Second,** we visited the Vietnam Veterans Memorial.
> **Exhausted,** we rested on the Mall.

▐▶ Use commas to separate the date and year. No comma is needed between the month and date or between the month and year.

> We arrived on September 1, 1999.
> We planned to leave on September 8.
> The last time we visited was April 1989.
> He knew that November 22, 1963, was the day JFK died.

▐▶ Use commas to separate parts of a play as well as in the name of a person or place.

For example, use a comma between an act and a scene; a person's last name and a title that follows it; a city and a state. (No comma is needed, however, between the state and the zip code.) In the middle of sentences, set these elements off with commas.

> Act III, scene vi Martin Gordon, Jr.
> Venice, California Schenectady, NY 12306
> I watched as Martin Gordon, Jr., addressed the senior class.
> We moved to Venice, California, when I was a freshman.

▐▶ Use a comma after the greeting and the closing of a friendly letter.

> Dear Alma,   Yours truly,   Love,   Sincerely,

▐▶ Use a comma to set off a direct quotation, but omit the commas with indirect quotations.

> "This is a beautiful city," Molly remarked.
> Jamey added, "There is so much to do and see here."
> "The museums alone," said Mr. Tanaka, "are well worth the trip."
> They all said they were glad they came.

Enriching Your Vocabulary

The origin of the word *bastion* is the old French word for "build," *bastir*. Literally, *bastion* means "fortification," but it is often used figuratively to indicate strength. One might consider a school or university to be a *bastion* against ignorance and superstition.

WRITING HINT

Different conventions apply to friendly letters and business letters (see Lesson 4.6). For example, friendly letters have no heading (usually, the writer gives only the date of the letter) and no inside address. In a friendly letter, a comma (not a colon) follows the greeting. The signature is always handwritten instead of typewritten.

Exercise 8 Using Commas Correctly

Add missing commas to the following sentences. If a sentence uses correct punctuation, write *C* after it.

1. I read as far as Act I scene v last night.
2. Tania Swerdlow Ph.D. addressed our world history class.
3. Their home is in Taos New Mexico.
4. No I have never seen torch ginger plants in a rain forest.
5. The first moon walk occurred on July 20 1969.
6. "That is a sweet dog" said Bobby.

Exercise 9 Proofreading a Friendly Letter

Add commas where they are needed in the following friendly letter. Delete any unnecessary commas.

> September 5 2013
>
> Dear Evan
>
> [1]Well it's been a long time since I've written. [2]I'm looking back at your letter dated July, 10 and asking myself, how I could have let so much time go by.
>
> [3]One reason was the trip our family took on August 12 to Phoenix Arizona. [4]First we visited my Great-Uncle Nick. [5]Second we traveled north to the Grand Canyon. [6](Yes it is as awesome as everyone says it is!)
> [7]We even crossed over the border to visit Mesa Verde National Park near Durango Colorado. [8]Tired but happy we arrived home on August 22.
>
> [9]Since I've been home I've been busy getting ready for the soccer season. [10]"Practice hard" says Coach Clark and I have been. [11]Hope all is well with you.
>
> Your pal
> Enrique

Exercise 10 Writing a Friendly Letter

Write a letter to a friend or relative, real or imagined. Using the letter above as a model, tell about a trip you took or might imagine taking. Name some dates and places, and include at least one quotation. When you are finished, check to be sure that you have used commas correctly.

Editing and Proofreading Worksheet 1

Edit the draft for errors in spelling, capitalization, punctuation, and usage. Write your edited version on a separate piece of paper. Compare your changes with those of a writing partner.

September 8 2013

Dear Jeff:

[1]How are you doing. [2]Yes it's been a long time since I wrote but I have been pretty busy.

[3]One thing that took up my time was reading *Gates of Fire* by S Pressfield. [4]I wonder whether you have read this book? [5]In my opinion this book is a total knockout. [6]Mainly this book is about a battle, that took place in 480 BC. [7]At that time the Persians were invading Greece. [8]With their squires and helpers and allies just three hundred Spartan warriors fought off an invading force of perhaps two million. [9]They fought to the death of the very last warrior. They lost the battle but they achieved glory. [10]As the historical note at the beginning says "They fought with bare hands and teeth before being at last overwhelmed." [11]This book is so moving. [12]So interesting. [13]I hope you will read it Jeff if you get the chance. [14]When my history teacher Ms Scalice recommended this book to me. [15]I didn't know what a treat I was in for.

[16]I've also been busy helping to plan our class trip to Nashville Tennessee. [17]Sally Jen and Marie are all on the committee so I said "Well I'll join too." [18]Some of the nicest funniest parents and teachers are chaperoning. [19]Including Dr Mullins whom you met last year when you visited. [20]This is going to be one great trip.

[21]Write back to me soon.

Your friend

Chuck

Editing and Proofreading Worksheet 2

Edit the draft for errors in spelling, capitalization, punctuation, and usage. Write your edited version on a separate piece of paper. Compare your changes with those of a writing partner.

[1]Are people eating more nutritious or less nutritious meals these days. [2]Depends on where they eat. [3]At least according to one US government study.

[4]When they cook at home people are in fact tending to consume food with less fat and more calcium iron and fiber. [5]Based on food consumption surveys that were taken between 1977 and 1995. [6]The USDA reports that people who cook at home are doing a good job of making meals with a high nutrient content.

[7]A problem arises however when people dine out. [8]Which they are doing more frequently than ever before. [9]In fact the proportion of meals eaten outside the home is almost twice what it was just twenty short years ago, this trend is incidentally expected to continue.

[10]What happens when people eat out. [11]For one thing the fat content of their meals goes up. [12]Perhaps by as much as six percent. [13]At the same time the fiber content goes down. [14]To about twenty-five percent below the recommended amount. [15]Calcium too falls, along with iron. [16]Calcium and iron being key nutrients that most Americans do not get enough of.

[17]How can people become better smarter eaters when they are away from home? [18]They need to study the menu and make smart choices, they also need to ask for changes. [19]Such as holding the salad dressing or serving it on the side. [20]Most of all they should change their attitudes. [21]Some people think eating out is a time to indulge themselves. [22]It isn't. [23]It shouldn't be.

Chapter Review

EXERCISE A Proofreading Jokes and Riddles

Proofread the following jokes and riddles. Add commas and end punctuation marks as needed.

1. Did you hear the one about the rope Skip it

2. What month has twenty-eight days: January February or March They all do

3. A father said "Johnny go faster I need to catch a train." Johnny said "Are you sure you're strong enough"

4. How do you keep a rhinoceros a bull or an alligator from charging Take away its credit cards

5. What did the shore say to the ocean "Hi Tide!"

6. If you are hiking on a hot day what should you take with you Well you should bring a thirst-aid kit

7. What did Mason say to Dixon? You know Dixon we've got to draw the line somewhere.

8. I am a father's child and I am a mother's child but I am no one's son. Who am I (a daughter)

9. I have leaves but I am not a tree; I have pages but I am not a king or queen; I have a spine but I am not an animal. What am I (a book)

10. At night they appear without an invitation and by day they disappear without a command What are they (stars)

EXERCISE B Using Commas and End Marks Correctly

In the following sentences, insert all missing commas, periods, and end marks.

1. When was the term *First Lady* first used

2. Rutherford B Hayes was inaugurated on March 5 1877.

3. A newspaper reporter used the term then but it didn't catch on.

4. It wasn't until *The First Lady in the Land* a play about Dolley Madison opened in 1911 that the term caught on.

5. For example while her husband was in office Mrs Lincoln was not called the First Lady.

6. Martha Washington or Lady Washington was never called the First Lady in her own day.

7. At the Smithsonian you can visit an exhibit on the First Ladies.

8. You can learn about their lives see some of their belongings and view some of their gowns.

9. My favorite teacher Dr Marilyn Lynch volunteers as a guide there.

10. Go see the exhibition and if she's there say hello to her for me

EXERCISE C Revising Sentences

Revise each sentence by inserting the words shown in parentheses at the caret mark. Add commas and end punctuation where necessary. Check to see that your sentences are punctuated correctly.

1. In an old song, two bits∧is the cost of a haircut and shave. (or one quarter)

2. ∧Did you know that a "C note" is worth one hundred dollars? (Otis)

3. The motto *e pluribus unum* first appeared on a U.S. coin∧ (in 1786)

4. The first woman to appear on American paper currency was∧Martha Washington. (of course)

5. ∧The dollar bill came to be known as a buck. (Because buckskins were used as currency on the frontier)

EXERCISE D Editing Sentences

On a separate piece of paper, write two corrected versions for each fragment or run-on sentence.

1. We were in Pasadena, California, we saw the Rose Bowl Parade.

2. Hundreds of floats made of thousands of fresh flowers.

3. The smell is so sweet, you can smell it for miles!

4. On New Year's Day Pasadena holds a flower festival, it is called the Tournament of Roses.

5. The Tournament of Roses Parade began in 1886, it celebrated the ripening of the oranges.

6. Adding the football game to the parade in 1902.

7. The Rose Bowl Parade also used for community events.

Punctuation: All the Other Marks

STUDENT WRITING
Expository Essay

Just Winging It: Future Dreams Take Flight
by Sara Detmering
high school student, Gig Harbor, Washington

"All clear for takeoff," the air traffic controller said to the pilot on the runway. The plane is not a massive Boeing 747 jumbo jet taking off from SeaTac. It is a Cessna 152 piloted by junior Garth Rydell, who is about to take off on a solo flight from Tacoma Narrows Airport.

Rydell has been interested in planes for a long time. He likes everything about them. He doesn't mind washing them or doing other maintenance work around them as long as he is around his passion: flying. "Ever since I can remember," Rydell said, "I have wanted to fly. I saw planes in the sky, and I decided that one day that would be me."

Rydell started taking flying lessons last July at Tacoma Narrows Airport after coming of age. When he began his lessons, he knew what he had to do to become a pilot. "There were so many requirements that had to be fulfilled," Rydell said. "The requirements vary based on the type of flying that you want to do. There are different requirements for flying cross-country and for flying at night."

Some of the requirements include ground schooling, book work, and a certain amount of hours in the air. All of this doesn't come at a cheap price either. The price of a pilot's license is around $3,000. The price may vary from company to company. "You have to pay for everything," Rydell said. "The books are about $160. To rent the plane and to pay the flight instructor comes to about $20 an hour, and your final exams cost money too. It would be a lot cheaper if you owned your own plane."

In order to obtain a pilot's license, the student must fly with an instructor and fly solo. At first, young students fly with an instructor. Then, as they learn more, they are able to gain more confidence and fly alone. Rydell said that after about a month of instruction, he was flying solo. "You have to have ten hours of solo flying time to obtain your license," Rydell said. . . .

Rydell has flown solo numerous times and admits he was nervous the first time he flew alone. "I haven't had anything really bad happen yet," Rydell said. "The door of my plane opened once while I was in the air, though."

Rydell spends as much time as possible in the air. He loves aviation so much he plans on having a future in it later on in life. "I think I might fly when I am older," Rydell said. "I'd love to fly commercial planes or own my own business someday."

Having the opportunity to start flying at a young age has broadened Rydell's horizons. Flying can be a lifelong activity, and it is a possible career that Rydell is looking forward to.

Sara Detmering has narrowed the topic of her expository essay to focus on the hobby of a single person. Such a narrow focus allows her to give details and examples that bring out the person's character.

As you reread the essay, notice how Sara has used punctuation around quotations. In this chapter, you'll practice the rules for writing dialogue and for punctuating your own essays accurately.

Colons

A **colon** (:) is a signal: It alerts the reader to the information that follows it. This may be a list, a long quotation, a formal statement, or any information that explains what precedes the colon.

▐▐▐➤ Use a **colon** before a list of items, especially after the words *the following* or *the following items*.

> Robert Frost's most famous poems are perhaps the following works: "Birches," "Mending Wall," and "Stopping by Woods on a Snowy Evening."

Exception: Do not use a colon when the list follows the main verb of a sentence or a preposition.

> Among Frost's themes **are** nature, rural life, and human relationships.
> I have read **about** his early poems, some of his letters, and his life.

▐▐▐➤ Use a colon before a formal statement or quotation, before any statement that explains what precedes it, and before a long quotation that is set off as a block (any quotation of more than three lines). Capitalize the first word after a colon in this case.

> Many people have the same opinion of Frost: He is the greatest American poet of all time.
> This may be the most famous opening line in American poetry: "Whose woods these are I think I know."

When a long quotation (more than three lines) is set off as a block, indent the quotation, and don't use quotation marks.

> Writing about "Stopping by Woods on a Snowy Evening," one critic states:
>> Probably no other of Frost's lyrics, perhaps no other English-language poem in this century, has been more often anthologized, dissected, and commented upon than this poem. Yet it retains its capacity to engage the reader and, what is more remarkable, to surprise and even perplex him.

▐▐▐➤ Use a colon to emphasize a word or phrase.

> This poem is built on two soundless images: snow and sleep.

▐▐▐➤ Use a colon in these situations: (1) between the hour and minutes, (2) between the chapter and verse in a reference to the Bible, and (3) after the greeting of a business letter.

> 2:45 P.M.   Ruth 1:4–8   Dear Ms. Yamamoto:

> **WRITING HINT**
>
> Colons and semicolons have similar names but very different purposes. Don't mix them up. Learn the rules for using semicolons. (See Lesson 14.2.)

EXERCISE 1 Adding Colons to Sentences

Insert colons where they are needed in the following sentences. If a sentence is correct, write *C* after it.

1. I think Robert Frost's most famous line is this one "Good fences make good neighbors."

2. Many people have questioned the meaning of that line is it straightforward or ironic?

3. I have the greatest respect for Frost's language, rhyme, and imagery.

4. My favorite poems by Frost are "After Apple-Picking," "Fire and Ice," and "The Oven Bird."

5. Along with Robert Frost, these are my favorite poets W. B. Yeats, Emily Dickinson, and Langston Hughes.

6. Lauren has just one favorite book *The Little Prince*.

7. Mark quoted a passage from Proverbs 19 1.

8. This is what it says "Better to be poor and above reproach than rich and crooked in speech."

9. At 4 00 P.M. today, Kyung will attend her poetry class.

10. The following classes are most important to Kyung English, history, and math.

EXERCISE 2 Writing Sentences

Working Together

On a separate piece of paper, write complete sentences that include the following items. Insert colons wherever they are needed. Exchange papers with classmates, and check for the correct use of colons.

1. a list of three foods you especially like

2. a short quotation from someone you admire

3. a long quotation from any source, including one of your textbooks

4. a formal statement that follows an independent clause

5. the date and the time of a meeting or other event

Semicolons

A **semicolon** (;) separates sentence elements. It signals a pause that is longer than a comma's pause but shorter than a period's.

▶ Use a semicolon to join closely related independent clauses in a compound sentence without a coordinating conjunction.

> John Singer Sargent is an important American artist; he painted many famous portraits.

▶ Use a semicolon before a conjunctive adverb or transitional phrase that appears between two independent clauses. Also, use a comma after the conjunctive adverb or transitional phrase.

> Sargent was an inspired portrait painter; in addition, he painted landscapes and murals.

▶ Use a semicolon to separate items in a series when one or more of the items contain a comma.

> Among the famous people Sargent painted were John D. Rockefeller, the oil tycoon; Robert Louis Stevenson, the novelist; and Isabella Stewart Gardner, the art patron.

EXERCISE 3 Using Semicolons and Colons

Some of the following sentences need a semicolon; others require colons. Review the rules for colons in Lesson 14.1, and then add the proper punctuation marks.

1. Museums often spotlight a single artist; a show on a popular artist can draw thousands of visitors.

2. Often, more than one museum shows the same exhibit; accordingly, the same show travels to different cities.

3. For example, one show started out at the National Gallery in Washington, D.C.; traveled to the Museum of Fine Arts in Boston, Massachusetts; and ended up at the Tate Gallery in London.

4. Some of the most popular shows have focused on the following artists; Picasso, Monet, and Sargent.

5. These shows sometimes draw huge crowds; some people buy tickets months in advance.

6. These shows often have good results for the museum; for example, some museums increase their membership during a big show.

Common Conjunctive Adverbs

accordingly	meanwhile
also	moreover
besides	nevertheless
consequently	otherwise
furthermore	still
however	then
indeed	therefore

Common Transitional Phrases

as a result	in fact
for example	in other
for instance	words
from that	on the other
point on	hand
in addition	that is

7. It is exciting to see so many works by one famous artist; however, long lines and crowds can be a problem.

8. Some people avoid such shows; the crowds are just too annoying.

9. Some people go to these shows for just one reason: to see the artwork.

10. Some share the following complaints: crowded, overheated rooms long, slow-moving lines and annoying, loud conversations.

EXERCISE 4 Using Punctuation in Compound Sentences

Combine each pair of sentences into a compound sentence, using punctuation, conjunctive adverbs, or transitional phrases. Check your combined sentences for proper punctuation.

1. We visited the Metropolitan Museum of Art. It is in New York City.

2. It has more than three million works of art; Several hundred thousand works are on public view.

3. My mother loved the Egyptian collection there; My brother loved the arms and armor collection.

   it's

4. The Egyptian collection is huge. It is as big and as complete as any other Egyptian collection outside Cairo.

5. The arms and armor in the museum's collection were not chosen for their technical or military interest. They were chosen for their design and decoration.

6. In the European paintings gallery, you can see works by Gauguin, Cézanne, and Renoir. You can see works by Monet and van Gogh.

7. My favorite room is the room of musical instruments; It displays the oldest piano in the world.

   too.

8. The old harpsichords and violins are fun to look at. The old instruments from Asia and Africa are even more interesting.

   it's

9. For example, in the collection is an Indian sitar called a *mayuri*. It is shaped like a peacock and has peacock feathers!

   well

10. There were many collections we did not get to. Next time, we will visit the costume collection and the Islamic art collection.

Underlining (Italics)

When you write by hand, use **underlining** to indicate **italics**. When you write on a computer, select italics from your program's tool bar (sometimes represented as a slanted *I*) or format menu. (*Italic type looks like this*.) Do not use both underlining and italics.

⟶ Use underlining (or italics) for the following kinds of titles and names.

BOOKS	*The Sea Wolf Travels with Charley The Great Gatsby*
MAGAZINES	*Vogue Time Atlantic Monthly*
NEWSPAPERS	*Austin Ledger Detroit Free Press Philadelphia Inquirer*
PLAYS	*Hamlet Arcadia A Raisin in the Sun*
MOVIES	*North by Northwest Lady and the Tramp City Lights*
TV/RADIO SERIES	*20/20 All Things Considered Talk of the Nation*
LONG MUSICAL WORKS/MUSIC COLLECTIONS	*Graceland The Four Seasons The Magic Flute*
WORKS OF ART	*Mona Lisa The Scream The Thinker*
SHIPS, PLANES, SPACECRAFT	*Viking U.S.S. Arizona Air Force One*

Note that abbreviations such as H.M.S., S.S., and U.S.S., which form the beginning of the names of many ships, are *not* italicized.

⟶ Use italics for foreign words and expressions that are not commonly used, as well as for words, letters, and numbers referred to as such.

FOREIGN WORDS	These students were the best in the state, the *crème de la crème*. [*Crème de la crème* means "the best of the best"; because this French phrase is not commonly used, it is italicized.] Some of them are rather blasé about their mental abilities. [*Blasé* is French for "unmoved by" or "getting no enjoyment from," but it is commonly used and recognized; therefore, it is not in italics.]
WORDS AS WORDS	Did you know that the word *squab* refers to the young of a pigeon?
LETTERS	He's the kind of guy who dots all his *i*'s and crosses all his *t*'s.
NUMBERS	The new player chose the number *26* for his jersey.

EDITING TIP

Not all titles are italicized. Many kinds of titles (short stories, poems, TV episodes, songs, and chapters of a book) belong in quotation marks. The shorter parts of longer works are often not italicized. (See Lesson 14.4 for more on quotation marks.)

EXERCISE 5 Editing Sentences

Edit the following sentences by underlining words and phrases that should be italicized where they are needed.

1. We switched on Biography to see who would be featured.

2. Mariner 2 was the first interplanetary probe to fly by Venus.

3. Representatives of Japan signed the formal surrender documents ending World War II while on board the U.S.S. Missouri.

4. The Marriage of Figaro is considered one of the most popular operas of all time.

5. Do you know anyone who has ridden the European luxury train called the Orient Express?

6. Our drama club is staging The Wizard of Oz.

7. Close Encounters of the Third Kind is an electrifying movie.

8. What will the topic be on Nature tonight?

9. My favorite classical guitar selection is Recuerdos de la Alhambra.

10. I listen to it on a double-CD set called Guitar Classics.

EXERCISE 6 Editing a Report

Read the following report. Add underlining to indicate italics.

¹Have you ever seen the book called The Shock of the New? ²The Shock of the New is also the title of an eight-part television series produced by the BBC and Time-Life. ³In the book, as in the series, art critic and historian Robert Hughes explores modern art. ⁴He traces the development of the avant-garde from early works by Pablo Picasso, such as Les Demoiselles d'Avignon, through fairly recent works, such as David Hockney's A Bigger Splash. ⁵From Vincent van Gogh's Starry Night to Andy Warhol's Marilyn Monroe Diptych, some of the greatest works of the twentieth century are represented.

Quotation Marks

▐▶ Use **quotation marks** for titles of short works.

POEMS	"The Raven" "Dover Beach" "Stopping by Woods on a Snowy Evening"
SHORT STORIES	"The Gold-Bug" "Big Two-Hearted River"
ARTICLES	"Stress and Longevity" "Is Homework Good for Young Children?"
SONGS	"Oh, Susanna" "America, the Beautiful"
SINGLE TV/RADIO PROGRAMS	"The Watergate Era" "The Homecoming"
PARTS OF BOOKS	Chapter 2, "War Divides the Nation"

> See Lesson 14.5 for more on punctuating dialogue.

▐▶ Use quotation marks at the beginning and end of a direct quotation.

When a direct quotation is an entire sentence, begin it with a capital letter. Introduce a short, one-sentence quotation with a comma.

A French proverb says**,** "**N**othing is so burdensome as a secret."

When you quote only a word or two and place those words somewhere other than at the beginning of the sentence, use a lowercase letter.

A French proverb calls secrets "**b**urdensome."

▐▶ Introduce a quotation that is a long sentence or more than one sentence with a colon. (See Lesson 14.1 on colons.) Do not use quotation marks for a quotation of more than three lines that is set off as a block.

In *Stride Toward Freedom*, his book about the events in Montgomery, Alabama, Dr. Martin Luther King, Jr., argues against violence**:**

> Violence as a way of achieving racial justice is both impractical and immoral. It is impractical because it is a descending spiral ending in destruction for all. The old law of an eye for an eye leaves everybody blind. It is immoral because it seeks to humiliate the opponent rather than win his understanding; it seeks to **annihilate** rather than to convert.

▐▶ Use single quotation marks for a quotation within quoted material or for the quoted title of a work within a quotation.

The defense attorney said, "We all heard the witness say, 'I'm not sure.'"
The children begged, "Please play 'This Old Man' again!"

Do not use quotation marks with an indirect quotation.

DIRECT	"Leave the dog alone for now," Jill said.
INDIRECT	Jill told me to leave the dog alone for now.

EDITING TIP

Remember to finish what you start—or even to start what you finish. Careless writers may omit the beginning or ending quotation mark. Always proofread to be sure you have included both.

Enriching Your Vocabulary

The word *annihilate* comes from *nihil*, the Latin word for *nothing*. When a building is *annihilated*, it is reduced to a pile of rubble.

P.S. No one can remember every rule relating to punctuation, italics, quotation marks, and other mechanics. For help when you can't remember, use an English handbook (such as this book) or a standard reference work on this subject, such as *Words into Type*.

EXERCISE 7 Editing Sentences

Edit the following items by adding quotation marks where they are needed. Add capital letters, commas, colons, and other appropriate punctuation where they are needed. If an item is correct, write *C* after it.

1. The American architect Frank Lloyd Wright once said Television is chewing gum for the eyes.

2. The name of the article is To Save a Falcon.

3. We were assigned Chapter 3 Early Egyptian Empires.

4. If I Had a Hammer is a famous folk song enjoyed by many children.

5. My favorite short story is The Open Window by Saki (H. H. Munro).

6. Tonight's episode of *Biography* is Cartier: Jewelers to the Kings.

7. When he stepped onto the moon, Neil Armstrong said That's one small step for a man, one giant leap for mankind.

8. Velma remarked I heard the teacher say don't spend more than thirty minutes on this.

9. Wesley said my favorite song on that CD is Moonlight.

10. In her autobiography, Helen Keller compared herself to a ship lost in a fog at sea.

    Have you ever been at sea in a dense fog, when it seemed as if a tangible white darkness shut you in, and the great ship, tense and anxious, groped her way toward the shore with plummet and sounding-line, and you waited with beating heart for something to happen? I was like that ship before my education began, only I was without compass or sounding-line, and had no way of knowing how near the harbor was.

11. Raffi asked me to close the door so that the hamster couldn't get out.

12. Luella said, "Marvin insisted, You stay right here and wait, and I did

13. Did Mark Twain write The Celebrated Jumping Frog of Calaveras County Nico asked.

14. What do you think this quotation means I asked my mother. You must lose a fly to catch a trout.

15. We listened to Where Have All the Flowers Gone?

Punctuating Dialogue

Dialogue is the words that characters speak in stories, poems, and plays. Follow these rules for punctuating dialogue and for punctuating other direct quotations.

IIII➤ Place quotation marks at the beginning and end of a speaker's exact words. Begin a new paragraph every time the speaker changes.

> "Which computer game are you playing?" asked Robin.
> "It's a new geography game," Zohra replied.

IIII➤ For clarity's sake, dialogue requires **dialogue tags**, words such as "he said" and "she remarked" that identify who's talking. When a dialogue tag interrupts a quoted sentence, begin the second part of the quotation with a lowercase letter.

> "Did you know that the first computer game," **asked Sean**, "**w**as created in 1962?"

If the second part of a divided quotation is a complete sentence, it should begin with a capital letter.

> "Students at Harvard created it," he said. "**T**hey played it on the room-size computers of that time."

IIII➤ When a direct quotation comes at the beginning of a sentence, use a comma, question mark, or exclamation point—but not a period—to separate it from the dialogue tag that follows.

> "Video games for television were developed in the mid-1960s**,**" Sean added.

IIII➤ Commas and periods always go *inside* the closing quotation marks.

> "Perhaps you have heard of Pong®**,**" Barbara said.
> She explained, "It was the first truly successful video game**.**"

IIII➤ When the speaker's words are a question or an exclamation, place the question mark or exclamation point *inside* the closing quotation marks. Place a period after the dialogue tag that follows.

> "Do you remember a company called Atari™**?**" Barbara asked.
> "What a lot of money that company made**!**" she exclaimed.

IIII➤ When the quotation itself isn't a question or an exclamation, place the question mark or exclamation point *outside* the closing quotation marks.

> Does your mom often say, "I wish you wouldn't play those games"**?**
> How I wish my mom would say, "Please play just once more"**!**

Quotation Marks with Other Punctuation Marks

Periods and **commas** always go inside closing quotation marks.

Semicolons and **colons** always go outside closing quotation marks.

Question marks and **exclamation points** go inside the quotation if the quotation is a question or an exclamation. They go outside if the whole sentence is a question or an exclamation.

WRITING HINT

It isn't often that people speak to each other in complete sentences and formal language. To write dialogue that sounds natural, use sentence fragments, contractions, and slang words and expressions. Also, don't overuse *said*. Try to use verbs that express the speaker's tone of voice, such as *grumbled*, *shouted*, *whimpered*, and *begged*.

EXERCISE 8 Punctuating Dialogue

Add all the appropriate punctuation marks to the dialogue below. Insert a paragraph sign (¶) to show where a new paragraph should begin. Add other punctuation where it is needed. Write your revised dialogue on a separate piece of paper.

¹Rodney this is simply the best barbecue sauce I ever tasted gushed Sherry. ²It's the perfect blend of spicy and sweet. ³That recipe has been in my family Rodney explained for a couple of generations now. ⁴My grandma was always pretty proud of it. ⁵I can see why said Sherry. ⁶I've tasted a lot of barbecue sauces in my life she added but I really do think this one could win a prize. ⁷Flattered, Rodney boasted And you're just having this sauce on chicken. ⁸You've really got to try it on ribs. ⁹Well I'd like to Sherry replied. ¹⁰Would you be willing to give me the recipe? ¹¹Well hesitated Rodney that's not so easy. ¹²We Washingtons have been making that sauce the same way for years—with a little of this and a little of that. ¹³I can't say that the recipe's ever been written down. ¹⁴Seeing Sherry's disappointment, he quickly added But I'll check with my dad on that.

Working Together

EXERCISE 9 Writing a Dialogue

With a partner or a small group, write a dialogue. Choose one of the following scenarios, or create one of your own. Write the dialogue on a separate piece of paper, and proofread it carefully for correct punctuation and capitalization.

- One friend wants to borrow something from another friend. The object has great value, and the owner is reluctant to lend it.

- A dog has gotten loose, entered a neighbor's garage, and torn up and scattered the trash. The neighbor finds the mess and calls the dog's owner.

- During the intermission of a concert, two old friends meet who have not seen each other since they went to camp together several years ago.

Apostrophes

Apostrophes (') are used in contractions, in the possessive forms of nouns and pronouns, and in three kinds of plurals.

▸ Use an apostrophe in contractions and in other places where letters, words, or numbers have been omitted.

we're   I've   you'll   darlin'   ma'am   o'clock   spring of '47

▸ To show possession, add an apostrophe and -*s* ('*s*) to singular nouns and to indefinite pronouns that stand on their own or are combined with a modifier.

boy's   boss's   the musician's   Dickens's
someone's   nobody's   each other's   everyone else's

Exception: Not every name adds an apostrophe and -*s* to show possession. With the names Jesus and Moses and with some names from classical history and mythology, add only an apostrophe. (Adding only an apostrophe makes it easier to pronounce these names.)

Jesus' teachings   Moses' mother   Odysseus' exploits

▸ To show possession in a plural noun that ends in -*s*, add only an apostrophe (').

girls' club   two cents' worth   the Donahues' garage

▸ To show possession in a plural noun that does not end in -*s*, add an apostrophe and -*s* ('*s*).

sheep's wool   children's ideas   men's book group

▸ To show possession of one thing owned jointly by two people, add an apostrophe and -*s* ('*s*) only to the second of the two names. To show ownership when two or more persons each own something, add an apostrophe and -*s* ('*s*) to each name.

JOINT OWNERSHIP   Chip and Nancy's home is the blue one.
INDIVIDUAL OWNERSHIP   We painted both Judy's and Dane's rooms.

▸ Use an apostrophe and -*s* ('*s*) to form plurals in these three cases: (1) to form the plurals of letters, (2) to form the plurals of numbers, and (3) to form the plurals of words that are referred to as words.

There are two *c*'**s** and two *r*'**s** in *occurred*.
Alexandra is learning to multiply by *6*'**s** and *7*'**s**.
Henry's arguments are always so full of *but*'**s**!

EDITING TIP

Here are the two most common mistakes that writers make with apostrophes.

1. Don't put apostrophes in possessive personal pronouns.

   hers   his   yours
   its   ours   theirs

2. Don't use apostrophes to form the plurals of common or proper nouns.

   SINGULAR
   The Gomez twins

   PLURAL
   The Gomezes

   NOT
   The Gomez's

⫸ When you use numerical representations of decades or centuries, you may add an apostrophe and -s ('s) or leave the apostrophe out. But consistently use whichever style you choose.

      1900s, 1900's   1860s, 1860's   '90s, '90's

EXERCISE 10 Proofreading Sentences

Add or delete apostrophes and s's as needed in the following sentences. If a sentence is correct, write *C* after it.

  1. My daughters name is Camille; its spelled with one *m* and two *l*s.

  2. The first names of the Joneses are Fred, Delilah, Jamey, and Rob.

  3. My father graduated from high school in the 70's; my grandmother graduated from high school in the 50's.

  4. Isn't Krysta's and Michelle's room too small for two people?

  5. My parents are staying overnight with the O'Neill's.

  6. Isnt it correct to spell *traveled* with two *l*'s?

  7. I'm sure I gave you Debs phone number and not someone elses.

  8. Both Franks uniform and Lisas T-shirt have shrunk.

  9. We're learning about Jesus's life in our mens Bible study group.

10. We've already learned about Moses' leadership of the Jews.

11. Its time for the Garden Club to hold it's annual barbecue.

12. The number on Scooters dog license has two *7*s and two *2*s in it.

13. Youre invited to the Collinses annual holiday open house.

14. After Charles and Jen read each others reports, they decided Charles'paper needed revision.

15. "Weve followed deer tracks before," said Stuarts sister.

Hyphens, Dashes, and Parentheses

▶ Use **hyphens** to join some compound nouns and for written numbers from *twenty-one* to *ninety-nine*.

> When it comes to sports, John has an unpredictable mind-set.
> I have fifty-three pages left to read in this book.

▶ Use a **dash** to signal an abrupt break or an unfinished statement.

> Leo yelled, an instant too late, "Watch out for that——!"

▶ Also use a dash to mean *namely*, *that is*, or *in other words*, or to set off any interrupter that you want to emphasize.

> The resort developers had just one goal—to make money fast.
> Their philosophy—build it fast, sell it fast—was reflected in the slipshod construction.

▶ Use **parentheses** to enclose information that explains or supplements something in a sentence but is of less importance than other information in the same sentence.

> The film (which few people remember now) was a big hit when it was released in 1971.

WRITING HINT

Use dashes and parentheses when writing as you would use a salt shaker when dining—with care. Too many dashes or parentheses can fragment your writing and make it difficult to read.

EXERCISE 11 Writing Sentences

Write a complete sentence that contains each of the following elements.

1. an unfinished bit of dialogue that ends a sentence
2. an interrupting word, phrase, or clause in the middle of a sentence
3. information that is clearly secondary to the rest of the sentence
4. a compound noun
5. one or more numbers between twenty-one and ninety-nine

EDITING TIP

When you're writing quickly, you may remember an opening parenthesis but not the closing one. Always double-check parentheses during proofreading.

EXERCISE 12 Editing Sentences

Add parentheses, dashes, and hyphens where they are needed in the following sentences.

1. Mr. Johnson has a collection of twenty seven adventure videos.
2. The photograph on page 96 of the effects of the flood haunted me.

3. The last thing I heard as the train pulled out of the station was "Carol, wait for us at!"

4. Jason had one very clear look on his face anger.

5. DVRs digital video recorders are a common household item.

6. Chemicals called chlorofluorocarbons CFCs damage the ozone.

7. "I uh well just felt like it," confessed Leah.

8. "That is not what I" Leslie began.

9. The blessings of friends and family we cannot be thankful enough for them.

10. In the Mexican state of Chiapas chee•AH•pas , a peasant uprising occurred.

11. The ideals that General Douglas MacArthur emphasized duty, honor, country help explain much of his success.

12. Foreign investors own a large part thirty two percent of that company.

13. Eve has a great deal of self confidence at least on the dance floor.

14. This type of test item found in Lesson 6 should not prove difficult.

Working Together

Exercise 13 Using Parentheses and Dashes

A writer might add either parentheses or dashes to the following sentences. Underline the word, phrase, or clause in each sentence that might be punctuated in this way. Then get together with two other classmates, and discuss which choice you would make and why.

1. The algebra test the hardest test I ever took contained forty-five items.

2. OPEC declared an oil embargo a complete ban on trade.

3. The Hubble Space Telescope once known, unfortunately, more for its failures than its successes observes objects in remote regions of the universe.

4. Juan Perón's enemies the church and the military were powerful.

5. The rise of dictators especially Hitler and Mussolini helped lead to World War II.

Editing and Proofreading Worksheet 1

Edit the draft for errors in spelling, capitalization, punctuation, and usage. Write your edited version on a separate piece of paper. Compare your changes with those of a writing partner.

[1]In the early 70s, supermarket profits were at an all-time low. [2]Because markup on food is not high, supermarkets have only just so many ways of increasing prophets cutting labor costs is one of them. [3]This drive to cut the costs of retailers people who sell in small quantities directly to the consumers helped lead to an important invention the uniform product code UPC. [4]The UPC is also known as the bar code. [5]Among other things this symbol has brought about bigger stores and larger inventories.

[6]In an article entitled Bar Codes Reading Between the Lines, which appeared in the Smithsonian, author Ed Leibowitz traces the short and important history of this invention. [7]Of it's beginnings, Leibowitz writes, How strange that the checkout line this unhappy place, this technological backwater should have pioneered a symbol that has transformed not just the supermarket but also mass retail worldwide. [8]Leibowitz also notes that, in the twenty five years or so of its existance, the bar code has "blossomed by the thousands in every American household.

[9]Although theres now widespread use and acceptance of the bar code, that wasnt always the case. [10]Many 1970's consumers were angry about bar codes after all the price tag was now gone from many items. [11]When Stephen Brown wrote his insiders account of the UPC, Revolution at the Checkout Counter, he made it clear that consumers needs did not lead to the creation of the code. [12]Instead, he said, those who created the code "focused on improving business effitioncies," explaining that "any consumer benefit was a fortuitous by-product.

Editing and Proofreading Worksheet 2

Edit the draft for errors in spelling, capitalization, punctuation, and usage. Write your edited version on a separate piece of paper. Compare your changes with those of a writing partner.

Friday, March 5

- Theater Three presents The Dining Room at 800 P.M. Tickets are priced as follows in advance $9.00, at the door, $13.50.

- Acton Jazz Café presents the B. D. Magoon Trio. They're album Night Tide was just released and includes the single Watchtower which recently recieved critical praise in the Middlesex News.

- The Brighton Public Library will continue it's film festival with the classic Double Indemnity, showing at 330 P.M. and 730 P.M.

- Powers Gallery will present the work of Wade Hares, including his too most famous paintings, Electric Trains and Mowing Field.

- R. C. Whitestock will read at the Grover Memorial Library at 700 P.M. He plans to read, among other poems, Summer Light, from his recently published book, New and Selected Poetry.

- The Commonwealth Ballet presents Carmen at 800 P.M. in the Blanchard Auditorium. Theres no reserved seating for this performance.

- Historian Will Moretti will read Chapter 3, Faith in Crisis from his new book Voices of the Reformation.

- On Friday night only, in honor of its 25th anniversary, the Maynard Swing Dance Club will admit the first twenty five people free.

Chapter Review

EXERCISE A Using Colons and Semicolons

Insert colons and semicolons where they belong in the following sentences.

1. The train makes the following stops Providence, Rhode Island Stamford, Connecticut Penn Station, New York City.

2. Joseph Stalin began his climb to power in 1922 by 1928, he was in complete control of the Communist Party.

3. We studied these Civil War battles Chickamauga, Antietam, and Chancellorsville.

4. Mr. Parmenter is a specialist on just one thing vacuum cleaners.

5. The bumper sticker read, Save lives Donate blood.

6. *Deep Space 1* is the first spacecraft with an ion engine only it is practically a science fiction myth.

7. We read aloud Act I scene I Act 2 scene IV and the final act.

8. The sermon this week is on Deuteronomy 5 19–24.

9. The party started at 730 however Kesia refused to get there a moment before 815.

10. Virginia Woolf writes this "Most commonly we come to books with blurred and divided minds, asking of fiction that it shall be true, of poetry that it shall be false, of biography that it shall be flattering, of history that it shall enforce our own prejudices."

11. Every American should visit these three places Washington, D.C. Gettysburg, Pennsylvania and Chicago, Illinois.

EXERCISE B Using Italics, Quotation Marks, Apostrophes, Parentheses, Dashes, and Hyphens

Insert the appropriate punctuation marks in each item. Add underlining to indicate italics.

1. Ms. Kenyon assigned twenty two pages in a chapter called

   The Respiratory System in Biological Science.

2. Did you know that reruns of M*A*S*H a show about army doctors

   and nurses are a big hit in India?

3. The North Atlantic Treaty Organization NATO was formed in 1949.

4. Isnt Marisa just full of joie de vivre?

5. Kathie confused the films Its a Wonderful Life and Life Is Beautiful.

6. Come Together is the first cut on the Beatles CD Abbey Road.

7. Jorge ended his speech dramatically with and liberty and justice for all.

8. How many ss and ps are there in Mississippi?

9. Better muscle tone and increased endurance these are my reasons for joining the gym.

10. Some of the players eyes werent on the ball.

Exercise C Editing a Dialogue

Edit the following dialogue. Add quotation marks, other punctuation marks, and capitalization as needed. Insert paragraph symbols (¶) to show when a new paragraph begins.

[1]Have you ever read Walden by Henry David Thoreau asked Tammy. [2]No I haven't admitted Jeremy. [3]You really ought to she suggested. [4]In fact, everybody should read at least the chapter called Where I Lived, and What I Lived For. [5]With so much good stuff around to read replied Jeremy why should I read that? [6]Well, for one thing, it is full of wisdom. [7]My favorite line in the whole chapter although there are many is A man is rich in proportion to the number of things which he can afford to let alone. [8]That is a good line commented Jeremy and I see the wisdom in it, but, still, isnt it challenging to read Thoreau? [9]A little, yes, Tammy said. [10]But she quickly added it's so worth the effort!

Capitalization

STUDENT WRITING
Research Paper

Six Lanes, Five Miles, a Decade of Controversy:
**The Construction of the Massachusetts Turnpike
Extension Through the City of Newton**
by Toby Berkman
high school student, Newton, Massachusetts

The construction of the Massachusetts Turnpike Extension was a divisive issue that caused fear and anger among the citizens of Newton, Massachusetts, for more than a decade. The conflict, which began in 1952 and did not end until 1964, was heated and bitter throughout. From the moment it was first proposed, Newton citizens and politicians opposed the turnpike extension vehemently.

Newton residents saw the turnpike as more than just a strip of concrete that would displace numerous houses and businesses. They saw it as the end of a way of life—a divisive force that would destroy neighborhoods, divide Newton into two sections, and turn their city of parks and gardens a dull gray. Conversely, the Turnpike Authority, as well as many Boston politicians, viewed the turnpike as a necessary change. They observed the flight of many businesses to the suburbs, were afraid of losing new development, and concluded that only the extension of the turnpike could save Boston.

In this way, the turnpike extension represented a conflict of interest between Boston and Newton. Newton wanted to remain a quiet, peaceful suburb while Boston sought a convenient commute for suburbanites as a way to revitalize its economy. Because of Boston's larger population, prominent businesses, and political dominance, its interest prevailed while those of Newton were largely ignored. This paper will explore the reasons behind the construction of the turnpike extension, the history of Newton's battle against the Turnpike Authority, the explanation for Newton's eventual defeat, and the underlying issues at the heart of the conflict.

> The paragraphs above are the first three of a full-length research paper. This introduction is effective because it gives the reader just enough context to understand the main idea of the paper.
>
> Toby Berkman has many opportunities to utilize the rules of capitalization that are discussed in this chapter. Notice that the words requiring capital letters are official titles, highway names, organizations, and city names.

Proper Nouns and Proper Adjectives

▷ Both proper nouns and proper adjectives begin with a capital letter. Remember that a **proper noun** names a particular person, place, thing, or idea and that a **proper adjective** is the adjective form of a proper noun. (See Lessons 5.1 and 5.4 for more on proper nouns and proper adjectives.)

▷ Capitalize the names of people.

  Thurgood Marshall   Jane Austen   Pablo Picasso

▷ Capitalize the names of places.

PLANETS, CONSTELLATIONS	Venus the Pleiades the Big Dipper
ISLANDS	San Juan Islands Nantucket Hawaii
COUNTRIES	Sri Lanka Madagascar Brazil
STATES	Montana California Texas
CITIES	St. Louis Beijing Guadalajara
BODIES OF WATER, MOUNTAINS	Rio Grande the Blue Ridge Mountains
LOCALITIES, REGIONS	the Yucatán Peninsula the Southwest the Middle East the South
STREETS, HIGHWAYS	Rodeo Drive Route 66 Adirondack Northway Tamiami Trail Brooklyn-Queens Expressway
BUILDINGS	the Eiffel Tower the Empire State Building
PARKS, MONUMENTS	Yellowstone the Vietnam Veterans Memorial

Note: Do not capitalize articles (*a, an,* and *the*) and short prepositions (such as *in* and *of*) when they are part of a phrase that includes a proper noun. (See, for example, *the Middle East* and *the Pleiades* above.)

▷ Capitalize the adjective forms of proper nouns.

  Napoleonic weapons   Mexican restaurant
  Mesopotamian civilization   African trade routes

EXERCISE 1 Proofreading a Paragraph

Insert capital letters where they belong in the following paragraph. To indicate a capital letter, use the proofreading symbol, which is three underscores beneath the letter: (c).
                                                                    ≡

  [1]If you live in the south or the southwest, san antonio is a

perfect destination for you. [2]My friend matt and I traveled there

---

EDITING TIP

Don't capitalize words such as *north*, *south*, *east*, and *west* when you're talking about compass directions. Capitalize these words only when they refer to regions of a country.

I never like to head **north** except when we go to Maine.

Maine is my favorite state in the **Northeast**.

---

from the southern great plains of Oklahoma. ³To reach san antonio, we took the h. e. bailey turnpike south out of oklahoma city and then continued on route 281. ⁴It was a long trip just to the texas border, but we perked up once we hit the lone star state. ⁵After all, we were in the land of general santa anna, davy crockett, and jim bowie. ⁶Once we reached the city, of course, we visited the alamo. ⁷Then we went to the paseo del rio (or river walk), which runs along the san antonio river. ⁸We stopped in market square to ogle everything from leather crafts to pottery, and then we went to hemisfair plaza, which contains the san antonio convention center. ⁹We even rode the elevator to the top of the tower of the americas. ¹⁰From there, we had a great view of the whole city.

EXERCISE 2 Proofreading Sentences

Proofread the following sentences to correct all errors in capitalization. Again, use the proofreading symbol for capitalization. To show lowercase, put a slash through the capital letter, like this: (𝒞).

1. Mr. min taught us some Korean cooking.

2. Isn't the Thomas Jefferson memorial near the potomac river?

3. Charleston, south carolina, is my favorite city in the south.

4. When you reach atlanta, head North on peachtree street.

5. Be sure to visit the gateway arch and busch stadium in st. louis.

6. From the mauna kea observatory on hawaii, we saw saturn and its rings.

7. If you live South of the equator, the southern cross constellation is an important guide for you.

8. This constellation guided the first travelers around the south african Cape Of Good Hope.

9. Is the Strait of hormuz part of the persian gulf?

10. We learned how new products from north America affected european markets.

Titles; Greetings

||||➡ Capitalize titles and abbreviations of titles only when they are used before names. Also capitalize abbreviations of academic degrees after a name.

  Judge Salinas   Clara Duvall, Ph.D.
  Reverend Eunice Jefferson (*or* Rev. Jefferson)

||||➡ A few titles are capitalized even when the name of the person is not used with them.

  the President   the Pope
  the Chief Justice   the Prime Minister

||||➡ Capitalize a word that shows a family relationship only when you use it immediately before a name or as a name.

  Please say hello to Aunt Ruth, who is my favorite aunt.
  Tell me, Grandpa, how did you learn to swim?

||||➡ Capitalize the first and last words and all important words in the titles of works.

Note: Unless they appear as the first word in a title, do not capitalize the following short words: articles (*a*, *an*, *the*), coordinating conjunctions, and prepositions with fewer than five letters.

BOOKS	*The Old Man and the Sea* *Mythology*
PERIODICALS	the *Miami Herald* the *Los Angeles Times*
STORIES, ESSAYS	"Araby" "The Last Leaf"
POEMS	"My Last Duchess" "The Bells"
PLAYS	*Othello* *Death of a Salesman*
TV SERIES/EPISODES	*Mystery!* "The Case of the Missing Computer"
DOCUMENTS	the Declaration of Independence the Magna Carta
WORKS OF ART	*Ballet Rehearsal* *Black Iris*
MUSICAL WORKS	*The Barber of Seville* "Hey Jude" "Etude in C Major, Opus 10"
MOVIES	*Shakespeare in Love* *Rear Window* *On the Waterfront*

||||➡ Capitalize the salutation and the first word of the closing in friendly letters and business letters.

  Dear Dr. Ritter: Dear Nancy,   Yours truly,   Best wishes,

WRITING HINT

Remember that all forms of *be* are verbs. They require capitals in titles.

I memorized Wordsworth's poem "The World is Too Much with Us."

EXERCISE 3 Proofreading a Paragraph

Insert capital letters where they belong in the following paragraph. To indicate a capital letter, use the proofreading symbol, which is three underscores beneath the letter: (c̲).

¹Today aunt Laurie recommended the poet Mary Oliver to me. ²She loves Oliver's poems. ³She gave me *American primitive*, Oliver's Pulitzer Prize-winning volume. ⁴My favorite poems in this book are "A poem for the blue heron," "Postcard from flamingo," and "In the pinewoods, crows and owl." ⁵I am going to pass this book along to uncle Ned, grandma, and my cousins.

EXERCISE 4 Proofreading Sentences

Edit the following sentences to correct all errors in capitalization. Again, use the proofreading symbol for capitalization. To show lowercase, put a slash through the capital letter, like this: (C̸).

1. Last week grandma Clark recommended Truman Capote's story "a Christmas memory."
2. Juliana Pritchard, m.d., is our Doctor.
3. We studied senator John Glenn's congressional record.
4. President John Adams appointed John Marshall chief justice of the supreme court.
5. The press frequently quoted vice president Spiro Agnew.
6. Not many people are familiar with Beethoven's *fourth symphony*.
7. Van Gogh's *Landscape with sheaves of wheat and a windmill* is one of my favorite paintings.
8. I hope someone will decide to broadcast *The Marriage Of Figaro* on *Live From The Met*.
9. Have you ever tried the crossword puzzle in The *London Times*?
10. My stepbrother Phil and his Dad both read *Sports illustrated* from cover to cover.

EXERCISE 5 Writing About Favorites

On a separate piece of paper, list your all-time favorites in the following categories: books, movies, short stories, CDs, songs, TV series or episodes, and magazines. Provide a brief reason for each choice. Check to make sure you've used capital letters correctly in each sentence.

First Words, Groups, Organizations, Religions, School Subjects

▐▐▐▶ Capitalize the first word in every sentence. Capitalize the first word in a direct quotation when the quotation is a complete sentence, but do not capitalize the first word in an indirect quotation.

DIRECT   **O**ur history teacher said, "**R**ead the section called 'Alexander Defeats Persia.'"

INDIRECT   She said that Alexander is known historically as "the Great."

If a quoted sentence is interrupted, begin the second part with a lowercase letter.

"Alexander," said Ms. McGuire, "named many cities after himself."

Note: When you quote lines of poetry, capitalize the words as the poet did. In traditional poetry, every line begins with a capital letter, but most modern poets ignore this convention. Some poets, such as Emily Dickinson and E. E. Cummings, have deliberately flouted the conventions.

▐▐▐▶ Capitalize the names of groups, teams, businesses, institutions, and organizations.

Library of Congress	Milwaukee Brewers	Sunshine Juice Company
Beth Israel Hospital	University of Arizona	Oxfam
World Trade Organization		

▐▐▐▶ Capitalize the names of languages, nationalities, peoples, races, and religions.

My Pakistani classmate is Muslim and speaks Urdu, while my Indian classmate is Hindu and speaks Bengali.

▐▐▐▶ Capitalize the names of school subjects that are followed by a number. Capitalize the names of all languages.

Dirk's favorite classes are American government, History 102, and Latin.

Enriching Your Vocabulary

The word *flout* comes from the Middle English verb *flouten*, which means "to play the flute." Today, it has come to mean "to be scornful" or "to scoff." The Impressionists *flouted* the conventions of nineteenth-century academic painting.

EXERCISE 6 Proofreading Sentences

Use proofreading symbols to show where letters should be capitalized (a̲) or made lowercase (A̸) in the following sentences.

1. was it yeats who said, "education is not the filling of a pail, but the lighting of a fire"?

2. Nirupam speaks english in school and hindi at home.

3. Alex is taking algebra 1, Biology, and political science.

4. Liana is majoring in american studies at washington university.

5. The Shirazis give money to save the children and to the united way.

6. We have hired coppola construction, inc., to repair our roof.

7. We saw the Miami dolphins practice at summer camp.

8. Do you think the republican party will be able to work together with the democratic party on this issue?

9. Will said that he preferred "Classical music to popular music."

10. Our high school has both japanese and brazilian foreign exchange students.

11. It was thrilling to see halley's comet through the giant telescope.

12. "We are going to study," said Ms. Bolton, "the shinto religion."

13. Mary asked, "did you decide on algebra 2 or geometry?"

14. Buddhism and confucianism exist side by side in many asian countries.

15. The novelist draws inspiration from both his british and his west indian backgrounds.

16. Fernando has joined an organization called youth helping elders.

17. Of all the peoples of the world, the chinese are the most numerous.

18. Moira is a fan of the Dallas cowboys and the Denver broncos.

19. When Harley was a Freshman, he took photography 101.

20. "It is never too late," George Eliot wrote, "To be what you might have been."

I and *O*; Historical Events, Documents, and Periods; Calendar Items; Brand Names; Awards

▶ Capitalize the words *I* and *O*.

The first-person pronoun *I* is always capitalized. So is the poetic interjection *O*, which is rarely used today. The modern interjection *oh* is not capitalized unless it's the first word in a sentence.

> The line from Keats is "**O** what can ail thee, knight-at-arms?"
> Manuel and **I** went to that summer camp and, **oh**, what a great time we had there!

▶ Capitalize the names of historical events, documents, and periods.

HISTORICAL EVENTS	Gulf War Siege of Vicksburg Reformation
SPECIAL EVENTS	Cannes Film Festival Taste of Chicago World Series
DOCUMENTS	Universal Declaration of Human Rights Articles of Confederation
PERIODS	Golden Age of Greece the Enlightenment Mesozoic Era

▶ Capitalize calendar names but not seasons.

CALENDAR ITEMS	Labor Day New Year's Day Monday, December 13
SEASONS	spring fall colors a long winter

When you refer to a century, however, do not use capital letters.

> sixteenth-century literature   issues for the twenty-first century

▶ Capitalize brand names of manufactured products, but do not capitalize the common noun that follows the brand name.

> Ford Explorer   Kleenex tissues   Macintosh computers

▶ Capitalize the important words in the name of an award.

> Nobel Prize for Physics   Grammy Award
> Heisman Trophy   an Oscar

WRITING HINT

The names of seasons are capitalized under just one circumstance—when they are personified.

The hands of Autumn gently close the year's shutters.

EXERCISE 7 Proofreading Sentences

Use proofreading symbols to show where letters should be capitalized (m̲) or made lowercase (M̸) in the following sentences. If a sentence is correct, write *C* after it.

1. Do we have a break during spring semester?

2. Antonio Vivaldi was born during the Seventeenth Century.

3. Muffin got loose again, and, Oh, what a mess she made!

4. Esmeralda won the Kiwanis Junior Citizen Of The Year Award.

5. Nothing is more beautiful than Autumn leaves, but "o! what they herald!"

6. Our class is studying the paleolithic era.

7. Didn't the novel *Cold Mountain* win the national book award?

8. Charlene and i will go to New Orleans for mardi gras.

9. My family will hold its annual reunion on Independence day.

10. The second half of the Nineteenth century was a time of dramatic change.

Working Together

EXERCISE 8 Create Your Own Exercise

Work with a partner to create a history quiz based on what you have been learning in class this year or last year. Use a short-answer format, and construct all the questions so that their answers will include the names of historical events, special events, documents, and periods. When you are finished, exchange your quiz with another pair. Proofread the completed quiz for the correct use of capital letters.

Working Together

EXERCISE 9 Writing a Paragraph

Refer to **Composition,** Lesson 2.3, for a list of transition words to use in your paragraph.

With a partner, write a paragraph in which you compare and contrast three or more competing products. (Consider, for example, competing brands of frozen pizza or snack foods or different types of bicycles or smart phones.) Proofread your paragraph for the correct use of capital letters.

Editing and Proofreading Worksheet 1

Edit the draft for errors in spelling, capitalization, punctuation, and usage. Write your edited version on a separate piece of paper. Compare your changes with those of a writing partner.

[1]Are you interested in natural history, european, asian, and african history, as well as in cultural and political phenomena? [2]Then *Zarafa* is the book for you. [3]Written by michael allin,its a chronicle of a giraffe's journey from its home in africa to paris france. [4]Set in the Nineteenth Century. [5]This unusual little book weaves together information ranging from Charles Darwins mission on the ship the beagle to Champollions deciphering of the Rosetta stone. [6]It weaves all that together with wit and wisdom!

[7]Zarafa, the first giraffe ever seen in france, arrived in 1872 as a royal gift from muhammad ali, the ottoman viceroy of egypt to king charles X of france. [8]Zarafa (named after the word zerafa, which means "charming" or "lovely one" in arabic) was captured as a calf in the ethiopian highlands by arab hunters. [9]From their, she was shipped down the nile river and raised in khartoum, she traveled nearly two thousand miles from there to cairo and alexandria, and then she sailed across the mediterranean, she landed in marseilles and then walked to paris.

[10]This was, of course, no ordinary walk it was a procession a parade and a sideshow attraction. [11]It was led by Étienne Geoffroy Saint-Hilaire, who was a leading scientist and had helped found the national museum of natural history. [12](He had also started the paris zoo with animals saved from the mobs who attacked Louis XIV's home in versailles. [13]Everywhere, crowds gathered to see the first girafe in fact, it wasn't long until "Zarafamania" raged. [14]The giraffe began appearing on products, children ate gingerbread giraffes, and the Journal of women and fashion reported a new fashion: a giraffe necklace.

Editing and Proofreading Worksheet 2

Edit the draft for errors in spelling, capitalization, punctuation, and usage. Write your edited version on a separate piece of paper. Compare your changes with those of a writing partner.

[1]When you use the Internet don't ever forget these three words Narrow Your Search! [2]Heres what happened to me when I typed in galileo. [3]First, I got 116,063 items. [4]That's just a few too many! [5]Also, I got the most craziest stuff. [6]The first match was something from the bicycle helmet safety institute!

[7]There was an article from the journal of geophysical research and information from NASA, I certainly expected that kind of stuff. [8]But it wasn't really what I wanted. [9]I also landed a review of Michael Moriartys performance in Galileo. [10]Which appeared in a biography in the HBO series called the inventors's specials. [11](it tells among other things, about galileos trial, in which he was forced to say he was wrong about the sun being the center of the universe.

[12]I finally found a site that had a pretty good biography of Galileo by typing in "galileo galilei' and 'jupiter' this site called him an Astronomer, Mathematician and Physicist. [13]I found out that Galileo was born in pisa italy, in february 1564 and that he was the Son of a Musician. [14]He attended the university of pisa and later taught Mathematics at the university of padua. [15]Galileo is known for his astronomical work. [16]He invented a telescope with which he was able to see the four largest Moons of jupiter. [17]He could also tell that the milky way is made up of individual stars. [18]His biggest trouble, however was that he illegally taught the theory attributed to copernicus that the planets of our Solar System revolve around the sun. [19]This Theory was widely considered untrue, and even the teaching of it was a major offense. [20]Galileo spent the last eight years of his life under House Arrest for teaching copernican doctrine.

Chapter Review

EXERCISE A Proofreading Sentences

Insert the proofreading symbol for capitalization (f̲̲) wherever it is necessary in the following sentences.

1. is the constellation orion visible in the winter sky?

2. the hawaiian islands are in the pacific ocean.

3. a scientist from india won this year's nobel prize for chemistry.

4. during summer vacation, we will visit illinois and indiana.

5. hasn't rachel already been to the pacific northwest?

6. have you ever been to larimer square in denver?

7. the tyndall glacier is at the very edge of the continental divide.

8. we took the santa monica freeway to figueroa street.

9. randy was excited to see the statue of liberty in the harbor.

10. jill asked whether i caught the shakespearean allusion.

11. there will be a joint press conference with the french president and the british prime minister.

12. in the *phoenix sun*, I read an article entitled "officials face trial in alleged plot."

13. we enjoyed watching *lady and the tramp* at the beaumont theater.

14. "next tuesday," announced joelle, "is my birthday."

15. will the new england patriots go to the superbowl?

EXERCISE B Proofreading an Article

Proofread the following travel article for correct capitalization. Use the proofreading symbols for capitalization (c̲̲) and lowercase (ℓ̸).

¹England's capital city, London, is situated in southeast England and is divided by the Thames river. ²If you visit in the Summer, take a River excursion. ³Among the places you can visit in this way is hampton court,

an english renaissance building which is the former home of, among others, Henry VIII.

⁴One of the most important places to visit in London is westminster abbey, which dates from the Thirteenth century and is one of the most beautiful examples of gothic architecture in England. ⁵It is known as the burial place of the famous dead, including many poets. ⁶Among them is John Gay, author of *the Beggar's opera*. ⁷His Epitaph reads: "life is a jest, and all things show it; I thought so once, and now I know it."

⁸Moving away from the River, do not miss the chance to stroll down fleet street, with its memories of Dr. Samuel Johnson and the history of the press. ⁹From there, it is just a short walk to st. paul's cathedral, the masterpiece of sir christopher wren.

¹⁰Finally, don't fail to visit the tate gallery. ¹¹There you can see such famous paintings as Mark Rothko's *light red over black*; J. M. W. turner's *Petworth, sunset in the park*; and several of william blake's illustrations for dante's *divine comedy*.

Exercise C Writing Sentences

On a separate piece of paper, write a complete sentence about the topic of each numbered item. Check your sentences for correct capitalization.

1. a grandparent, uncle, or aunt

2. a piece of music you find soothing or enjoyable

3. the subjects you are taking in school

4. a book you have enjoyed reading

5. an organization you belong to

6. TV programs you watch every week

7. two movies you wish you hadn't seen

8. three places you want to visit

Spelling

STUDENT WRITING
Expository Essay

County-Funded Program Sponsors Activities for Disabled Students
by Fred Hernandez and Monica McNealy
high school students, Coral Gables, Florida

Jared Berger is the typical fourth grader—sports and competition are as much a part of his life as they are for the next kid. Only one thing sets him apart from others his age: He was born with a missing heart chamber.

Doctors warned Tracy Berger, Jared's mother, to keep him away from athletics. The thrill of winning a race or throwing a winning pass—the most important things for the average ten-year-old—was, in their opinion, beyond his ability. "They told me to just teach him to read and play the piano because he'd never be athletic," Berger said.

But Jared has been able to surpass his doctors' shortsighted expectations, becoming living proof that the human spirit can overcome any obstacle.

That is the goal of the Sports Program for Students with Disabilities: to give physically, visually, and hearing impaired students an opportunity to compete in sports to which they are otherwise not exposed. The county-funded program sponsors such events as track and field, tennis, basketball, and sailing for disabled students of all ages.

Students from Claude Pepper and Arcola Lake also received help from the Gables cross country, volleyball, and softball teams. Coaches Stephanie Hoffman and Nicki Brisson encouraged Gables athletes to take part in the event. Team members encouraged the children as they completed the races by offering a helping hand and by pushing the wheelchairs of the exhausted athletes.

The students began practicing early with their physical education teachers for their respective events. At Arcola Lake, Luisa Rodriguez and Jeff Niefeld began preparing by practicing calisthenics and conditioning students with running. "We've been doing this program for twenty years," Rodriguez said. "Last year we won region and county finals. We're so proud."

To the children, a sense of accomplishment is what made the day worthwhile. "The best part is the increase of self-esteem for the kids," Berger said.

Apparent excitement colored the faces of kids. Winning and losing was not as important as simply being there to participate. "Just being able to compete in the events is what's important," Soraya Ligonde, first place winner of the sixty-meter wheelchair race, said. "I feel happy."

So, what advice do these young athletes have for others who aspire to prove the naysayers wrong? "Just get out there," Jared Berger said. "Try to do the best you can."

> The authors of the expository essay begin with an interesting anecdote that highlights one of the participants in a sports program. They use quotations and examples to help explain the program. The ending quotation effectively recalls the anecdote from the first paragraph.
>
> This essay is effective partly because the words are spelled correctly. In this chapter, you'll learn strategies and rules to help you spell accurately as you write.

Using a Dictionary

Being able to spell correctly is an important skill—both in school and in the workplace. One sure way to improve your spelling is to refer to a print or digital dictionary whenever you're in doubt.

▥▶ If you don't know how to spell a word or if you're not sure about the spelling you've written, check a dictionary.

In addition to showing each entry word's definition and word history, a dictionary gives many kinds of spelling help.

entry word ⌐ pronunciation
⌐irregular noun plural   alternative plural form
¹**fo·cus** \'fō-kəs\ *n, pl* **fo·ci** \'fō-,sī *also* -,kī\ *also* **fo·cus·es**
  1a : a point at which rays (as of light, heat, or sound) converge or from which they diverge . . .

⌐ entry for word that is spelled the same but has different meaning
⌐alternative past participle
²**focus** *vb* **fo·cused** *also* **fo·cussed**; **fo·cus·ing** *also*
fo·cus·sing *vt* **1a** : to bring into focus—**fo·cus·able**⌐—syllable breaks
\-kə-sə-bəl\ *adj*—**fo·cus·er** *n*⌐—related words

alternative comparative forms
part of speech ⌐
¹**lit·tle** \'li-təl\ *adj* **lit·tler** \'li-təl-ər, 'lit-lər\ *or* **less**
\'les\ *or* **les·ser** \'le-sər\; **lit·tlest** \'li-təl-əst, 'lit-ləst\ ⌐—alternative pronunciation
or **least** \'lēst\ **1** : not big : as **a** : small in size or extent: TINY <has ~ feet>
b : YOUNG <was too ~ to remember>

Exercise 1 Using a Dictionary to Check Spelling

Work with a partner to circle the correctly spelled word in each numbered item. If you're not sure of the correct spelling of a word, take turns looking up the term in a dictionary.

1. a. publicly   b. publically   c. publichly

2. a. atheletics   b. athletics   c. athelletics

3. a. mischievous   b. mischievious   c. mischeivious

4. a. similar   b. similiar   c. similer

5. a. monsterous   b. monstrous   c. monsterouse

6. a. maintainance   b. maintenence   c. maintenance

7. a. disasterous   b. disastrous   c. desasterous

8. a. extraordinery   b. extrordinary   c. extraordinary

EDITING TIP

1. Learn what a new or unfamiliar word means. When dealing with two words that sound—or even look—similar but have different meanings, you need to know which meaning goes with which spelling.

   Is it *vial* (a small bottle), *vile* (evil), or *viol* (a musical instrument)?

2. Learn to pronounce and spell a new word by syllables or word parts. Mispronunciation leads to misspelling.

   Do you say *govenor* instead of *governor* or *mathmatics* instead of *mathematics*?

3. Whenever you misspell a word, add it (spelled correctly) to your proofreading log. Underline the letter or sequence of letters that you misspelled.

9. a. conscience   b. consience   c. consciense

10. a. siege   b. seige   c. ciege

EXERCISE 2 Using a Dictionary

On a separate piece of paper, answer the following questions by referring to a dictionary or by confirming your answers in a dictionary.

1. *Criteria* is a plural word. What is its singular form?

2. Assume you have to hyphenate the word *residential* at the end of a line. Show all of the points where you could place a hyphen.

3. Write the plural form or forms of these words.

   a. piano   d. salmon

   b. avocado   e. moose

   c. memento   f. bison

4. Spell the noun that is formed from the verb *occur*.

5. Spell the word that begins with *com-* and refers to the hue or appearance of skin, especially facial skin.

6. Spell the words that name these symbols—( )—and this one—(.

7. How do you spell the past tense and past participle of the verb *lie*, meaning "to recline"? Use each word in a sentence.

8. When a word has alternate spellings, the one listed first in the dictionary is the preferred form. Underline the spelling that is preferred in the United States for the following words.

   a. dialog or dialogue   d. harbor or harbour

   b. marvelous or marvellous   e. theater or theatre

   c. connexion or connection   f. advertise or advertize

9. If you have two married sisters, what do you call their husbands when you refer to both at once?

10. Change each of the following words to an adjective ending in *-able* or *-ible*. Write the correct new word.

   a. collapse   d. irritate

   b. defense   e. separate

   c. response   f. believe

Spelling Rules

English spelling is highly irregular. That's why learning a few rules—even rules with exceptions—is useful.

▶ Write *i* before *e* except after *c*.

Note that most of these words have a long *e* sound.

FOLLOW RULE	achievement	belief	field	grief	niece
AFTER *C*	ceiling	conceited	perceive	receive	
EXCEPTIONS	either	financier	neither	protein	seize

▶ Write *ei* when these letters are not pronounced with a long /*e*/, especially when the sound is a long /*a*/ as in *neighbor* and *weigh*.

	height	their	foreign	forfeit
SOUNDS LIKE AY	beige	eight	sleigh	vein

▶ For words with more than one syllable that end with the sound /*seed*/, only one word is spelled with *-sede*. Three words end in *-ceed*. All other words end in *-cede*.

-SEDE	supersede				
-CEED	exceed	proceed	succeed		
-CEDE	concede	intercede	precede	recede	secede

EXERCISE 3 Proofreading Sentences

Cross out each misspelled word, and write the correct word above it. If a sentence is completely correct, write *C* after it.

1. *Carpe diem* is Latin for "sieze the day."

2. A siege was a common battle tactic during the Crusades.

3. Filing the application should presede payment.

4. Did your freind see a yeild sign at that intersection?

5. Do you know your exact hieght and weight?

6. The tide began to receed at sundown.

7. The total weight should not excede forty-four pounds.

8. When the amendment passed, many senators were relieved.

9. Was South Carolina the first state to sesede?

Enriching Your Vocabulary

The Latin verb *intercedere* comes from *inter*, or "between," and *cedere*, or "to move or go." It is the source of the English verb *intercede*. Have you ever tried to *intercede* in an argument between friends?

WRITING HINT

A good way to remember something is to make up a mnemonic, or memory, device. Here's a nonsense sentence to help you remember some exceptions to the *i*-before-*e* rule.

Either w**ei**rd bird can s**ei**ze a lizard at l**ei**sure, but n**ei**ther does.

10. Robert E. Lee was a great general, but he did not succede at Gettysburg.

11. The cashier forgot to give a reciept to my neice.

12. Our nieghbors have an electric fence around there yard.

13. Either you or I must solve this problem, or niether of us will sleep tonight.

14. I believe Sarah let go of her horse's reins and then fell.

15. I can't concieve of getting fewer than eight e-mails in one day.

EXERCISE 4 Writing Sentences

Use the word listed in each item in a complete sentence. Make sure your sentence answers the question or questions in parentheses following each word.

1. intercede   (Why would someone intercede? When? How?)

2. proceed   (Where or with what would you proceed?)

3. supersede   (What might supersede something else? Why?)

4. recede   (What might recede? When?)

5. concede   (Who might concede? Why?)

EXERCISE 5 Sentence Imitation

With a partner, read the sentences below. Revise each sentence so that it is about a different topic, but maintain the same structure and use the same parts of speech. In addition, keep the boldface words from the lesson in your revision.

1. The students in the **foreign** exchange program knew the team would never **concede** to its opponent.

   EXAMPLE   The diplomats in the **foreign** policy department thought the politician would soon **concede** to his rival.

2. Despite **their** rivalry, all of the teams shared the **belief** that maintaining the playing **field** was needed if they were to **succeed**.

3. The **neighbors** agreed that **neither** the shady park nor the open playing **field** should be sold off as private land.

4. During the **height** of the housing boom, several powerful companies attempted to **seize** the valuable public lands.

5. However, the community resisted by making **their** voices heard at the ballot box, and the companies had to **forfeit** the proposal.

Prefixes and Suffixes

Prefixes and suffixes are groups of letters that change a word's meaning. A **prefix** (such as *be-*, *im-*, *over-*, and *under-*) is added to the beginning of a word; a **suffix** (such as *-ance*, *-hood*, *-ism*, and *-less*) is added to the end.

▶ Adding a prefix does not change the spelling of the original word.

belabor **im**possible **over**estimate **under**rate

▶ If a word ends in *-y* preceded by a consonant, change the *-y* to *i* before adding a suffix.

bur**ial** craz**iness** merr**iment** tid**iest** worr**isome**

Note: Some words ending in *-y* retain the *-y* when adding a suffix: *dryness, shyness, flying, spying, crying, prying, trying, ladylike, babyhood.*

▶ If a word ends in *-y* preceded by a vowel, keep the *-y*.

destro**yer** emplo**yment** essa**yist** stra**ying** ba**ying**

▶ Adding the suffix *-ly* or *-ness* does not change the spelling of the original word.

usual**ly** manual**ly** calm**ness** kind**ness**

Exception: If a word ends in two *l*'s, drop one of the *l*'s before adding *-ly*:

full + ly = ful**ly**

▶ Drop a word's final silent *-e* before adding a suffix that begins with a vowel.

assur**ance** domina**tion** grac**ious** lov**able**
respons**ible** termina**tor**

Note: American dictionaries give *likable, lovable, movable,* and *sizable* as preferred spellings but do also include *likeable, loveable, moveable,* and *sizeable.* Consistently use the spelling that you choose.

A few words do retain the *-e* before a vowel.

acr**eage** dy**eing** ho**eing** mil**eage** ther**ein**

▶ Keep the final silent *-e* if the word ends in *-ge* or *-ce* and the suffix begins with *a* or *o*.

advanta**geous** chan**geable** coura**geous** servi**ceable**

Some Prefixes and Their Meanings

Prefix	Meaning
circum-	around
dis-, un-	the opposite
il-, im-, in-, ir-	not
post-	after
pre-	before
re-	again
sub-	below
super-	above, beyond

Some Suffixes and Their Meanings

Suffix	Meaning
-able	capable of being
-ate, -en, -fy	become, make
-dom, -hood	state of being
-er, -or	a person who
-less	without
-ment	state or condition of
-ous, -ful	full of

WRITING HINT

When a prefix appears before a single proper noun, a proper adjective, or a compound proper noun, add a hyphen.

anti-Semitic
all-American
pan-Asian
pre-World War II
trans-Canadian

▐▶ Keep the final silent -e before adding a suffix that begins with a consonant.

advertis**ement** care**ful** hop**eless** stat**ement** tim**ely**

EXCEPTIONS   argu**ment** aw**ful** tru**ly** whol**ly**

Note: American dictionaries give *judgment* and *acknowledgment* as the preferred spellings but also include *judgement* and *acknowledgement*.

▐▶ Double the final consonant in some one-syllable words when the suffix begins with a vowel. Doubling occurs when the word ends in a consonant preceded by a single vowel.

bi**gger** dra**gged** hi**dden** stir**ring** sto**pping** wra**pper**

▐▶ Double the final consonant in some words of more than one syllable. Doubling occurs if the word ends in a single consonant preceded by a single vowel and the new word is accented on the second syllable.

commi**tted** begi**nning** occu**rred** regre**ttable**

▐▶ Do not double the final consonant when the new word is not accented on the second syllable: *lightened, reckoned, altered.* This rule helps you understand why we have these mysterious pairs of related words: *referred, reference; preferred, preference; inferring, inference; conferring, conference.*

EXERCISE 6 Adding Prefixes and Suffixes

Write the word that results when the following prefixes or suffixes are added.

1. im + patient _____

2. admit + ed _____

3. outrage + ous _____

4. wise + dom _____

5. manage + ment _____

6. defy + ance _____

7. duty + ful _____

8. pay + ment _____

9. dull + ly _____

10. lovely + er _____

11. regret + ed _____

12. state + hood _____

13. be + little _____

14. kid + ed _____

15. notice + able _____

16. guide + ance _____

17. worry + er _____

18. marriage + able _____

19. sly + ness _____

20. like + able _____

Noun Plurals

The chart below has directions for how to form the plurals of nouns.

Making Nouns Plural		
KINDS OF NOUNS	**WHAT TO DO**	**EXAMPLES**
Most nouns	Add -s to the singular.	crackers, bottles, stick shifts
Nouns that end in -s, -x, -z, -ch, -sh	Add -es to the singular.	gases, bosses, boxes, waltzes, benches, wishes
Nouns that end in -y preceded by a consonant	Change the -y to i, and add -es.	hobbies, bodies, duties, inventories
Nouns that end in -y preceded by a vowel	Add -s.	plays, donkeys, decoys, joys, trolleys
Family names	Follow the four preceding rules, except for a name ending in a -y preceded by a consonant. In that case, add -s.	the Masons, the Parishes, the Alvarezes, the Kotlowitzes, the Murrays, the Kerenskys
Most nouns that end with -f	Add -s.	sheriffs, staffs, puffs, serfs
A few nouns that end in -f or -fe	Change the -f to -v and add -s or -es.	shelves, wolves, halves, elves, lives, selves, thieves
Nouns ending in -o preceded by a vowel	Add -s.	studios, rodeos, videos, zoos
Most nouns ending in -o preceded by a consonant	Add -es.	buffaloes, echoes, potatoes, vetoes
Most musical terms ending in -o	Add -s.	altos, sopranos, cellos, concertos, pianos, banjos
Compound nouns	Make the most important word plural.	mothers-in-law, cross sections, passersby, surgeons general
Letters, numbers, and words referred to as words	Use an apostrophe (') + -s.	D's, 6's, &'s, three yes's and two no's
Irregular plurals, foreign plurals, and words that stay the same in the singular and plural	No rules apply. Memorize these forms.	men, mice, trout, species, crises, algae, feet, teeth, oxen, swine, formulae

WRITING 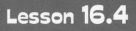 **HINT**

Spell-checkers are handy tools, and some are smarter than others, but no spell-checker takes the place of proofreading. That's because the computer won't know if you meant, say, *gas* or *gasp*, *has* or *as*, and *form* or *from*.

Note: There are some exceptions. Among them are *silos, avocados, Latinos, autos, pros,* and *memos*.

EXERCISE 7 Forming Plural Nouns

Write the plural form of each noun. If you're unsure of the correct form, check a dictionary to see if it lists irregular plurals or alternate plural forms. If no plural form is listed, follow the rules in the chart on page 297.

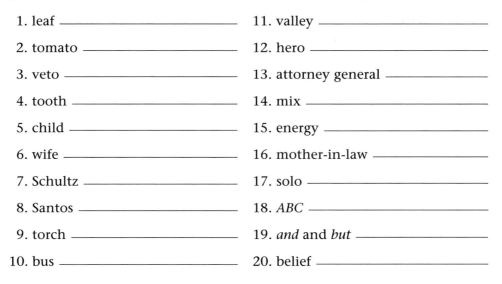

1. leaf _____

2. tomato _____

3. veto _____

4. tooth _____

5. child _____

6. wife _____

7. Schultz _____

8. Santos _____

9. torch _____

10. bus _____

11. valley _____

12. hero _____

13. attorney general _____

14. mix _____

15. energy _____

16. mother-in-law _____

17. solo _____

18. *ABC* _____

19. *and* and *but* _____

20. belief _____

EXERCISE 8 Finding More Than One Plural Form

Each of the following nouns has more than one acceptable plural form. Use a dictionary to find both and list them.

1. scarf _____ _____

2. volcano _____ _____

3. index _____ _____

4. syllabus _____ _____

5. mosquito _____ _____

6. hoof _____ _____

7. no _____ _____

8. radius _____ _____

9. zero _____ _____

10. fish _____ _____

Editing and Proofreading Worksheet 1

Edit the draft for errors in spelling, capitalization, punctuation, and usage. Write your edited version on a separate piece of paper. Compare your changes with those of a writing partner.

¹Todays big rigs are safer then ever. ²Due mainly to many new technological advancments. ³These allow companys to keep track of thier drivers, they also give drivers more options on the road.

⁴Like a Globeal Positionning System. ⁵This system, sends signalls to satellites, which then show the trucks position to whomever is monitorring that information. ⁶This keeps drivers on coarse. ⁷And on sckedule.

⁸Todays trucks are also equiped with radar. ⁹This system will cause alarms to go off when a truck gets too close to another vehicle. ¹⁰This has two important uses. ¹¹One is that it gives drivers time to avoid crashs. ¹²The second is that it gives the trucking company information on which truck drivers are regularily tailgateing.

¹³In the old days, CB radioes were indispensible on trucks, but these days, the truck driver stays in touch by e-mail. ¹⁴Wire-less modems enable drivers to have conversations with their dispatchers and others in corporate headquarters.

¹⁵The world of trucking is changeing in other ways, too. ¹⁶Devices for testing drowsyness are currently being developped. ¹⁷These devices would measure how drooppy a truckers eyelids are! ¹⁸(And how will they go about cureing this? ¹⁹Maybe by releaseing peppermint spray into the cab or shakeing the drivers seat.) ²⁰A lane tracker is also in developement that would beep if truckers were weaveing.

Editing and Proofreading Worksheet 2

Edit the draft for errors in spelling, capitalization, punctuation, and usage. Write your edited version on a separate piece of paper. Compare your changes with those of a writing partner.

[1]If you've got a few worrys about spelling, your not alone. [2]Even spelling experts conceed that English spelling is loaded with quirkes. [3]Much of the reason for this is that our language comes from such outragously varying sources. [4]Such as Latin, Greek, French, Scandanavian, just for starters. [5]For example, did you ever notice how you can pronounse *ch* as *ch*, *sh*, or *k*? [6]Well, the words with the *k* sound come from Greek, such as *anchor*, *chaos*, and *anarchy*. [7]The words with the *sh* sound come from French, like *chauffeur*, *chandeleir*, and *chef*. [8]And the one's with the *ch* sound? [9]Well. [10]They come from many sources, both foriegn and Old English.

[11]But *ch* isn't nothing compared with *sh*. [12]You can spell that sound about as many ways as you can concieve of, here are eight, *sheep*, *tissue*, *dominateion*, *permission*, *ocean*, *sure*, *suspicion*, and *mansion*. [13]Then theres even just plain *sh* (as in "be queit!").

[14]How should a person procede? [15]Just grit your tooths and bear it? [16]No! [17]Learn a few rules for the most common not the most wierd situations. [18]Like changeing -*y* to *i* to form words like *dutys* and *cherrys*. [19]And makeing nouns that end in -*o* preceeded by a consonnant plural by adding -*es*. [20]To make words such as *potatos* and *echos*. [21]And also learn all those decieving *i* before *e* excepttions, such as *sieze*, *niether*, and *liesure*. [22]Just take some time with these rules, and you will sucede!

Chapter Review

EXERCISE A Adding Prefixes and Suffixes

Write the word that results when the following prefixes or suffixes are added.

1. im + polite ——————
2. excite + ed ——————
3. rely + able ——————
4. courage + ous ——————
5. un + wise ——————
6. comply + ance ——————
7. bounty + ful ——————
8. arrange + ment ——————
9. dull + ly ——————
10. lovely + er ——————

11. commit + ed ——————
12. likely + hood ——————
13. mis + spell ——————
14. wed + ed ——————
15. manage + able ——————
16. recur + ence ——————
17. sorry + er ——————
18. dry + ness ——————
19. create + ive ——————
20. cohere + ence ——————

EXERCISE B Spelling Plural Nouns

In the space provided, write the plural form of each of the nouns listed below.
Use a dictionary to spell plurals you don't know.

1. ferry ——————
2. brother-in-law ——————
3. policy ——————
4. buffalo ——————
5. hippopotamus ——————
6. kangaroo ——————
7. cargo ——————
8. duty ——————
9. fax ——————
10. journey ——————

11. ratio ——————
12. pooch ——————
13. loaf ——————
14. industry ——————
15. reef ——————
16. peach ——————
17. chimney ——————
18. passerby ——————
19. waltz ——————
20. virus ——————

CHAPTER REVIEW

EXERCISE C Choosing the Correct Spelling

Look carefully at each choice, and then choose the correct spelling of each word. Write the letter of the correct spelling in the blank.

_____	1. (a) refered	(b) referred	(c) reffered
_____	2. (a) superceed	(b) supercede	(c) supersede
_____	3. (a) thiefs	(b) theives	(c) thieves
_____	4. (a) noteably	(b) notibly	(c) notably
_____	5. (a) oxes	(b) oxens	(c) oxen
_____	6. (a) moneys	(b) monys	(c) monnies
_____	7. (a) shelfs	(b) shelfes	(c) shelves
_____	8. (a) inference	(b) inferrence	(c) inferance
_____	9. (a) exceed	(b) excede	(c) exseed
_____	10. (a) arguement	(b) argument	(c) argumment
_____	11. (a) privelege	(b) privalege	(c) privilege
_____	12. (a) receed	(b) recede	(c) resede
_____	13. (a) recommendation	(b) reccommendation	(c) recomendation
_____	14. (a) dissapearance	(b) disapearance	(c) disappearance
_____	15. (a) temperment	(b) temperament	(c) tempermant
_____	16. (a) liesure	(b) leizure	(c) leisure
_____	17. (a) separate	(b) seperate	(c) separrate
_____	18. (a) imediately	(b) imediatly	(c) immediately
_____	19. (a) competant	(b) competent	(c) compatent
_____	20. (a) dissipline	(b) disciplin	(c) discipline

Cumulative Review

EXERCISE A Punctuation Marks

Add end marks and commas where they belong in the following paragraphs, and correct any spelling errors. Use the proofreading symbols shown below.

capital ≡	lower case /	apostrophe ⌄
period ⊙	semicolon ⨟	quotation marks ⌄⌄ ⌄⌄
comma ⌃	colon ⨢	parentheses ( )
hyphen =	dash ⊥/M	italics <u>mano-a-mano</u>

¹Some foriegners wonder why americans love cartoons so much? ²Whatever the reasons, cartoons are popular with all ages. ³No matter what age they are from two to ninety two people seem to enjoy cartoons. ⁴They remain the standard fare of saturday mornings. ⁵And other days and times too.

⁶Two of americas favorite cartoon heros are bugs bunny and daffy duck. ⁷The first bugs bunny cartoon was porkys hare hunt it appeared in 1937. ⁸You might wonder whether bugs asked his famous question whats up doc in that cartoon. ⁹In fact he didn't. ¹⁰Those well-known words didn't come out of bugs mouth until his fifth film appearance which occured in a wild hare in 1939.

¹¹Daffy Duck wasn't exactly daffy at first either. ¹²For example he didn't even have the name daffy until his second film appearance, in his first movie porkys duck 1936, he was refered to as "That darnfool duck. ¹³Well that darnfool duck or daffy has acheived just about as much fame as any duck in history. ¹⁴Along with bugs bunny, he's surely as fameous as the president.

EXERCISE B Capitalization

Add capital letters where they are needed in the following items. Use the proofreading symbol for capitalization: (c). Write C if the item is correct.

1. the *washington post*

2. the elizabethan age

3. the red river

4. the ship *old ironsides*

5. a spa in santa barbara

6. aunt chandra and uncle nanda

7. world literature and spanish

8. independence day

9. leo's bowlarama

10. the novel *tender is the night*

11. philip rowse, m.d.

12. at broadway and thirty-sixth

13. honda accord

14. yap island in the caroline islands

15. russian revolution

16. bill of rights

17. the song "michael, row the boat ashore"

18. the last days of summer

19. herculean efforts

20. internet explorer

EXERCISE C Spelling

On a separate piece of paper, rewrite each sentence, correcting the misspelled words.

1. Salim thought he saw elfs on the rooves of all the houses.

2. They are known for their relyable, courteyous busyness practices.

3. When were the first rodeoes held on the western fronteir?

4. Neither Mel nor Elena was promoted to cheif casheir.

5. At the conference, we recieved an update on endangered specieses.

6. They are conducting studys on the migrateion of Canadian gooses.

7. The Clancy's and the Cox's attended the reception.

8. There are two *c*s and two *m*s in *accommodate*.

9. At the begining of a party, people are serious; then they get sillyer and noisyer.

10. The boys spotted turkies and foxs in our nieghbor's woods.

Standardized Test Practice: Grammar and Usage

In addition to an essay component, standardized writing tests include a multiple-choice component that tests your understanding of standard written English. In this section of Level Orange, you will find four multiple-choice formats in four different sections. (For additional practice in standardized test formats with grammar feedback, go to www.grammarforwriting.com.) The four formats include:

- SAT Practice: Identifying Sentence Errors
- SAT Practice: Improving Sentences
- SAT Practice: Improving Paragraphs
- ACT Practice

Following these four sections is a practice test in which items from three formats are combined.

IDENTIFYING SENTENCE ERRORS

In this type of multiple-choice item, a sentence will have four words or phrases underlined and labeled **A** through **D**. Your task will be to identify an error, if there is one, and fill in the corresponding answer oval. If there is no error, your answer choice will be **E**, which is "No Error."

IMPROVING SENTENCES

In this section, your task will be not only to spot mistakes but fix them, too. In each test item, a sentence will be all or partly underlined. You must spot and fix an error, if there is one, within the underlined portion. Choices **B** through **E** each rephrase the underlined portion, serving as a possible replacement for it. Choice **A** repeats the underlined portion exactly as it is originally given. Choose **A** if you think the item is correct as is.

IMPROVING PARAGRAPHS

The test items in this section have the same structure as the ones in the Improving Sentences section but are keyed to a passage instead of an individual sentence. The items test your ability to revise and combine sentences within the context of an essay and improve its unity, organization and coherence, and word choice.

ACT PRACTICE

As its title suggests, this section is standardized test practice in ACT format. It includes two passages with grammar and usage items keyed to them. Like the Improving Paragraphs section, the test items ask you to revise and combine sentences within the context of an essay and improve its unity, organization and coherence, and word choice.

SAT Practice: Identifying Sentence Errors

Directions: In each item, one of the underlined words or phrases may contain an error in grammar, usage, word choice, or idiom. If there is an error, choose the underlined part that must be changed to make the sentence correct, and fill in the corresponding oval. If the sentence has no error, fill in oval E. In selecting answers, follow the requirements of standard written English.

Example

<u>Although</u> Jen had a keen interest in British history, <u>she spent</u>
  A   B

many hours in college <u>studying</u> the War of the Roses, a bloody
                    C

fifteenth-century struggle <u>traditionally seen</u> as the last dying
                                D

convulsion of the Middle Ages in England. <u>No error</u>
                                    E

Ⓐ Ⓑ Ⓒ Ⓓ Ⓔ

The correct choice is **A** because the subordinating conjunction, *Although*, is an illogical choice; it is *because* Jen had a keen interest in British history that she studied that violent period.

---

1. Neither the film's screenwriter, Nunnally Johnson, nor Henry Fonda,

<u>who was unforgettable</u> as Tom Joad, <u>was awarded</u> an Oscar for <u>their</u>
         A   B   C

work in *The Grapes of Wrath*, a movie regarded by many critics as

American cinema at <u>its</u> peak. <u>No error</u>
               D   E

Ⓐ Ⓑ Ⓒ Ⓓ Ⓔ

2. <u>Due to</u> the <u>immigration</u> patterns of recent decades, there <u>are</u> more
  A   B   C

Spanish speakers residing in Texas and California <u>than</u> New York.
                                               D

<u>No error</u>
 E

Ⓐ Ⓑ Ⓒ Ⓓ Ⓔ

3. To <u>whom</u> do you think the senator <u>was referring</u> when she <u>admitted</u>,
    A   B   C

somewhat reluctantly, that mistakes <u>were made</u> by some of her
                                   D

colleagues? <u>No error</u>   Ⓐ Ⓑ Ⓒ Ⓓ Ⓔ
          E

4. Frontier humor, <u>which</u> appeared <u>mainly</u> in tall tales of exaggerated
                   A   B

<u>feats</u> of strength and often included encounters with creatures such
 C

as snakes, panthers, and bears, <u>have reflected</u> the optimistic spirit of
                                      D

pre-Civil War America. <u>No error</u>   Ⓐ Ⓑ Ⓒ Ⓓ Ⓔ
                      E

5. *The Lottery*, Shirley Jackson's powerful <u>allegory</u> of brutality and
                                  A

social sacrifice, <u>recounts</u> the events in a small New England town
               B

<u>on the day of</u> <u>their</u> annual lottery. <u>No error</u>   Ⓐ Ⓑ Ⓒ Ⓓ Ⓔ
     C   D   E

6. Steven Spielberg's 2002 film *Catch Me If You Can* <u>focuses</u> on the
                                        A

escapades of an <u>illusive</u>, charismatic con artist <u>who manages</u>
                B   C

for quite some time to stay one step ahead of the detectives

<u>entrusted with his capture.</u> <u>No error</u>   Ⓐ Ⓑ Ⓒ Ⓓ Ⓔ
         D   E

7. The <u>length</u> of the Mississippi River, 3,740 miles, <u>which includes</u>
      A   B

its largest feeder, the Missouri River, <u>is</u> definitely shorter
                              C

<u>than either the Nile nor the Amazon.</u> <u>No error</u>   Ⓐ Ⓑ Ⓒ Ⓓ Ⓔ
        D   E

8. <u>Without barely</u> any recognition from art critics and unknown to his
     A

neighbors, some of <u>whom were</u> artists in <u>their</u> own right, the
            B   C

reclusive, self-taught sculptor <u>slowly</u> produced a formidable body of
                         D

extraordinary work. <u>No error</u>
              E

Ⓐ Ⓑ Ⓒ Ⓓ Ⓔ

9. <u>Because</u> the peanut, a legume once <u>commonly known</u> as a "goober,"
   A   B

<u>comes</u> from a prehistoric plant, <u>it</u> is a comparatively modern snack
 C   D

food. <u>No error</u>
      E

Ⓐ Ⓑ Ⓒ Ⓓ Ⓔ

10. In 1520, Ferdinand Magellan, <u>sailing</u> for <u>Spain, discovered</u> <u>near the</u>
                        A   B   C

southernmost tip of South America a strait that <u>soon became</u> a key
                               D

passageway to the Pacific Ocean. <u>No error</u>
                       E

Ⓐ Ⓑ Ⓒ Ⓓ Ⓔ

11. <u>Compared to</u> the challenging standards of <u>today's</u> crossword puzzles,
     A   B

the first of these mental exercises, <u>which</u> appeared in December of
                          C

1913, was trivially easy, containing <u>only</u> well-known words and
                          D

straightforward clues. <u>No error</u>
              E

Ⓐ Ⓑ Ⓒ Ⓓ Ⓔ

12. Entries at the crafts fair <u>were judged</u> <u>according to</u> how original
                        A   B

they were, how well they <u>made use of</u> everyday materials, and
                     C

<u>for their utility.</u> <u>No error</u>
  D   E

Ⓐ Ⓑ Ⓒ Ⓓ Ⓔ

13. <u>Although</u> this year's annual fundraising event <u>had been well attended,</u>
   A   B

the organizers noted, grudgingly, that there <u>were less people</u> there
                                               C

than <u>had shown</u> up in previous years. <u>No error</u>   Ⓐ Ⓑ Ⓒ Ⓓ Ⓔ
       D   E

14. The Pledge of Allegiance to the American flag <u>is</u> <u>neither</u> an old
                                              A   B

English verse <u>or</u> one created by the Founding Fathers; <u>it was, rather,</u>
           C   D

written in 1892 to commemorate that year's Columbus Day. <u>No error</u>   Ⓐ Ⓑ Ⓒ Ⓓ Ⓔ
                                                         E

15. Paleontologists have to work <u>carefully and meticulously</u>, and <u>you</u>
                                     A   B

also need patience to unearth <u>precious, ancient</u> artifacts
                               C

<u>without damaging</u> them in any way. <u>No error</u>   Ⓐ Ⓑ Ⓒ Ⓓ Ⓔ
        D   E

16. <u>In constant demand</u> as an inspirational speaker at corporate events,
           A

the former college football coach <u>had never been</u> <u>more busier</u>, even
                                       B   C

during his hectic days <u>pacing</u> the sidelines. <u>No error</u>   Ⓐ Ⓑ Ⓒ Ⓓ Ⓔ
                 D   E

17. <u>Anyone</u> today <u>who</u> sees photographs of dead Civil War soldiers must
      A   B

keep in mind how much <u>those images</u> <u>must of shocked</u> the nation
                          C   D

when they first appeared in 1862, after the bloody Battle of Antietam.

<u>No error</u>   Ⓐ Ⓑ Ⓒ Ⓓ Ⓔ
  E

18. For people who take their Gothic cathedrals serious, France is the
                             A   B

place to visit: The Cathedrals at Chartes, Reims, Rouen, and Amiens

are among the world's most spectacular examples of that
  C   D

architectural style. No error   Ⓐ Ⓑ Ⓒ Ⓓ Ⓔ
            E

19. Tanzania, which is the name they chose for the federation of
                A   B

Tanganyika and Zanzibar, the island off the east coast of Africa,

is one of the poorest countries in the world. No error   Ⓐ Ⓑ Ⓒ Ⓓ Ⓔ
  C   D   E

Directions: In each of the following items, all or part of the sentence is underlined. Beneath each sentence are five ways of phrasing the underlined part. Choice (A) is the same as the original; the other four choices are different. Select the answer choice that best expresses the meaning of the original sentence. Your goal is to produce the most effective sentence, one that is clear and not wordy. Choose (A) if the original sentence is better than any of the other answer choices.

Example

The countries of southern Europe, Portugal, Spain, Italy, and Greece, are mountainous and tend to depend more on agriculture <u>than the rest of Europe</u>.

(A) than the rest of Europe

(B) then the rest of Europe

(C) than the rest of Europe does

(D) than on the rest of Europe

(E) then does the rest of Europe

Ⓐ Ⓑ Ⓒ Ⓓ Ⓔ

The correct choice is **C**. The original sentence contains an incomplete comparison. Affixing "does" to the end of the sentence correctly completes the comparison. Choice **B** retains the incomplete comparison and incorrectly uses the adverb "then," a word commonly confused with the conjunction "than." Choice **D** does not correct the faulty comparison, and choice **E** incorrectly uses "then" to introduce the subordinate clause.

1. Rose Bertin, the first fashion designer to achieve fame and recognition, <u>dressing not only Marie Antoinette but also many in the French aristocracy</u>.

   (A) dressing not only Marie Antoinette but also many in the French aristocracy

   (B) dressing not only Marie Antoinette but many others in the French aristocracy

   (C) dressed not only Marie Antoinette but also many in the French aristocracy

(D) dressing not only Marie Antoinette but also dressed many in the French aristocracy

(E) dressed not only Marie Antoinette but did so with many others in the French aristocracy, too

Ⓐ Ⓑ Ⓒ Ⓓ Ⓔ

2. John Brown was a great hero to some, such as Frederick Douglass and Herman Melville, to others he was a villainous traitor, fully deserved of the noose.

(A) John Brown was a great hero to some, such as Frederick Douglass and Herman Melville, to others he was a villainous traitor, fully deserved of the noose.

(B) John Brown was a great hero to some, such as Frederick Douglass and Herman Melville, since to others he was a villainous traitor, fully deserved of the noose.

(C) John Brown was a great hero to some, such as Frederick Douglass and Herman Melville; therefore, to others he was a villainous traitor, fully deserved of the noose.

(D) John Brown was a great hero to some, such as Frederick Douglass and Herman Melville, but to others he was a villainous traitor, fully deserved of the noose.

(E) John Brown was a great hero to some, such as Frederick Douglass and Herman Melville; he was a villainous traitor, fully deserved of the noose.

Ⓐ Ⓑ Ⓒ Ⓓ Ⓔ

3. Fortunately, when the avalanche began, I remembered everything I had been taught that moment about cross-country skiing.

(A) Fortunately, when the avalanche began, I remembered everything I had been taught that moment about cross-country skiing.

(B) Fortunately, when the avalanche began, I remembered everything about cross-country skiing I had been taught that moment.

(C) Fortunately, at the moment when the avalanche began, I remembered everything I had been taught about cross-country skiing.

(D) Fortunately, when the avalanche began, I remembered everything I had been taught about cross-country skiing the moment it happened.

(E) When the avalanche began, I fortunately remembered everything that I had been taught about it.

Ⓐ Ⓑ Ⓒ Ⓓ Ⓔ

4. <u>Neither Agatha Christie nor P. D. James hold a candle to Dorothy Sayers; her witty and charming Lord Peter Wimsey runs circles around Miss Marple and Adam Dalgliesh.</u>

(A) Neither Agatha Christie nor P. D. James hold a candle to Dorothy Sayers; her witty and charming Lord Peter Wimsey runs circles around Miss Marple and Adam Dalgliesh.

(B) Neither Agatha Christie or P. D. James holds a candle to Dorothy Sayers; her witty and charming Lord Peter Wimsey runs circles around Miss Marple and Adam Dalgliesh.

(C) Neither Agatha Christie nor P. D. James hold a candle to Dorothy Sayers; her witty and charming Lord Peter Wimsey run circles around Miss Marple and Adam Dalgliesh.

(D) Neither Agatha Christie nor P. D. James holds a candle to Dorothy Sayers; her witty and charming Lord Peter Wimsey is running circles around Miss Marple and Adam Dalgliesh.

(E) Neither Agatha Christie nor P. D. James holds a candle to Dorothy Sayers; her witty and charming Lord Peter Wimsey runs circles around Miss Marple and Adam Dalgliesh. Ⓐ Ⓑ Ⓒ Ⓓ Ⓔ

5. <u>After diving for more than an hour, the shipwreck finally came into view.</u>

(A) After diving for more than an hour, the shipwreck finally came into view.

(B) Although diving for more than an hour, the shipwreck finally came into view.

(C) After they dived for more than an hour, the shipwreck finally came into view.

(D) After diving for more than an hour, the divers finally spotted the shipwreck.

(E) After the shipwreck finally came into view, they had been diving for more than an hour. Ⓐ Ⓑ Ⓒ Ⓓ Ⓔ

6. <u>In Ambrose Bierce's *In the Midst of Life*, he</u> includes the gripping short story, "An Occurrence at Owl Creek Bridge," which later appeared as a memorable episode on the TV series, *The Twilight Zone*.

(A) In Ambrose Bierce's *In the Midst of Life*, he

(B) In his book, *In the Midst of Life*, Ambrose Bierce

(C) In Ambrose Bierce's *In the Midst of Life*, the author

(D) In Ambrose Bierce's *In the Midst of Life*, the volume

(E) In writing *In the Midst of Life* Ambrose Bierce Ⓐ Ⓑ Ⓒ Ⓓ Ⓔ

7. In 1901, Sam Crawford, playing for the Cincinnati Reds, hit sixteen home runs, more <u>than anybody that season</u>.

(A) than anybody that season

(B) then anybody that season

(C) then anybody hit that season

(D) than anybody hit that season

(E) than anybody else hit that season

Ⓐ Ⓑ Ⓒ Ⓓ Ⓔ

8. Consuming several small meals each day <u>rather than to eat a few large ones are a healthier way to eat</u>.

(A) rather than to eat a few large ones are a healthier way to eat

(B) rather than to eat a few large ones is a healthier way to eat

(C) rather than eating a few large ones are a healthier way to eat

(D) rather than eating a few large ones is a healthier way to eat

(E) rather than to eat a few large ones are most likely healthy

Ⓐ Ⓑ Ⓒ Ⓓ Ⓔ

9. <u>No one eats more slow than Daniel, who routinely sifts</u> through his food to make sure no vegetables get into his mouth by mistake.

(A) No one eats more slow than Daniel, who routinely sifts

(B) No one eats more slow than Daniel, whom routinely sifts

(C) No one eats slower than Daniel, whom routinely sifts

(D) No one eats more slowly than Daniel does; he routinely sifts

(E) No one eats as slow as Daniel, who routinely sifts

Ⓐ Ⓑ Ⓒ Ⓓ Ⓔ

10. According to *The New Book of Lists* by David Wallechinsky and Amy Wallace, <u>you burn 500 calories an hour when making mountains out of molehills but only 75 calories</u> an hour by turning the other cheek.

(A) you burn 500 calories an hour when making mountains out of molehills but only 75 calories

(B) somebody burns 500 calories an hour when making mountains out of molehills but only 75 calories

(C) one burns 500 calories an hour when making mountains out of molehills but only 75 calories

(D) they burn 500 calories an hour when making mountains out of molehills but you only burn 75 calories

(E) one burns 500 calories an hour after making mountains out of molehills but is burning only 75 calories

Ⓐ Ⓑ Ⓒ Ⓓ Ⓔ

11. In 2003, Shirin Ebadi, an Iranian lawyer and human rights activist, became the first Muslim woman to have won the Nobel Peace Prize.

   (A) became the first Muslim woman to have won the Nobel Peace Prize

   (B) became the first Muslim woman having won the Nobel Peace Prize

   (C) becomes the first Muslim woman to have won the Nobel Peace Prize

   (D) became the first Muslim woman to win the Nobel Peace Prize

   (E) had become the first Muslim woman winning the Nobel Peace Prize

Ⓐ Ⓑ Ⓒ Ⓓ Ⓔ

12. Introducing readers to the personal and collective alienation typically found in postcolonial countries, V. S. Naipaul won critical acclaim for *A House for Mr. Biswas*.

   (A) Introducing readers to the individual and collective alienation typically found in postcolonial countries, V. S. Naipaul won critical acclaim for *A House for Mr. Biswas*.

   (B) Introducing readers to *A House for Mr. Biswas*, the individual and collective alienation typically found in postcolonial countries, V. S. Naipaul won critical acclaim.

   (C) V. S. Naipaul won critical acclaim for *A House for Mr. Biswas*, in which he introduced readers to the individual and collective alienation typically found in postcolonial countries.

   (D) V. S. Naipaul, in introducing readers to the individual and collective alienation typically found in postcolonial countries, won critical acclaim for *A House for Mr. Biswas*.

   (E) In *A House for Mr. Biswas*, introducing readers to the individual and collective alienation typically found in postcolonial countries, V. S. Naipaul won critical acclaim.

Ⓐ Ⓑ Ⓒ Ⓓ Ⓔ

13. Delivering messages by horseback for the Boston Committee of Safety was no doubt far more exciting for Paul Revere <u>than to be a practicing dentist, which he was from 1768 to 1775.</u>

(A) than to be a practicing dentist, which he was from 1768 to 1775

(B) than practicing dentistry, which he did from 1768 to 1775

(C) than to be a practicing dentist, which he did from 1768 to 1775

(D) than to practice being a dentist, which he did from 1768 to 1775

(E) than to be a practicing dentist from 1768 to 1775

Ⓐ Ⓑ Ⓒ Ⓓ Ⓔ

14. <u>The aging ballplayer, back for his fourteenth season, aims to compete vigorously, if not more vigorously, than he had in past seasons.</u>

(A) The aging ballplayer, back for his fourteenth season, aims to compete vigorously, if not more vigorously, than he had in past seasons.

(B) The aging ballplayer, back for his fourteenth season, aims to compete as vigorously as, if not more vigorously than, he had in past seasons.

(C) The aging ballplayer, back for his fourteenth season, aims to compete more vigorously as he had in past seasons.

(D) Back for his fourteenth season, the aging ballplayer aims to compete vigorously, if not more so than in past seasons.

(E) Back for his fourteenth season, the aging ballplayer aims to compete not as vigorously as, if not more vigorously that he had competed in past seasons.

Ⓐ Ⓑ Ⓒ Ⓓ Ⓔ

15. Johan Vaaler, a Norwegian, invented the paper clip in 1899; in Oslo, ninety years later, <u>a huge paper clip statue has been erected in his honor.</u>

(A) a huge paper clip statue has been erected in his honor

(B) a huge paper clip statue will be erected in his honor

(C) a huge statue of a paper clip was erected in his honor

(D) a huge paper clip statue had been erected in their honor

(E) a huge statue of a paper clip has been erected in his honor

Ⓐ Ⓑ Ⓒ Ⓓ Ⓔ

SAT Practice: Improving Paragraphs

ONLINE COMPONENTS
www.grammarforwriting.com

Directions: The passage that follows is an early draft of an essay. Some parts need to be rewritten. Read the passage carefully and answer the questions that follow. Cho ose the answer that most clearly and effectively expresses the writer's intended meaning. In making your decisions, follow the conventions of standard written English. After you have chosen your answer, fill in the corresponding oval.

(1) Places, like people, may not be what they seem to be at first glance. **(2)** Take New York City, the "Big Apple," for example. **(3)** People who have never had the pleasure of visiting this extraordinary city may be under the misperception that it is a dangerous, noisy, crowded, impersonal place. **(4)** However, a closer look tells a different story all together.

(5) First, it is a myth that New York is unsafe. **(6)** Statistics drawn from recent studies indicate that the Big Apple is one of the country's safest large cities. **(7)** It is safe day and night, thanks in part to one of the largest and best-trained police forces anywhere.

(8) Second, I know that New York may appear to you to be crowded, noisy, and impersonal. **(9)** But whereas Times Square, Wall Street, and the posh Fifth Avenue are always bustling, these are actually very small areas. **(10)** This city of more than 8 million residents consists of dozens and dozens of small, distinct neighborhoods, each with their own unique stores, galleries, restaurants, and personalities. **(11)** Together, these friendly, diverse neighborhoods create the rich tapestry that gives this great city its incomparable energy and style.

(12) Third, it's that style that sets New York apart, that keeps this venerable, historic American city young at heart. **(13)** Although some of its buildings hail from earlier eras, what goes on in them is often very modern indeed. **(14)** From within 100-year-old warehouses come new ideas in art, fashion, and food that have had repercussions in Paris, London, and Rome. **(15)** From small studios tucked away in 200-year-old downtown streets comes some of the most influential new music in the world. **(16)** From within its many top-notch colleges and conservatories comes the next wave of world-class dancers, singers, filmmakers, painters, and poets.

1. In context, what is the best way to deal with sentence 4 (reproduced below)?

However, a closer look tells a different story all together.

(A) Delete it.

(B) Switch it with sentence 3.

(C) Insert "on the other hand" after "However."

(D) Change "all together" to "altogether."

(E) Change "however" to "nonetheless."

2. In context, which of the following is the best version of the underlined portion of sentence 8 (reproduced below)?

Second, I know that New York may appear to you to be crowded, noisy, and impersonal.

(A) Secondly, I know that New York can appear to you

(B) Second, to people who do not know the city well, New York may appear

(C) I know that New York may appear to most

(D) Next, to a few people New York may appear

(E) And apparently, New Yorkers are known

Ⓐ Ⓑ Ⓒ Ⓓ Ⓔ

3. Which of the following is the best way to revise the underlined portion of sentence 10 (reproduced below)?

This city of more than 8 million consists of dozens and dozens of small, distinct neighborhoods, each with their own unique stores, galleries, restaurants, and personalities.

(A) each with their own unique stores, galleries, restaurants, and people

(B) each distinguished by their own stores, galleries, restaurants, and personality

(C) all with its own unique stores, galleries, restaurants, and personalities

(D) each having their own unique stores, galleries, restaurants, and personalities

(E) each with its own unique stores, galleries, restaurants, and personality.

Ⓐ Ⓑ Ⓒ Ⓓ Ⓔ

4. In context, which of the following is the best revision of sentence 14 (reproduced below)?

From within 100-year-old warehouses come new ideas in art, fashion, and food that have had repercussions in Paris, London, and Rome.

(A) (As it is now)

(B) From within 100-year-old warehouses and factories comes new ideas in art, fashion, and food that will have immediate repercussions in Paris, London, Rome, and, of course, all across America.

(C) From within 100-year-old warehouses and factories came new ideas in art, fashion, and food that will have immediate repercussions in Paris, London, Rome, and Milan. of course, all across America.

(D) From within 100-year-old warehouses and factories come new ideas in art, fashion, and food that will have repercussions in Paris, London, and Rome.

(E) From within 100-year-old warehouses and factories come new ideas in art, fashion, and food having immediate repercussions in Paris, London, and Rome.

Ⓐ Ⓑ Ⓒ Ⓓ Ⓔ

5. Which is the best way to revise and combine sentences 5 and 6 (reproduced below)?

First, it is a myth that New York is unsafe. Statistics drawn from recent studies indicate that the Big Apple is one of the country's safest large cities.

(A) First, it is a myth that New York is unsafe, but statistics drawn from recent studies indicate that the Big Apple is one of the country's safest large cities.

(B) First of all, it is a myth that New York is unsafe, and statistics drawn from recent studies indicate that the Big Apple is one of the country's safest large cities.

(C) First, it is a myth that New York is unsafe; statistics drawn from recent studies indicate that the Big Apple is one of the country's safest large cities.

(D) First of all, even though it is a myth that statistics drawn from recent studies indicate that the Big Apple is one of the country's safest large cities, New York is safe.

(E) It is a myth that New York is unsafe first of all; statistics drawn from recent studies indicate that the Big Apple is one of the country's safest large cities.

Ⓐ Ⓑ Ⓒ Ⓓ Ⓔ

6. Which of the following would make the most logical final sentence for the essay?

(A) It's the Big Apple: take a big hearty bite.

(B) You talkin' to me?

(C) So, wouldn't you agree that New York deserves, not a glance, but a long, close look?

(D) New York is a safe, clean, special modern city.

(E) This sums up what I have to say about New York.

Ⓐ Ⓑ Ⓒ Ⓓ Ⓔ

ACT Practice

Directions: You will find two reading passages in the left column and questions in the right column. In each of the passages, some words and phrases are underlined with a number underneath. The numbers refer to the questions at the right. Most questions ask you to choose the answer that best expresses the idea in standard written English or in the style of the passage. If you think the original wording is best, choose answer A, "NO CHANGE."

Other questions, indicated by a small number in a box, ask about the passage as a whole or about a particular section of the passage.

For each question, choose what you think is the best answer, and fill in the corresponding oval at the bottom of the page. Sometimes you will need to read several sentences beyond the numbered point in the passage to answer the question correctly.

Passage I

The Elevator Boy Poet

[1]

Paul Laurence Dunbar, poet, essayist, fiction writer, songwriter, and linguistic innovator, was born in 1872 in Dayton, Ohio, to two former slaves. He learned homespun wisdom from his mother, whom also taught him to read, and from
₁
his father, who escaped from enslavement and joining the Union Army during the
₂
Civil War.

1. **A.** NO CHANGE
   B. that
   C. who
   D. she

2. **F.** NO CHANGE
   G. will join the Union Army
   H. joined the Union Army
   J. was joining the Union Army

I. Ⓐ Ⓑ Ⓒ Ⓓ   2. Ⓕ Ⓖ Ⓗ Ⓙ

[2]

Dunbar, who himself was never enslaved, had ongoing contact with those who had been. He grew up steeped in oral tradition; and he would go on to become an influential interpreter of the African American experience and to champion civil rights as well as higher education for blacks. His writings, particularly his poems, in which he attempted to recreate authentic African American dialect, was considered militant by the standards of his time.

[3]

The only student of color at his high school in Dayton, Dunbar distinguished himself by his erudition and scholarly achievements. There, he had been reading the poetry of Keats, Wordsworth, Coleridge, and Burns; he also read the American poets Whittier and Longfellow. But it was not just the reading of those poets that influenced Dunbar. The body of

3. **A.** NO CHANGE
   B. tradition, and then he
   C. tradition, and he
   D. tradition, but he

4. **F.** NO CHANGE
   G. had been considered militant
   H. is considered militant
   J. were considered militant

5. **A.** NO CHANGE
   B. read
   C. had read
   D. had been reading

6. **F.** NO CHANGE
   G. Burns, he also
   H. Burns; and he also
   J. Burns; also

3. Ⓐ Ⓑ Ⓒ Ⓓ
4. Ⓕ Ⓖ Ⓗ Ⓙ

5. Ⓐ Ⓑ Ⓒ Ⓓ
6. Ⓕ Ⓖ Ⓗ Ⓙ

literature written in the plantation tradi-tion—works that romanticized plantation life—also helped him develop his own poetic voice.

[4]

Upon graduating from high school in 1891, Dunbar took a job as an elevator operator in a hotel. <u>Because he became</u> <u>known as the "elevator boy poet," he</u> <u>wrote on the job when time allowed.</u> Dunbar published his first volume of poetry just two years later, and <u>not hardly wasting</u> any time, Dunbar attended the World's Columbian Exposition in Chicago to sell copies of his book there. <u>It</u> soon <u>catched</u> the attention of Frederick Douglass, Booker T. Washington, and other influen-tial African Americans. Within the com-munity of black writers and literary critics, reactions to his writing were mixed. <u>Many praised his poetry for its</u> <u>righteous anger, some criticized Dunbar</u> <u>for not fully transcending the plantation</u> <u>tradition.</u> In 1972, with many prominent

7. Which of the following is the best version of this sentence?

   A. Because he wrote on the job when time allowed, he was becoming known as the "elevator boy poet."

   B. Because he wrote on the job when time allowed, he became known as the "elevator boy poet."

   C. When he wrote on the job when time allowed, he became known as the "elevator boy poet."

   D. When time on the job allowed for writing, he became known as the "elevator boy poet."

8. **F.** NO CHANGE
   G. not scarcely wasting
   H. not to be wasting
   J. not wasting

9. To what does "It" refer to in this sentence?

   A. World's Columbian Exposition
   B. Dunbar
   C. Dunbar's attendance
   D. His writing

10. **F.** NO CHANGE
   G. caught
   H. had been catching
   J. catches

11. Which word would be best to join the two independent clauses in this sentence?

   A. nevertheless,
   B. however,
   C. because
   D. but

7. Ⓐ Ⓑ Ⓒ Ⓓ
8. Ⓕ Ⓖ Ⓗ Ⓙ
9. Ⓐ Ⓑ Ⓒ Ⓓ

10. Ⓕ Ⓖ Ⓗ Ⓙ
11. Ⓐ Ⓑ Ⓒ Ⓓ

black poets and novelists in attendance, conferences were held at two universities to honor the centennial of his birth. What followed was a rebirth of appreciation of this gifted poet and his body of work, which was groundbreaking.
12

12

Passage II

Coyote and the Trader

[1]

Tales about tricks and pranks, especially when played by the lowly and poor on the mighty and rich, delighting audiences since the dawn of storytelling. In Native American legends, the trickster, an impish rebel and a breaker of taboos, appears in the form of Coyote. The exploits of this mischief-maker have been recounted from Alaska to Florida. When a tribe has a trickster of its own, Coyote often shows up in stories as his sidekick.
13
13
13
13
14
14
14
14
14

12. F. NO CHANGE
G. his groundbreaking body of work
H. his work, which was a ground-breaking body
J. his body of pioneering work, which was groundbreaking

13. Which of the following is the best version of this group of words?
A. Tales about tricks and pranks, especially when played by the lowly and poor on the mighty and rich, are delighting audiences since the dawn of storytelling.
B. Tales about tricks and pranks, especially when played by the lowly and poor on the mighty and rich, have delighted audiences since the dawn of storytelling.
C. Tales about tricks and pranks, especially when played by the lowly and poor on the mighty and rich: delighting audiences since the dawn of storytelling.
D. Tales about tricks and pranks played by the lowly and poor on the mighty and rich, especially, delighted audiences since the dawn of storytelling.

14. Which is the best way to combine these two sentences?
F. The exploits of this mischief-maker have been recounted from Alaska to Florida, although when a tribe has a trickster of its own, Coyote often shows up in stories as his sidekick.

---

12. Ⓕ Ⓖ Ⓗ Ⓙ
13. Ⓐ Ⓑ Ⓒ Ⓓ

14. Ⓕ Ⓖ Ⓗ Ⓙ

[2]

In one tale told by the Sioux, there is a clever trader who claims that he always got the better of anyone he deals with.
$\overline{15}$
Then one day, when the trader is boasting about his cheating skills, a customer tells him that there is indeed somebody who can outsmart him and then points to
$\overline{16}$
Coyote, who happens to be in the store at the time. The trader approaches Coyote and confidently challenges him.

[3]

Calm, the trickster tells the trader that,
$\overline{17}$
although he would like to help out, he can't do any outsmarting at the moment because he doesn't have his cheating medicine with him. Laughing, the trader suggests that Coyote should go and get it. In response, Coyote points out that he lives far away but that, if the trader will

G. The exploits of this mischief-maker have been recounted from Alaska to Florida, however, when a tribe has a trickster of its own, Coyote often shows up in stories as his sidekick.

H. The exploits of this mischief-maker have been recounted from Alaska to Florida; and when a tribe has a trickster of its own, Coyote often shows up in stories as his sidekick.

J. The exploits of this mischief-maker have been recounted from Alaska to Florida; even when a tribe has a trickster of its own, Coyote often shows up in stories as his sidekick.

15. A. NO CHANGE
　　B. gets
　　C. will get
　　D. will have gotten

16. F. NO CHANGE
　　G. the customer
　　H. the trader
　　J. Coyote

17. A. NO CHANGE
　　B. Calmly,
　　C. Calmingly,
　　D. Cleverly,

---

15. Ⓐ Ⓑ Ⓒ Ⓓ
16. Ⓕ Ⓖ Ⓗ Ⓙ

17. Ⓐ Ⓑ Ⓒ Ⓓ

permit him to borrow his fast horse, he
                         ___
                         18
can gallop home and get the medicine.

The trader hesitates, but then agrees to

loan Coyote his horse.
____
19

[4]

Coyote then adds that he is a poor

rider, that he is afraid of the horse, and so
                                  _____
                                      20
the horse might be afraid of him, too. He

suggests that, if the trader will lend him

his clothes, he can fool the horse into

thinking that he, Coyote, is the trader.

Reluctantly, but still quite confident that

he will in the end get his victory, the

trader agrees to give his clothes to Coyote.

So he does. As the trader stands there in
            _____
                      21
his underwear, Coyote rides away with his
_____
                 21
fast horse and fine clothes.
_____
          21

18. Who or what is the antecedent of
    "his"?
    F. the horse
    G. Coyote
    H. the trader
    J. the customer

19. **A.** NO CHANGE
    B. lend
    C. loan him
    D. sell

20. **F.** NO CHANGE
    G. horse, but
    H. horse, and even if
    J. horse, and that

21. Which would make the best choice as
    a concluding sentence to add after
    this one?
    A. There you have it.
    B. That was the last time anyone
           tried to outcheat Coyote.
    C. And that is how Coyote
           outsmarted the trader.
    D. And that was the last time the
           trader tried to cheat anybody.

18. Ⓕ Ⓖ Ⓗ Ⓙ
19. Ⓐ Ⓑ Ⓒ Ⓓ

20. Ⓕ Ⓖ Ⓗ Ⓙ
21. Ⓐ Ⓑ Ⓒ Ⓓ

Practice Test

Time—25 Minutes

You have 25 minutes to write an essay on the topic below.

DO NOT WRITE AN ESSAY THAT ADDRESSES ANY OTHER TOPIC. AN ESSAY ON A DIFFERENT TOPIC WILL NOT BE ACCEPTED.

Plan and write an essay on the assigned topic. Present your thoughts clearly and effectively. Include specific examples to support your views. The quality of your essay is more important than its length; but to express your ideas on the topic adequately, you will probably want to write more than one paragraph. Keep your writing to a reasonable size, and be sure to make your handwriting legible.

Consider the following statement. Then write an essay as directed.

"In the realm of ideas it is better to let the mind sally forth, even if some precious preconceptions suffer a mauling."

—Robert F. Goheen, Commencement speech, Princeton University, 1966

Assignment: Write an essay in which you agree or disagree with the statement above, using examples from history, current events, science, art, music, or your own experience to support your position.

WRITE YOUR ESSAY ON A SEPARATE SHEET OF PAPER.

Time—35 Minutes (49 questions)

Directions: In each item, one of the underlined words or phrases may contain an error in grammar, usage, word choice, or idiom. If there is an error, choose the underlined part that must be changed to make the sentence correct, and fill in the corresponding oval. If the sentence has no error, fill in oval E. In selecting answers, follow the requirements of standard written English.

Example

<u>As</u> her mother did before <u>her</u>, Anna, <u>who</u> is very interested
A   B   C

in medicine, <u>will have gone</u> to medical school. <u>No error</u>
                    D   E

Ⓐ Ⓑ Ⓒ Ⓓ Ⓔ

1. All members of the bobsled team <u>believe</u> that <u>their</u> chances
                                              A   B

   <u>of winning</u> a medal at the upcoming games <u>were</u> better than
       C   D

   fifty-fifty. <u>No error</u>
                     E

Ⓐ Ⓑ Ⓒ Ⓓ Ⓔ

2. <u>Either</u> a junior or a senior <u>will be chosen</u> to represent <u>our</u> school in
       A   B   C

   the poetry contest that <u>will be taking place</u> later this semester.
                                  D

   <u>No error</u>
       E

Ⓐ Ⓑ Ⓒ Ⓓ Ⓔ

3. <u>Whomever</u> else decides to run for mayor <u>will encounter</u> a very
       A   B

   strong field of worthy candidates, each of <u>whom</u> <u>boasts</u> outstanding
                                                    C   D

   credentials and deep pockets. <u>No error</u>
                                         E

Ⓐ Ⓑ Ⓒ Ⓓ Ⓔ

4. Accustomed to <u>being</u> <u>complemented</u> for his <u>impeccable</u> taste in
             A   B   C

clothing, Jed was quite surprised at the modest reaction to what he

<u>had thought</u> was a very stylish new jacket. <u>No error</u>   Ⓐ Ⓑ Ⓒ Ⓓ Ⓔ
    D   E

5. <u>Known</u> for his adroit manipulation of traditional genres,
    A

E. L. Doctorow, the author of *The March*, <u>wrote, among other things,</u>
                                               B

The Book of Daniel, a fictionalized account of the Rosenberg trial;

Billy Bathgate, a coming-of-age story set during the Great Depression;

and <u>he also wrote</u> *Ragtime*, a novel set in early <u>twentieth-century</u>
       C   D

America. <u>No Error</u>   Ⓐ Ⓑ Ⓒ Ⓓ Ⓔ
        E

6. <u>What</u> novel <u>begins</u> with the line, "When he was nearly thirteen, my
    A   B

brother Jem got his arm <u>badly</u> broken at the <u>elbow</u>"? <u>No error</u>   Ⓐ Ⓑ Ⓒ Ⓓ Ⓔ
                         C   D   E

7. Bolivia <u>has a</u> gross domestic product per capita of $2,400, <u>which</u>
         A   B

<u>is less than</u> <u>any country</u> in South America. <u>No error</u>   Ⓐ Ⓑ Ⓒ Ⓓ Ⓔ
   C   D   E

8. When Jonas told his <u>cousin Salim</u> that James Joyce's *Dubliners* was
                                 A

rejected by twenty-two publishers before it <u>was finally published</u> by
                                                       B

Grant Richards in 1914, <u>his</u> facial expression showed how
                                    C

astonishing that fact <u>was.</u> <u>No error</u>   Ⓐ Ⓑ Ⓒ Ⓓ Ⓔ
                      D   E

9. According to legend, Gilgamesh, king of Uruk, <u>who</u> was half man,
                                                        A

half beast, <u>sought</u> the secret of eternal life but <u>couldn't never</u> find <u>it.</u>
                B   C   D

<u>No error</u>   Ⓐ Ⓑ Ⓒ Ⓓ Ⓔ
  E

10. The acceptance of railroads came quickly in the <u>1830s, although</u>
                                                 A

there <u>was</u> some <u>opposition: ministers</u> preached against the "iron
          B   C

horse," doctors warned of <u>excessive</u> speed, and canal and turnpike
                                    D

companies were hostile. <u>No error</u>   Ⓐ Ⓑ Ⓒ Ⓓ Ⓔ
                       E

11. The Iran-Contra affair, <u>which</u> <u>they</u> said was fraught with numerous
                                 A   B

violations of federal laws, <u>grew</u> out of a series of covert actions by
                           C

National Security Council <u>officials.</u> <u>No error</u>   Ⓐ Ⓑ Ⓒ Ⓓ Ⓔ
                            D   E

12. Economist and social critic Thorstein Veblen <u>wrote about what he</u>
A

<u>believed</u> to be an unstable dichotomy in modern <u>society</u>,
  A   B

<u>differentiating</u> <u>among</u> industrial occupations, <u>which</u> involved the
      B   C   D

machine production of goods, and business occupations, which

involved sales of goods in the pursuit of profit. <u>No error</u>
E

Ⓐ Ⓑ Ⓒ Ⓓ Ⓔ

13. Maxim Gorky, the Russian <u>short-story</u> writer and novelist who
A

<u>first attracted</u> attention with <u>their</u> sympathetic stories of vagrants
      B   C

and other social outcasts, <u>was himself once</u> an impoverished and
D

bitter wanderer who meandered throughout southern Russia.

<u>No error</u>
E

Ⓐ Ⓑ Ⓒ Ⓓ Ⓔ

14. Neither the steady rain nor the near-frigid temperature <u>were</u> enough
A

to prevent the game from <u>being completed</u> that bitter Sunday
B

evening; <u>the umpires were</u> steadfast <u>in their determination to get</u> the
          C   D

game in. <u>No error</u>
         E

Ⓐ Ⓑ Ⓒ Ⓓ Ⓔ

15. I think that ham and cheese sandwiches taste <u>badly</u> when
A

<u>they are made</u> with mayonnaise <u>as well as</u> with mustard and that
      B   C

they are particularly <u>inedible</u> when they are made on any kind of
D

bread other than rye. <u>No error</u>
                     E

Ⓐ Ⓑ Ⓒ Ⓓ Ⓔ

16. Because he is a legend today, Geronimo's courage and determination
                    A

sustained the spirits of the Chiricahua Apaches during the last days
        B

of the Indian wars that took place in the late nineteenth century.
                        C   D

No error   Ⓐ Ⓑ Ⓒ Ⓓ Ⓔ
    E

17. Although the game of squash is often compared with the game of
        A   B

racquetball, squash players liken the strike of the ball more to a
                            C

fencing thrust than to a racquetball swing. No error   Ⓐ Ⓑ Ⓒ Ⓓ Ⓔ
                D   E

18. The term *tuxedo* has glamorous and formal connotations, but it
                                            A

actually derives from a mispronunciation of an Algonquian word
        B

being employed by those early inhabitants of the area in New York
        C

known as Tuxedo Park. No error   Ⓐ Ⓑ Ⓒ Ⓓ Ⓔ
        D   E

Directions: In each of the following items, all or part of the sentence is underlined. Beneath each sentence are five ways of phrasing the underlined part. Choice (A) is the same as the original; the other four choices are different. Select the answer choice that best expresses the meaning of the original sentence. Your goal is to produce the most effective sentence, one that is clear and not wordy. Choose (A) if the original sentence is better than any of the other answer choices.

Example

Upon returning from his scouting mission during the Battle of Chancellorsville, Confederate soldiers accidentally shot General Thomas "Stonewall" Jackson.

(A) Upon returning from his scouting mission during the Battle of Chancellorsville, Confederate soldiers accidentally shot General Thomas "Stonewall" Jackson.

(B) Upon returning from his scouting mission during the Battle of Chancellorsville, Confederate soldiers accidentally shot general Thomas "Stonewall" Jackson.

(C) Upon returning from his scouting mission during the Battle of Chancellorsville, General Thomas "Stonewall" Jackson was accidentally shot by Confederate soldiers.

(D) Upon returning from his scouting mission during the Battle of Chancellorsville, Confederate soldiers were shot accidentally by General Thomas "Stonewall" Jackson.

(E) Confederate soldiers shot general Thomas "Stonewall" Jackson accidentally upon returning from his scouting mission during the Battle of Chancellorsville.

Ⓐ Ⓑ ● Ⓓ Ⓔ

19. When Poe's "The Pit and the Pendulum" was first published in *The Gift* (a yearly book of verse and stories) in 1843, it secured his reputation as a master of graphic gothic tension.

(A) it secured his reputation as a master of graphic gothic tension

(B) his reputation as a master of graphic gothic tension was secured

(C) it was securing his reputation as a master of graphic gothic tension

(D) his reputation for graphic gothic tension mastery was being secured

(E) it secured his reputation for being a master of graphic gothic tension   Ⓐ Ⓑ Ⓒ Ⓓ Ⓔ

20. The Volga is the <u>fifth-longest river in Russia, it is the sixteenth longest in the world</u>.

(A) fifth-longest river in Russia, it is the sixteenth longest in the world

(B) fifth-longest river in Russia, nonetheless, it is the sixteenth longest in the world

(C) fifth-longest river in Russia; and it is the sixteenth longest in the world

(D) fifth-longest river in Russia and the sixteenth longest in the world

(E) fifth-longest river in Russia it is the sixteenth longest in the world   Ⓐ Ⓑ Ⓒ Ⓓ Ⓔ

21. Miracle plays, which were popular vernacular dramas in Europe during the Middle Ages, <u>have been banned in England by Henry VIII in the sixteenth century</u>.

(A) have been banned in England by Henry VIII in the sixteenth century

(B) having been banned in England by Henry VIII in the sixteenth century

(C) were banned in England by Henry VIII in the sixteenth century

(D) but were banned in England by Henry VIII in the sixteenth century

(E) have been banned by Henry VIII in England in the Sixteenth Century   Ⓐ Ⓑ Ⓒ Ⓓ Ⓔ

22. For many minor league stars, the inability to successfully hit major league pitchers' curveballs <u>are what keeps them in the minors</u>.

(A) are what keeps them in the minors

(B) are what's keeping them in the minors

(C) is what keeps them as minors

(D) is what keeps them in the minors

(E) are keeping them in the minors   Ⓐ Ⓑ Ⓒ Ⓓ Ⓔ

23. <u>Dams were built along the Klamath River that diverted water to the farmers inland.</u>

(A) Dams were built along the Klamath River that diverted water to the farmers inland.

(B) Dams that diverted water to the farmers inland were built along the Klamath River.

(C) Diverting water to the farmers inland, dams were built along the Klamath River.

(D) Inland dams were built along the Klamath River to divert water to the farmers.

(E) Dams were built along the Klamath River, which diverted water to the farmers inland.

Ⓐ Ⓑ Ⓒ Ⓓ Ⓔ

24. <u>Along with a number of other players, Guerrero's fine play in the tennis tournament caught the attention of several sportswriters and commentators.</u>

(A) Along with a number of other players, Guerrero's fine play in the tournament caught the attention of several sportswriters and commentators.

(B) Along with the fine play of a number of other players in the tournament, Guerrero caught the attention of several sportswriters and commentators.

(C) The fine play of Guerrero and that of a number of other players in the tournament caught the attention of several sportswriters and commentators.

(D) The fine play of Guerrero and of a number of other players caught the attention of several sportswriters and commentators in the tournament.

(E) Guerrero's fine play in the tournament, along with a number of other players, caught the attention of several sportswriters and commentators.

Ⓐ Ⓑ Ⓒ Ⓓ Ⓔ

25. <u>In Giuseppe Tomasi di Lampedusa's *The Leopard*, he provides a psychological study of how one prince comes to terms with the loss of the Bourbon aristocracy's power in Italy.</u>

(A) In Giuseppe Tomasi di Lampedusa's *The Leopard*, he provides a psychological study of how one prince comes to terms with the loss of the Bourbon aristocracy's power in Italy.

(B) In *The Leopard*, by Giuseppe Tomasi di Lampedusa, he provides a psychological study of how one prince comes to terms with the loss of the Bourbon aristocracy's power in Italy.

(C) In *The Leopard*, Giuseppe Tomasi di Lampedusa provides a psychological study of how one prince comes to terms with the loss of the Bourbon aristocracy's power in Italy.

(D) In *The Leopard*, a psychological study of how one prince came to terms with the loss of the Bourbon aristocracy's power in Italy, is provided by Giuseppe Tomasi di Lampedusa.

(E) In Giuseppe Tomasi di Lampedusa's *The Leopard*, a psychological study of one prince coming to terms with the loss of the Bourbon aristocracy's power in Italy is provided. Ⓐ Ⓑ Ⓒ Ⓓ Ⓔ

26. Trying to look as calmly as I could despite the fear I felt, I slowly negotiated my way backward, away from the menacing rattler that was sunning itself on a rock.
   (A) Trying to look as calmly as I could
   (B) Trying to look calm, if I could
   (C) Looking to be calm
   (D) Trying to look as calm as I could
   (E) Trying as I could to look calmly Ⓐ Ⓑ Ⓒ Ⓓ Ⓔ

27. Spelunkers take lanterns, food, and water with them when they descend into a cave, and you also wear sturdy shoes and warm clothing.
   (A) descend into a cave, and you also wear sturdy shoes and warm clothing
   (B) descend into a cave, and they also wear sturdy shoes and warm clothing
   (C) dissent into a cave, and they also wear sturdy shoes and warm clothing
   (D) descend into a cave, and also you wear sturdy shoes and warm clothing
   (E) decent into a cave, wearing sturdy shoes and warm clothing Ⓐ Ⓑ Ⓒ Ⓓ Ⓔ

28. When several angry protestors greeted him as he emerged from his office, the embattled mining company executive remarked that he should of seen it coming.

(A) that he should of seen it coming

(B) that he should of saw it coming

(C) that he should have seen it coming

(D) that he should see it coming

(E) that he had seen it coming

Ⓐ Ⓑ Ⓒ Ⓓ Ⓔ

29. No one who witnessed the firing on Fort Sumter that April morning could have foreseen they would suffer four full years of bloody war.

(A) No one who witnessed the firing on Fort Sumter that April morning could have foreseen that they would suffer

(B) No one whom witnessed the firing on Fort Sumter that April morning could have foreseen that they would suffer

(C) No one that witnessed the firing on Fort Sumter that April morning could have foreseen that he or she would be suffering

(D) No one who witnessed the firing on Fort Sumter that April morning could have foreseen that the nation would suffer

(E) No one who witnessed the firing on Fort Sumter that April morning could have foreseen that it would suffer

Ⓐ Ⓑ Ⓒ Ⓓ Ⓔ

30. Upon leaving the court for the final time late in the fourth quarter, the appreciative fans gave the basketball star a rousing standing ovation.

(A) Upon leaving the court for the final time late in the fourth quarter, the appreciative fans gave the basketball star a rousing standing ovation.

(B) Upon leaving the court for the final time late in the fourth quarter, the basketball star gave the appreciative fans a rousing standing ovation.

(C) Upon the appreciative fans giving the basketball star a rousing standing ovation, he left the court for the final time late in the fourth quarter.

(D) Upon leaving the court the appreciative fans gave the basketball star a rousing standing ovation for the final time late in the fourth quarter.

(E) Upon leaving the court for the final time late in the fourth quarter, the basketball star got a rousing standing ovation from the appreciative fans.

31. The fleeing outlaw galloped out of town, followed a trail along the river bank, and rode on to his hideout in the mountains.

(A) The fleeing outlaw galloped out of town, followed a trail along the river bank, and rode on to his hideout in the mountains.

(B) The fleeing outlaw galloped out of town, and followed a trail along the river bank, and he rode on to his hideout in the mountains.

(C) The fleeing outlaw gallops out of town, follows a trail along the river bank, and he rides on to his hideout in the mountains.

(D) The fleeing outlaw galloped out of town, followed a trail along the river bank; and then he rode on to his hideout in the mountains.

(E) The fleeing outlaw galloped out of town following a trail along the river bank, and he rode on to his hideout in the mountains.

32. Because it was bitterly cold in the apartment during winter's last blast, the window had been opened wide.

(A) Because it was bitterly cold in the apartment during winter's last blast, the window had been opened wide.

(B) Because it was bitter cold in the apartment during winter's last blast, the window had been opened wide.

(C) Because of winter's last blast, it was bitterly cold in the apartment, and the window was wide open.

(D) Because it was so bitterly cold during winter's last blast, the window in the apartment had been opened wide.

(E) Because the window had been opened wide during winter's last blast, it was bitterly cold in the apartment.

Directions: The passage that follows is an early draft of an essay. Some parts need to be rewritten. Read the passage carefully and answer the questions that follow. Choose the answer that most clearly and effectively expresses the writer's intended meaning. In making your decisions, follow the conventions of standard written English. After you have chosen your answer, fill in the corresponding oval.

(1) In any President's administration, the composition of the cabinet is a key issue. (2) Some Presidents choose to surround themselves with people who think the same way they do. (3) Other Presidents fill cabinet posts with the most capable people they were able find, regardless of those people's political views. (4) In my opinion, that second approach is the one that works best, hands down.

(5) A President who chooses the first approach is likely to pick men and women who have worked in or contributed substantially to their election campaigns or who think exactly as they do. (6) These team members loyally support the President's views and policies. (7) When crises occur, this kind of administration speaks with one voice. (8) I believe that by ignoring opposing views, such an administration does not represent the thinking of many Americans.

(9) But when our nation faced its greatest challenge, the crisis of civil war, there was an all together different kind of administration in office. (10) When Lincoln picked his cabinet, he chose the best people he could find. (11) That group included his political opponents as well as his supporters. (12) He actively sought conflicting viewpoints and encouraged honest, substantive debates about the serious issues facing the country. (13) Lincoln listened to everyone, heard all the different arguments, and then made his decisions. (14) It served the country very well during those troubled times.

(15) When a government faces great challenges, as all governments do, it is far better for its leaders to be looking at all sides of the issues before acting. (16) It is far better for the country when Presidents listen to a variety of opinions from keen minds across the political spectrum. (17) How would an administration composed solely of like minds have performed had it faced the critical choices that faced Lincoln's?

33. In context, which of the following is the best way to deal with sentence 3 (reproduced below)?

Other Presidents fill cabinet posts with the most capable people they were able to find, regardless of those people's political views.

(A) Other Presidents are filling cabinet posts with the most capable people they were able to find, regardless of those people's political views.

(B) Other Presidents, regardless of their political views, fill cabinet posts with the most capable people they are able to find.

(C) In contrast, other Presidents fill cabinet posts with the most capable people they can find, regardless of those people's political views.

(D) Because other Presidents fill cabinet posts with the most capable people they can find, regardless of those people's political views.

(E) Nevertheless, other Presidents filled cabinet posts with the most capable people they were able to find, regardless of those people's political views.

Ⓐ Ⓑ Ⓒ Ⓓ Ⓔ

34. In context, which of the following is the best revision of sentence 5 (reproduced below)?

A President who chooses the first approach is likely to pick men and women who have worked in or contributed substantially to their election campaigns or who think exactly as they do.

(A) A President who chooses the first approach is likely to pick men and women who have worked in or contributed substantially to his or her election campaigns or who think exactly as he or she does.

(B) A President who chooses the first approach is likely to pick men and women whom have worked in or contributed substantially to their election campaigns or who think exactly as they do.

(C) A President who chooses the first approach is likely to pick men and women who have worked in or contributed substantially to his or her election campaigns or who have thought exactly as they do.

(D) A President choosing the first approach is likely to pick men and women that have worked in or contributed substantially to their election campaigns or who think exactly as he or she does.

(E) Presidents who choose the first approach are likely to pick men and women who have worked in or contributed substantially to his or she election campaigns or who think exactly as he or she does.

Ⓐ Ⓑ Ⓒ Ⓓ Ⓔ

35. Which of the following is the best revision of the underlined portion of sentence 9 (reproduced below)?

But when our nation faced its greatest challenge, the crisis of civil war, there was an all together different kind of administration in office.

(A) there was an all together different sort of administration

(B) there is an altogether different kind of administration

(C) it was an altogether different kind of administration

(D) there was an altogether different kind of administration

(E) they were a totally different kind of administration

36. In context, which of the following is the best way to revise and combine sentences 10 and 11 (reproduced below)?

When Lincoln picked his cabinet, he chose the best people he could find. That group included his political opponents as well as his supporters.

(A) When Lincoln picked his cabinet, he chose the best people he could find, including a group of his political opponents and supporters.

(B) When Lincoln picked his cabinet, he chose the best people he could find, assembling a group that included his political opponents as well as his supporters.

(C) When Lincoln picked his cabinet, he chose the best people he could find: his political opponents as well as his supporters.

(D) When Lincoln picked his cabinet from among the best people he could find, it included his political opponents as well as his supporters.

(E) When Lincoln picked his cabinet, he chose the best people he could find; his political opponents as well as his supporters.

37. In context, which of the following most logically replaces "It" in sentence 14 (reproduced below)?

It served the country very well during those troubled times.

(A) (As it is now)

(B) They

(C) That way of thinking

(D) This way of acting

(E) This approach to governing

38. In context, which of the following revisions is necessary in sentence 15 (reproduced below)?

When a government faces great challenges, as all governments do, it is far better for its leaders to be looking at all sides of the issues before acting.

(A) Change "to be looking" to "to have looked."

(B) Delete "as all governments do."

(C) Insert "As you can see" at the beginning.

(D) Change "to be looking" to "to look."

(E) Delete "all sides of" and insert "both domestic and foreign," after "issues."

Ⓐ Ⓑ Ⓒ Ⓓ Ⓔ

39. Which of the following is best to add after sentence 17 as a concluding sentence?

(A) Fabulously!

(B) Perhaps it would have performed rather poorly and inefficiently.

(C) The answer to that question, I contend, would be "Not very well at all."

(D) Unfortunately, we will never know.

(E) It would have failed; these men would not know anything about historical issues.

Ⓐ Ⓑ Ⓒ Ⓓ Ⓔ

Commonly Confused Words

▸ **accept, except** *Accept* is a verb that means " to receive" or "to agree to." *Except* is a preposition that means "but."

Please **accept** my apology.

I have considered every issue **except** that one.

▸ **advice, advise** *Advice* is a noun that means "recommendation" or "words of council." *Advise* is a verb that means "to give advice."

The guidance counselor gave me some **advice** on classes.

Can you **advise** me on what college to visit?

▸ **affect, effect** *Affect* is a verb that means "to influence." The noun *effect* means "the result of an action." The verb *effect* means "to cause" or "to bring about."

Changing the temperature will **affect** the baking time.

No one knows the full **effect** of the recent floods.

With these new rules, we hope to **effect** some changes in behavior.

▸ **all ready, already** Use *all ready* to mean "completely ready." Use *already* to mean "previously."

The lawyers are **all ready** for the impending trial.

I have **already** spoken to my parents about this.

▸ **all right** Spell *all right* as two separate words. The word *alright* is not acceptable in formal written English.

I think I did **all right** on the test.

▸ **all together, altogether** Use *All together* to refer to a group that is in the same place or in unison. Use *altogether* to mean "wholly, entirely."

We spent forty dollars **all together**.

Henry was **altogether** ashamed of what he had done.

▸ **amount, number** Both words refer to a quantity. Use *amount* with nouns that cannot be counted (for example, *water* or *sand*). Use *number* with nouns that can be counted (for example, *books* or *calories*).

The **amount** of junk mail that we receive is staggering.

The **number** of people at the party kept increasing.

▸ **bad, badly** Use *bad* as an adjective and as a predicate adjective after linking verbs. **Remember:** A predicate adjective describes the subject. Use *badly*, an adverb, to modify an action verb.

We feel **bad** about the mess we made.　　The room smelled **bad**.

Unfortunately, the actor played his part **badly**.　　He **badly** needs to practice.

beside, besides *Beside* means "by the side of." *Besides* as a preposition means "in addition to." *Besides* as an adverb means "moreover."

>We rested **beside** the falls. **Besides** me, John and Dolores were there.
>We were hungry; **besides**, we were tired of lugging our packs.

between, among Use *between* when you are comparing two people or things. You can also use *between* when discussing three or more things if you think only two will be compared at a time. Use *among* to refer to a group or to three or more people or things.

>I cannot choose **between** that bicycle and this one.
>Matt divided the remaining water **among** the three of us.

could (might, should, would) of Use *have*, not *of*, with these helping verbs.

>I **could have** listened to that music all night.
>Jen **should have** practiced her speech in front of her friends.

different from Use *from*, not *than*, after *different* when a noun, pronoun, or noun phrase follows. When you are introducing a clause, *different than* is acceptable.

>This pattern is **different from** that one.
>This quilt looks **different than** that quilt looks.

farther, further *Farther* refers to a physical distance. *Further* means "to a greater degree or extent."

>Today, I ran almost one mile **farther** than Jackie.
>We need to discuss this matter **further**.

fewer, less *Fewer* refers to nouns that can be counted. *Less* is used with nouns that cannot be counted.

>We have **fewer** flowers this year than we had last year.
>There is **less** chance of my going if it rains.

good, well *Good* is always an adjective, never an adverb. *Well*, however, can be both. The adverb *well* means "done in a satisfactory way." The adjective *well* means "in good health."

>Rena got a **good** grade on her test; she did **well** on it.
>I can't play tennis **well** when I don't feel **well**.
>I felt **good** when my puppy began to get **well**.

imply, infer Use *imply* to mean "hint"; use *infer* to mean "draw a conclusion."

>Are you trying to **imply** that I didn't do my job well?
>From her expression, I could **infer** that Ms. Kang was pleased with my essay.

▶ **irregardless, regardless** Always use *regardless*; *irregardless* isn't a word.

> Will the manager be fired, **regardless** of his track record?

▶ **lay, lie** *Lay* is a verb that means "to place" or "to put." *Lay* always takes an object. *Lie* means "to recline" or "to say something that is not true." *Lie* never takes an object. (See Lessons 9.2 and 9.3 for the principal parts of these verbs.)

> I will **lay** the first row of bricks for the fireplace.
> Jennifer **lies** down to take a nap.
> Did Joan **lie** about taking the money?

▶ **off, off of** Don't use *of* after the prepositions *inside, outside,* and *off.* Also, use *from*, not *off* or *off of*, when you're referring to the source of something.

> The Wyzickis live just **outside** [not *outside of*] Detroit.
> I got the information **from** [not *off* or *off of*] the Internet.

▶ **raise, rise** *Raise* means "to cause to move upward." It always takes an object. *Rise* means "to get up." It never takes an object.

> Please do not **raise** your voice to me.
> My mother and father **rise** before dawn every day.

▶ **set, sit** *Sit* means "to place oneself in a sitting position." It does not take an object. *Set* means "to place" or "to put"; it often takes an object.

> Eartha and I were hoping to **sit** in the first row of the concert hall.
> Did you **set** the vase down carefully?

▶ **than, then** *Than* is a conjunction that introduces a subordinate clause. *Then* is an adverb meaning "therefore" or "next in order or time."

> Lily is older **than** I am. If she is older, **then** she will be eligible for a driver's license before me.
> First, we will celebrate her birthday; **then** we will celebrate mine.

▶ **that, which, who** Use *that* to introduce an essential clause (one that is needed to complete the intended meaning of a sentence; see Lesson 8.2) that refers to things. Use *which* to introduce a nonessential clause (one that adds additional information to an already complete sentence; see Lesson 8.2). Use *who* to introduce a clause that refers to people.

> Here is the dog **that** followed us home.
> We talked about pets, **which** is one of my favorite subjects.
> Rico, **who** owns four dogs, loves to chat with me.

▶ **those, these, them** Don't use *them* as an adjective. Use *those* or *these*.

> I like **those** [not *them*] jeans the best.
> I am proud of **these** [not *them*] horses.

Index

A

a, an, 103, 277
abbreviations, 241
   of academic degrees, 279
   capitalization of, 279
   in dictionaries, 242
   and exclamation points, 241
   for government agencies, 241
   metric, 241
   periods after, 241
   in ship names, 261
   for states, 241
   for time, 241
   of titles, 279
absolute adjectives, 225
abstract nouns, 97
accept, except, 342
acronyms, 241
action verbs, 101, 127
active voice, 181
adjective(s), 103. *See also* adverb(s);
  modifiers
   absolute, 225
   articles as, 103
   commas to separate two or
     more, 243
   commas to set off single-word,
     249
   defined, 103
   degrees of comparison in, 223,
     225
   distinguishing from adverbs,
     105
   infinitive/infinitive phrases as,
     145
   participles/participal phrases as,
     141
   phrases, 145
   position in sentence, 103
   predicate, 103, 129
   present participles as, 141
   proper, 103, 277
adjective clauses, 99, 155, 247
   in combining sentences, 40, 155
   elliptical, 155
   essential, 155, 247
   introductory words for, 155
   nonessential, 155
   commas to set off, 247
adjective phrases, 137
adverb(s), 105. *See also* adjective(s);
  modifiers
   conjunctive, 125, 259

defined, 105
degrees of comparison in,
   223, 225
distinguishing from
   adjectives, 105
distinguishing from
   prepositions, 107, 137
infinitive/infinitive phrases
   as, 145
intensifiers as, 105
listing of common, 105
phrases, 137
position in sentence, 105
relative, 155
adverb clauses, 157, 245
   in combining sentences, 40
   elliptical, 157
   introductory, 157, 245
     commas to set off, 157, 245
   misplaced, 157
adverb phrases, 137
advice, advise, 342
affect, effect, 342
agreement. *See* pronoun-antecedent
  agreement; subject-verb agreement
alliteration, 63
all ready, already, 342
all right, 342
all together, altogether, 342
already, all ready, 342
already, placement of, in sentence,
  229
altogether, all together, 342
among, between, 343
amount, number, 342
amounts, and subject-verb
  agreement, 197
an, a, 103, 277
anecdotes
   in persuasive writing, 56
   supporting details with, 23
antecedent agreement, 99, 213
antecedents, 99. *See also* pronoun-
  antecedent agreement
apostrophes, 267–68
   in contractions, 267
   in forming plurals of letters,
     numbers, or words referred to
     as such, 267
   with numerical representations
     of decades or centuries, 267
appositive(s), 139–40, 211
   essential, 139

nonessential, 139, 247
nouns as, 139
pronouns as, 139
appositive phrases, 139–40
   in combining sentences, 139
   nonessential, 247
argument, 53, 55–60, 76–78
articles, 103, 277
   definite, 103
   indefinite, 103
artworks
   capitalization of important
     words in, 279
   italics for titles of, 261
   titles of, and subject-verb
     agreement, 197
attention grabber in persuasive
  writing, 30
audience, consideration of. *See also*
  reader
   in drafting, 13
   in persuasive writing, 58
autobiographies, chronological
  order for, 25
auxiliary verbs, 101

B

bad, badly, 105, 342
be, forms of, 101
   capitalization of, in titles, 279
   and predicate nominative, 205
   present tense of, 189
beside, besides, 343
between, among, 343
Bible, colon to separate chapter and
  verse in reference to, 257
biographical essays, 48–52
   body in, 52
   chronological order in, 50
   conclusion in, 52
   drafting, 52
   editing, 52
   introduction in, 52
   publishing, 52
   revising, 52
   tone in, 50
biographies, chronological order
  for, 25
block quotations, 257, 263
body
   in essays, 31, 32, 52, 73
   in business letter, 88
   in literary analysis, 64
   in persuasive writing, 59–60

books
    capitalization of important
      words in, 279
    italics for titles of, 261
    quotation marks for parts
      of, 263
brackets, 211
brainstorming, as prewriting
  strategy, 10, 12
business letters, 86–90
    capitalization of salutation and
      first word of closing in, 279
    clarity of, 89
    colon after greeting of, 257
    differences between friendly
      letters and, 249
    parts of, 88
    style for, 88

C

call to action, 30, 57
capitalization
    of abbreviations, 279
    of artwork titles, 279
    of awards, 283
    of book titles, 279
    of brand names, 283
    in business letters, 279
    of calendar items, 283
    of closings in business and
      friendly letters, 279
    for compound proper
      nouns, 103
    of documents, 279, 283
    of essay titles, 279
    of first word in direct
      quotations, 281
    of first word in sentences,
      117, 281
    of geographic names, 278
    of historical events, documents,
      and periods, 283
    of interjection *O*, 283
    of languages, 281
    of lines of poetry, 64, 281
    of magazine titles, 279
    of movie titles, 279
    of names of groups, teams,
      businesses, institutions, and
      organizations, 281
    of names of people, 278, 281
    of nationalities, 281
    of periodical titles, 279
    of place names, 278
    of play titles, 279
    of poem titles, 279
    of pronoun *I*, 283
    of proper adjectives, 103, 277

    of proper nouns, 97, 277
    of races, 281
    of religions, 281
    of salutation in letters, 279
    of school subjects, 281
    of time periods, 283
    of titles of books, 279
    of titles of musical works, 279
    of titles of TV series/
      episodes, 279
    of words showing family
      relationships, 279
cause-and-effect essays, 67–73
    chronological order in, 73
    editing, 73
    publishing, 73
    revising, 73
    signal words in, 71
    subordinating conjunctions
      showing, 40
    transitions to show, 26
causes, in expository writing, 67
-cede, spelling rules for, 293
-ceed, spelling rules for, 293
centuries
    apostrophes with numerical
      representations of, 268
    capitalization of references
      to, 283
chronological order, 25
    in biographical essays, 50
    in cause-and-effect essays, 73
    in narrative writing, 28
    transitional words showing, 26
claim,
    as part of argument, 55
    as part of informative/
      explanatory writing, 31–32, 69
    as part of literary analysis, 65
    as part of research papers, 82
    See also thesis statements
clarity
    and punctuating dialogue, 265
    as writing strategy, 25
clauses, 155
    adjective, 155, 247
    adverb, 157, 245
    commas to set off
      nonessential, 155
    in correcting run-on
      sentences, 125
    dependent, 153
    essential, 155, 247
    independent, 153, 161, 243, 259
    main, 153
    nonessential, 155, 247
    noun, 159

    subordinate, 40, 153, 155,
      157, 161
clincher sentences, 21, 22
closing, 88
    capitalizing, in friendly
      letters, 279
cluster diagram, 11
coherence in writing, 25–26
collective nouns, 97
    listing of common, 197
    subject-verb agreement
      and, 197
colons, 257
combination research paper, 74
combining sentences. *See* sentence
  combining
commas
    after abbreviations, 241
    with adjective clauses, 155, 247
    in combining sentences, 245
    with compound sentences, 245
    in correcting run-on
      sentences, 125
    with introductory elements, 245
    in letters, 249
    with nonessential elements, 247
    to prevent misreading, 245
    with quotation marks, 265
    with sentence interrupters, 247
    to separate acts and scenes in
      plays, 249
    to separate date and year, 249
    to separate direct quotation
      from dialogue tag, 265
    in a series, 243
    to set off appositive phrases, 139
    to set off direct quotations, 249
    to set off indirect
      quotations, 249
    to set off introductory adverb
      clauses and phrases, 137,
      157, 245
    to set off mild interjections, 109
    to set off nonessential
      appositives/appositive
      phrases, 247
    to set off nonessential
      clauses, 156
    to set off noun of direct
      address, 242
    to set off parenthetical
      expressions, 247
    to set off transitional
      expressions, 247
    to set off *well, yes, first, second,*
      no, 249
common nouns, 97, 197

comparative as degree of comparison, 223

comparisons
degrees of, 223, 225

comparisons (*continued*)
double, 223, 225
illogical, 227
incomplete constructions in, 211
subordinating conjunctions to show, 40
as supporting detail, 23

complements, subject, 129

complete predicates, 119

complete sentences, 117

complete subjects, 119

complex sentences, 161

compound-complex sentences, 161

compound nouns, 97, 243
hyphens in, 269

compound objects, 137

compound prepositions, 107

compound sentences, 161
commas with, 245
independent clauses in, 153
semicolons to join independent clauses in, 259

compound subjects, 36
in combining sentences, 36
and coordinating conjunctions, 36
and pronoun-antecedent agreement, 213
subject-verb agreement with, 195

compound verbs, 36
in combining sentences, 36
and coordinating conjunctions, 36

computers
as research tool, 79

concept, explaining, 24

conclusions, 31, 32, 52, 60, 64, 73

concrete nouns, 97

conjunctions, 109
coordinating, 36, 109, 125, 163, 243
correlative, 36, 109, 163
defined, 109
subordinating, 109, 157

conjunctive adverbs
in combining sentences, 259
commas after, 259
listing of common, 259
semicolons before, 259

connotations, 53

constructions, incomplete, 211

contractions, 101, 227
apostrophes in, 267

contrast, transitions to show, 26

controlling idea in essays, 31

coordinating conjunctions
in combining sentences, 36
in correcting run-on sentences, 125
listing of common, 36, 109
in parallel structure, 163
in series, 243

correlative conjunctions
in combining sentences, 36
listing of common, 36, 109
in parallel structure, 163

could of, might of, should of, would of, 343

counterargument, 53, 54, 56–59, 81. *See also* counterclaim

counterclaim, 53, 56–57. *See also* counterargument

criteria, 61

D

dangling modifiers, 231

dashes, 269

dates, commas to separate year and, 249

decades, apostrophes with numerical representations of, 267

declarative sentences, 117, 241
punctuation with, 117, 241

definite articles, 103, 277

degrees of comparison, 223
comparative, 223
decreasing, 223
forming, 223
positive, 223
superlative, 223
using, 225

demonstrative pronouns, 99

denotative meanings, 53

dependent clauses, 153

descriptive writing, 28

dialogue
adding to biographical essays, 50
punctuating, 265
sentence fragments in, 117

dialogue tags, 265

dictionary, 291
abbreviations in, 242
compound nouns in, 97
irregular verbs in, 175
preferred spelling in, 291, 295–96

different from, 343

direct address
commas to set off, 247

directions, capitalization of words referring to, 277

direction statement, 83

direct objects, 101, 127

direct questions, 241

direct quotations
capitalization in, 281
commas to set off, 249
quotation marks at beginning and end of, 263, 265

double comparisons, 223, 225

double negatives, 227

drafting, 64, 66, 90
of business letters, 90
defined, 13
in essays, 52, 73
revising and editing in, 85
strategies in, 13–14

E

editing, 18–19. *See also* proofreading
of business letters, 90
in cause-and-effect essays, 73
defined, 18
letters, 90

Editing and Proofreading Worksheets, 251–52, 271–72, 285–86, 299–300

Editing Tip, 127, 129, 137, 143, 153, 173, 189, 193, 195, 207, 209, 223, 225, 241, 243, 245, 261, 263, 267, 269, 277, 291

editorials, 53–60
analyzing opinion statements, 57–58
audience for, 58
body for, 59–60
choosing topic for, 57
conclusion for, 60
drafting arguments for, 58–60
editing, 60
introduction to, 59
publishing, 60
revising, 60
writing strategies for, 55–57

"E. E. Cummings and Cubism," by Wendy R. Diskin, 61–62

effect, affect, 342

effects, in expository writing, 67

-*ei*, spelling rules for, 293

elements, 61
commas with nonessential, 247

elliptical clauses, 155, 157

emotional appeals in persuasive writing, 53, 56

emphasis, transitions to show, 26

emphatic form of verb, 179
encyclopedia articles, in gathering information, 72
end marks, 241. *See also* exclamation points; periods; question marks
essays, 31–32, 48–50, 67–72, 74
  body in, 32
essays (*continued*)
  capitalization of titles of, 279
  conclusion in, 32
  introduction in, 31
  personal response, 61
  persuasive, 53
  thesis statement, or claim, in, 31
essential adjective clauses, 155, 247
essential appositives, 139
evaluations, 61, 74
"Evolution Shortens Tusks," 67–68
except, accept, 342
exclamation points
  after abbreviations, 241
  to end exclamatory sentences, 117, 241
  to end imperative sentences, 117, 241
  with quotation marks, 265
  to separate direct quotation from dialogue tag, 265
  to set off strong interjections, 109
exclamatory sentences, 117, 241
explanations in expository writing, 74
expository writing, 29, 31–32, 67–73, 74–85. *See also* cause-and-effect essays; research papers
eyewitness accounts, chronological order for, 25

F

farther, further, 343
fewer, less, 225, 343
fiction, chronological order in, 25
figurative language, 63, 65
first draft, writing, 84
5-W and How? questions
  as prewriting strategy, 11, 12
  in writing a biographical essay, 50
flexibility as drafting strategy, 14
focusing, 32
foreign words and expressions, italics for, 261
fragments, sentence, 117, 145, 153
freewriting, 10
friendly letters

capitalization of salutation and first word of closing in, 279
commas after closing, 249
differences between business letters and, 249
further, farther, 343
future perfect tense, 179
future tense, 179

G

gerund phrases, 143
gerunds, 143
good, well, 343
greeting in friendly letters, commas after, 249
groups, capitalization of names of, 281

H

heading in letters, 88
helping verbs, 101, 173
here, beginning sentences with, 123
hyphens, 269
  in compound nouns, 97
  in compound numbers, 269

I

I, capitalization of, 283
ideas and unity, as revising strategy, 15
-ie, spelling rules for, 293
illogical comparisons, 227
imperative sentences, 117
  punctuation after, 117, 241
  subject in, 123
imply, infer, 343
incomplete constructions, 211
indefinite articles, 103, 277
indefinite pronouns, 99
  agreement with antecedent, 213
  and subject-verb agreement, 193
independent clauses, 153
  in complex sentences, 161
  in compound-complex sentences, 161
  in compound sentences, 153, 161, 259
  in series, 243
  in simple sentences, 161
indirect objects, 127
indirect questions, 241
indirect quotations, 263, 281
  commas to set off, 249
infer, imply, 343
infinitive(s), 145
infinitive phrases, 145
  commas to set off introductory, 245

informative/explanatory writing, *See also* cause-and-effect essays; expository writing; research papers
inside address, 88
intensifiers, 105
intensive pronouns, 99
interjections, 109
  capitalization of *O,* 283
  comma to set off mild, 109
  exclamation point to set off strong, 109
Internet in gathering information, 72, 79–80
interrogative pronouns, 99
interrogative sentences, 117
  punctuation with, 117, 241
interrupters
  commas to set off, 247
  dashes to set off, 269
intervening phrases and subject-verb agreement, 191
interviews in gathering information, 72
introductions, 31, 52, 59, 64, 73
introductory adverb clauses, commas to set off, 157, 245
introductory elements, commas with, 245
introductory infinitive phrases, commas to set off, 245
introductory participles, commas to set off, 245
introductory prepositional phrases, commas to set off, 245
inverted sentences, subject in, 123
irregardless, regardless, 344
irregular verbs, 175, 177
I-search paper, 74
italics, 261
items in a series
  commas to separate, 243
  semicolons to separate, 259

L

lay, lie, 177, 344
less, fewer, 225, 343
letters. *See* business letters; friendly letters
letters as letters
  apostrophes to form plurals of, 267
  italics for, 261
letters to the editor
  revising, 16–17
  lie, lay, 177, 344
linking verbs, 101, 127, 129
lists, use of colon to introduce, 257

literary analysis,
     analyzing fiction, 61–66
     analyzing nonfiction, 91–94
literary present tense, 64
loaded words, 53, 56
logical appeals in persuasive
  writing, 53
logical order, 25
     in expository writing, 29

M

main clauses. *See* independent
  clauses
main ideas, 29
     turning into paragraphs, 32
metric abbreviations, 241
*might of, could of, should of, would
  of,* 343
misplaced adverb clauses, 157
misplaced modifiers, 229
*MLA Handbook for Writers of
  Research Papers, The,* 82
mnemonics, 293
Modern Language Association, in
  documenting sources, 82
modifiers. *See also* adjective(s);
  adverb(s)
     dangling, 231
     irregular, 223
     misplaced, 229
     one-syllable, 223
     single-word, 91
     two-syllable, 223
moods, 28

N

narrative writing, 28–29, 48–52.
  See also biographical essays
negatives, double, 227
no, commas to set off, 249
nominatives, predicate, 129, 205
none, and subject-verb
  agreement, 193
nonessential adjective clauses, 155
     commas to set off, 155, 247
nonessential appositives, 139
     commas to set off, 247
nonessential elements, commas
  with, 247
No Ordinary Time, by Doris Kearns
  Goodwin, 21–22, 48–49
noun(s), 97
     abstract, 97
     as adjectives, 103
     appositives/appositive phrases
       as, 139
     clauses, 159
     collective, 97, 197
     common, 97, 197

compound, 97, 103, 269
concrete, 97
gerunds/gerund phrases as, 143
infinitive/infinitive phrases
  as, 145
plural, 189, 267, 297
possessive, 143
proper, 97, 277
     capitalization of, 103
subject-verb agreement and
  collective, 197
noun clauses, 159
noun of direct address, commas to
  set off, 247
number, amount, 342
number in subject-verb
  agreement, 189
numbers
     apostrophes to form plurals
       of, 267
     italics for, 261

O

O, capitalization of, 283
object of preposition, 207
object pronouns, 207, 209, 211
objects
     compound, 137
     direct, 101, 127
     indirect, 127
observations in gathering
  information, 72
off, off of, 344
only, placement of, in sentence,
  229
"Opposition to Female Suffrage in
  the United States," by Nicole Herz,
  75–78
order of importance, in cause-and-
  effect essays, 73
organization and coherence, as
  revising strategy, 15
organization of writing
     chronological, 25, 28
     of importance, 25, 30
     logical, 25, 29
     spatial, 25, 28
     transitions to show importance
       of, 26
original research, 74
outlines, 13, 84

P

paragraphs
     clincher sentence in, 21, 22
     coherence in, 25–26
     topic sentence in, 21, 22
     types of, 28–30
     unity in, 21–22

varying sentences in
  effective, 34
parallel structure in effective
  sentences, 163
paraphrasing in note taking, 81
parentheses, 269
parenthetical documentation, 82
participial phrases, 141
     commas to set off, 245
     position in sentence, 141
participles, 141
     as adjectives, 141
     past, 141, 173
     present, 141, 173
part of speech. *See* adjective(s);
  adverb(s); conjunctions;
  interjections, noun(s);
  preposition(s); pronoun(s); verb(s)
parts of books, quotation marks for
  titles of, 263
passive voice, 181
past participles, 141, 173
past perfect tense, 179
past tense, 179
perfect tenses, 179
periods
     after abbreviations, 241
     to end declarative sentences,
       117, 241
     to end imperative sentences,
       117, 241
     with quotation marks, 265
person, 189
     describing, 24
     in subject-verb
       agreement, 189
personal pronouns, 99
personal response essay, 61
personification, 283
persuasive writing, 30, 53–60.
  See also editorials
     anecdotes in, 56
     attention grabber in, 30
     body in, 59–60
     call to action in, 30
     conclusion in, 60
     introduction in, 59
     opinion statement in, 30
     writing strategies for, 55–57
phrases
     adjective, 137
     adverb, 137
     appositive, 139–40
     colons to emphasize, 257
     gerund, 143
     infinitive, 145
     inserting, in combining
       sentences, 145

intervening, and subject-verb agreement, 191
participial, 141
prepositional, 107, 137
verb, 101
plagiarism, 81
planning, importance of, in drafting, 13
plural nouns, 189, 297
apostrophes in forming, 267
plural pronouns, 213
plural subjects, 189
plural verbs, 189
position statement, 55
positive as degree of comparison, 223
possession, apostrophes to show, 267
possessive forms, 99
possessive nouns in modifying gerunds, 143
possessive pronouns, 267
in modifying gerunds, 143
practical writing, 86–90. *See also* workplace writing
predicate adjectives, 103, 129
predicate nominatives, 129, 205
predicates
complete, 119
defined, 119
simple, 119
prefixes, 295–96
prepositional phrases, 107, 137
introductory, 245
commas to set off, 137, 245
prepositions, 107
commonly used, 107
compound, 107
distinguishing from adverbs, 107, 137
object of, 207
position of, in sentence, 107
present participles, 141, 173
present perfect tense, 179
present tense, 179
literary, 64
subject-verb agreement in, 189
prewriting, 9–12, 83, 89
brainstorming in, 10, 12
and business letters, 89
clustering in, 11
defined, 9
5-W and How? questions, 11, 12
freewriting in, 10
for literary analysis, 64, 65
major points and supporting details, 65

writer's notebook in, 9
primary sources, 79
progressive form, 179
pronoun(s), 99
appositives/appositive phrases as, 139
capitalization of *I*, 283
defined, 99
demonstrative, 99
first-person, 189
indefinite, 99
and subject-verb agreement, 193
intensive, 99
interrogative, 99
object, 207, 209, 211
personal, 99
plural, 213
possessive, 143
possessive personal, 267
reflexive, 99
relative, 99, 155
second-person, 190
singular, 213
subject, 205, 209, 211
subject-verb agreement with indefinite, 193
third-person, 189
pronoun-antecedent agreement, 99, 213
pronoun reference, clear, 215
proofreading, 18–19. *See also* editing
for capitalization, 18
defined, 18
symbols for, 19
proper adjectives, 103, 277
capitalization of, 103, 277
proper nouns, 97, 277
capitalization of, 97, 103, 277
compound, 103
publishing, 52, 60, 66, 73
suggestions for, 19
punctuation marks. *See also* specific marks in editing, 18
purpose, 13
subordinating conjunctions to show, 40

Q
question(s)
asking, in writing biographical essays, 50
direct, 241
5-W and How?, 11, 12
indirect, 269
question marks
after abbreviations, 241
to end interrogative sentences, 117, 241

with quotation marks, 265
to separate direct quotation from dialogue tag, 265
quotation(s)
adding to biographical essays, 50
block, 257, 263
capitalization of first words of, 281
colons to introduce formal, 257, 263
commas to set off direct, 249
indirect, 263, 281
introducing, by naming author of, 81
in note taking, 81
from poem, in literary analysis, 64
in supporting detail, 23, 29
quotation marks, 263
at beginning and end of direct quotations, 263
enclosing single words, phrases, and lines in, 64
for parts of book titles, 263
in punctuating dialogue, 265
single, 263
for titles of short works, 261, 263

R
raise, rise, 177, 344
reader. *See also* audience
guiding, as writing coherently strategy, 25
Readers' Guide to Periodical Literature, The, 79
reflexive pronouns, 99
regardless, irregardless, 344
regular verbs, 173
relative adverbs, 155
relative pronouns, 99, 155
reports, drafting part of, 14
research, evaluating, 84
research papers, 74–85. *See also* expository writing
types of, 74
writing strategies for, 78–82
revising, 15–17, 52, 60, 66, 73, 90
defined, 15
stranded infinitive phrases in, 145
strategies in, 15
writing partner, 16
Revising and Editing Worksheets, 46, 112, 131–32, 147–48, 165–66, 183–84, 199–200, 217–18, 233–34
rise, raise, 177, 344
run-on sentences, correcting, 125

S

salutation, 88
  capitalizing, in business
    letters, 279
secondary sources, 79
-sede, spelling rules for, 293
semicolons
  in combining sentences, 259
  before conjunctive adverbs, 259
  in correcting run-on
    sentences, 125
  in joining independent
    clauses, 259
  to separate items in a series, 259
  before transitional
    expressions, 259
sensory details, 28
sentence(s)
  capitalization of first words of,
    117, 281
  clincher, 21, 22
  complete, 117
  complex, 161
  compound, 153, 161, 245, 259
  compound-complex, 161
  correcting run-on, 125
  declarative, 117, 241
  defined, 117
  eliminating short, choppy
    sentences, 42
  exclamatory, 117, 241
  imperative, 117, 241
  interrogative, 117, 241
  placement of subject and verb
    in, 119
  position of preposition in, 107
  predicates in, 119
  punctuation of, 117
  simple, 161
  subject in, 119
  topic, 21, 22
  types of, 161
  varying, in effective
    paragraphs, 34
sentence combining. *See also*
 complex sentences; compound-
 complex sentences; compound
 sentences
  adjective clauses in, 40, 155
  adverb clauses in, 40, 41, 157
  appositives in, 139
  commas in, 245
  compound subjects in, 36
  compound verbs in, 36
  conjunctive adverbs in, 259
  eliminating short, choppy
    sentences, 42

noun clauses in, 159
phrases in, 145
subordinate clauses in, 40
sentence fragments, 117, 145, 153
  in dialogue, 117
sentence interrupters, commas
 with, 247
series
  commas in a, 243
  semicolons to separate items
    in, 259
set, sit, 177, 344
short stories
  capitalization of important
    words in title, 279
  punctuating dialogue in, 265
  quotation marks for titles
    of, 263
*should of, could of, might of, would
 of*, 343
simple predicates, 119
simple sentences, 161
simple subjects, 119
simple tenses, 179
single quotation marks, 263
singular pronouns, 213
singular subject, 189
singular verb, 189
sit, set, 177, 344
slashes, in quotations, 64
sources
  documenting, 80, 82
  evaluating, 79–80
  primary, 79
  secondary, 79
spatial order, 25
  in descriptive writing, 28
spell checkers, 18, 89, 297
spelling, 293
  with *-cede, -ceed,* and *-sede*, 293
  of gerunds, 143
  for *-ie* and *-ei*, 293 of past parti-
    ciples, 173
  preferred, in dictionary, 291,
    295–96
  with prefixes, 295–96
  as editing strategy, 18
  with suffixes, 295–96
split infinitives, 145
Step by Step, 42, 105, 121, 123, 127,
 205, 211, 223, 243, 247
style,
  for business letters, 88
  formal, 32, 57, 73
subject complement, 129
subject pronouns, 205, 209, 211
subjects

complete, 119
compound, 36, 213
defined, 119
finding, 123–24
placement in sentence, 119
plural, 189
simple, 199
singular, 189
you as understood, 123
subject-verb agreement
  and collective nouns, 197
  with compound subjects, 195
  with indefinite pronouns, 193
  with intervening phrases, 191
  in person and number, 189
  problems in, 197
  and titles of artwork, 197
subordinate clauses, 153, 155, 157
  beginning sentences with, 34
  in combining sentences, 40
  in complex sentences, 161
  in compound-complex
    sentences, 161
  in correcting run-on sentences,
    125
subordinating conjunctions, 40,
 109, 157
suffixes, 295–96
summarizing
  in expository writing, 74
  in note taking, 80
summary paper, 74
superlative degrees of
 comparison, 223
symbols, proofreading, 19
synthesizing, in expository
 writing, 74

T

tag, dialogue, 265
technology, 19, 79–80, 86
tense. *See* verb tenses
Test-Taking Tips, 105, 109, 143, 161,
 163, 179, 195, 213, 215, 225, 231
than, then, 344
that, which, who, 344
the, 103, 277
them, these, those, 344
then, than, 344
there, beginning sentences with, 123
these, them, those, 344
thesis statements, or claim, 55, 82
  analyzing, 72
  in expository writing, 31, 69, 71
  writing, 73
those, them, these, 344
thoughts, putting in order, as
 writing strategy, 25

time
  abbreviations for, 241
  colon to separate hour and
    minute in, 257
  and subject-verb
    agreement, 197
time (*continued*)
  subordinating conjunctions to
    show, 40
  transitions to show, 26
time order. *See* chronological order
timed essay, 91–94
titles, 279
  capitalization of, 279
  italics for, 261
  quotation marks for, 263
tone
  in biographical essay, 50
  in persuasive writing, 57
  objective, 32, 57, 73
topics
  choosing, 50, 57, 78–79, 83
  exploring, 71
  in expository writing, 69
  finding, 12
  limiting, 78–79, 83
  narrowing, 9, 12
topic sentences, 21, 22
transitional words and
  expressions, 59
  cause-and-effect, 26
  list of common, 26
  order of importance, 26
  semicolons before, 259
transitive verbs, 127

U

underlining, 261
understood subject, 123
unity, 21–22

V

verb(s), 101
  action, 101, 127
  auxiliary, 101

compound, 36
defined, 101
emphatic form, 179
forms of *to be*, 101
helping, 101, 173
irregular, 175, 177
linking, 101, 127, 129
placement of, in sentence,
  119
plural, 189
regular, 173
singular, 189
transitive, 127
verbals, 141
  gerunds as, 143
  infinitives as, 145
  participles as, 141
verb phrases, 101
verb tenses, 101, 179
  future, 179
  future perfect, 179
  past, 179
  past perfect, 179
  present, 179
  present perfect, 179
  of *to be*, 189
voice
  active, 181
  passive, 181
"Voters' Ed," by John B. Anderson
  and Ray Martinez III, 53–54

W

webbing, 11
well, comma to set off, 249
well, good, 343
which, that, who, 344
who/whom?, 209
word choice
  as revising strategy, 15
  for biographical essays, 50
words
  colons to emphasize, 257
  connotations of, 53
  denotations of, 53

determining part of speech
  of, 111
loaded, 53, 56
prefixes for, 295–96
suffixes for, 295–96
words as words
  apostrophes to form plurals
    of, 267
  italics for, 261
workplace writing, 86–90
  writing strategies for, 88–89
works cited, 82
*would of, could of, might of, should
  of*, 343
writer's notebook, 9, 12
writing. *See also* cause-and-effect
  essays; editorials; research papers
  descriptive, 28
  expository, 29, 31–32, 67–73,
    74–85
  narrative, 28–29, 48–52
  persuasive, 30, 53–60
  practical, 86–90
  workplace, 86–90
Writing Hint, 69, 81, 97, 101, 103,
  107, 117, 119, 125, 137, 141, 145,
  157, 159, 175, 177, 179, 205, 211,
  213, 227, 229, 245, 249, 257, 265,
  269, 279, 283, 293, 295, 297
writing process
  drafting in, 13–14
  editing and proofreading in,
    18–19
  prewriting in, 9–12
  revising in, 15–17

Y

year, commas to separate date
  and, 249
you, as understood subject, 124